W9-CGV-513

COPING WITH HUNGER

COPING WITH HUNGER: TOWARD A SYSTEM OF FOOD SECURITY AND PRICE STABILIZATION

DAVID BIGMAN
The Hebrew University of Jerusalem

BALLINGER PUBLISHING COMPANY
Cambridge, Massachusetts
A Subsidiary of Harper & Row, Publishers, Inc.

International Standard Book Number: 0-88410-371-4

Library of Congress Catalog Card Number: 81-22908

Printed in the United States of America

Library of Congress Cataloging in Publication Data

Bigman, David.
  Coping with hunger.

  Includes bibliographical references and index.
  1. Food supply. 2. Agricultural prices. I. Title.
HD9000.5.B48   338.1'9   81-22908
ISBN 0-88410-371-4   AACR2

To Eyal and Galya

CONTENTS

LIST OF FIGURES

LIST OF TABLES

xvii

PREFACE

The Malthusian verdict of a losing race between food and mouths to feed gave economics its reputation as a dismal science. Since Malthus published his work in 1798 the world has undergone a technological revolution, in industry and then in agriculture, that has brought perhaps the most profound changes in the course of history. Production has grown to levels never imagined before; income and living standards have risen sharply, and almost everyone has been affected. It was then believed that in the Malthusian race human ingenuity, imagination, and inventiveness would ever win. In the wake of the Keynesian revolution and the prosperity enjoyed after World War II, economics changed its image, to become in the eyes of many the key to a better world, with no unemployment and no inflation, no poverty and no hunger.

Today, nearly two centuries since the publication of *Essays on the Principles of Population,* Malthus's dismal prophecy seems more relevant than ever. In Malthus's time the world population was 900 million people; today there are almost 4.5 billion. If present trends continue, the world population will double itself every 35 years; meticulous statisticians have determined the date at which there will be no room left for all the world's inhabitants even if they stand shoulder to shoulder. Equally dismal, in the last decade the science of economics has lost much confidence in its ability to guide the policymakers and navigate the world to stability and affluence.

Some time ago I read a report about the Latin American World Model, a global study examining the most favorable scenario to cope with the food problem. Instead of projecting future conditions on the basis of present policies and trends, this model asks: "How can global resources best be used to meet basic human needs for all people?" Even under near-Utopian assumptions whereby all resources are mobilized for the sole purpose of solving the food problem, however, the model projects a major crisis in Asia by the year 2010 because of the failure of food production to keep pace with population growth.

As I was reading these gloomy projections, which apparently surprised even their authors, it dawned on me that this is yet another example, and a very illuminating one at that, of how we economists and model builders go wrong. In our adherence to analytical tools, we follow the trajectories injected by a model into the future and thus become captives of its inherent rigidities and inability to accommodate changes. All that a model tells us is how an economy has performed; it does not tell us what an economy *is*. It ignores the most powerful force that drives the economy—the human spirit and ingenuity—and thus cannot predict how people will behave in the future when confronted with new obstacles never encountered before.

Nevertheless, I did not come to bury model building but to praise it. Once we accept its limitations we can appreciate and take full advantage of a model's capacity to summarize the intricacies of an economy, to illustrate the connections and interactions between its various sectors, and to demonstrate the direct and indirect effects of policy actions on exogenous events.

A model that is capable of depicting all the complexities of the economy, Joan Robinson once remarked, will be of no more use than a map of one to one. Simplifying assumptions is the essential initial step in model building, and while its long-range projections should therefore be taken with a grain of salt, especially as we ignore factors that cannot be quantified,[1] it is still highly useful in alerting us to the likely consequences of different actions and trends, and in policing the decision-making process.

A large part of this book consists of analysis of various food policies based on a rather complex simulation model of an economy. The model has evolved over more than a decade and was originated by Shlomo Reutlinger, with whom I have collaborated for the past six years. Much of my thinking on the subject has its origin in our joint work, in his own writings, and in our many discussions. I am greatly indebted to him for his contribution to my work and for my very interest in this subject. In fact, If I were to have chosen a godfather for this book, I would have chosen him.

Over the years very many individuals have invested their skills and ingenuity in the development and programming of this model. David Blum, David Eaton, Bruce Arentzen, Keith Knapp, Yoni Levy, Miron Livni, Yitzhak Weksler, Eli Greenboim, and Ziv Bar-Shira all have their share in the model, and their contribution is gratefully acknowledged.

During my work on this book many colleagues assisted me with comments and advice, offering their own works for reference as well as taking time for endless discussions. I am especially indebted to Haim Shalit, who took the lion's share of this burden. I am also indebted to Gurushri Swami, John Wall, Ernst Lutz, Yoav Kislev, and Shlomo Yitzhaki.

I would like to thank Shirley Smith for her excellent and very careful editing work and Niha Gestetner for her meticulous art work. Special thanks are due to the secretaries of the Agricultural Economics Department of the Hebrew University of Jerusalem, particularly to Nitza Sadeh and Celina Gross for their superb typing job and for taking care of all the logistics that this work at times involved. Finally, I would like to thank the people of Ballinger, whose patience and pleasantness is commendable.

The research was supported in part by a grant from the United States—Israel (Binational) Agricultural Research and Development Fund (BARD).

A work on the subject of hunger and malnutrition cannot possibly leave one aloof, however analytical it may be. It is my deep conviction that a solution to the food problem is within the reach of mankind and my belief that we economists can make a substantial contribution towards that end. I hope that I have been able to convey these feelings in the writing of this book.

NOTE

1. To paraphrase Descartes, it sometimes seems that for us economists and model builders, if something is not measurable then it does not exist.

INTRODUCTION

In the 1970s food scarcity became the overriding concern of governments in the developing countries and the most pressing item on the international agenda. More than a billion people, almost one-quarter of the world's population, live on the verge of hunger; half of them suffer from chronic undernutrition. The number of hungry and malnourished people is likely to double by the year 2000, and the food crisis may well soar out of control.

Droughts, floods, and other natural or man-made calamities are only part of the problem. The central and most intransigent cause of hunger today is poverty. Hundreds of millions of people, not only in the developing countries, but also in the industrial nations, live in such poverty that their income cannot provide enough food to maintain health. Old remedies that focus on increasing global food supply, mostly via technological progress, will therefore not suffice to solve the problem since they will not materially change the status of the great majority of the people who are hungry and malnourished.

Widely recognized is the need for more equitable development and a comprehensive change in the distribution of the available food supply on the one hand and of the economic resources, particularly land, on the other hand. Only if poor people (and poor nations) are provided with the necessary means of production and a larger share in the nation's (and the world's) income and wealth, will they be able to take part in the growth process and ultimately reach the base line of self-reliance.

The aim of this book is to take a step beyond the mere outlining of general strategies for coping with the food problem and proceed to the details of specific tactics and precise policy measures that jointly make up an overall strategy in the war against hunger. What are the policies and practices in different countries in their attempts to deal with the food problem? How effective are they in meeting the pressing needs of today? What will their long-range effects be? What alternative policies exist that could serve the nation's short-term and long-term goals with respect to food? What are the direct and indirect effects of each policy and program on the various consumer groups in urban and rural areas, on producers, on the government, and on the balance of payments? These are the questions considered in this book.

Chapters 1 and 2 examine a number of conceptual issues that underlie all discussions on the subject. Chapter 1 considers the various characteristics of today's food problem across different population groups, across different geographical regions, and across time. It distinguishes between difficulties arising from temporary aberrations in supply and the more acute problem of chronic undernutrition caused by poverty; it categorizes the population according to their degree of vulnerability to hunger and analyzes the short-range and long-range aspects of the food problem, with special reference to the proposed solutions. A typology of hunger and an unequivocal definition of *food security* are needed not only for analytical purposes but even more so because the remedies vary according to the nature of the problem.

Chapter 2 examines the methodological framework for evaluating food policies. The main practical measure for policy evaluation put forward by welfare economics is the economic surplus. In a stochastic world most theoretical studies seek to assess the desirability of stabilization policies on the basis of the analytical framework advanced by Waugh, Oi, and Massell, which is based on the economic surplus concept. The chapter reviews this methodology and some of its more recent ramifications, and examines its usefulness in evaluating food policies. It concludes that in the assessment of the overall gains from a stabilization policy, a measure based solely on the economic surplus may be seriously deficient and only partly relevant because it disregards a number of very important aspects. Thus, for instance, the economic loss that the country may suffer as a result of a stabilization policy could be looked on as an insurance premium paid in order to achieve higher stability and to prevent sharp falls in price or acute supply shortages. The loss in itself cannot therefore indicate whether the policy is indeed undesirable.

Chapter 3 reviews the policies being used in many developing countries to cope with their specific food problems and to secure price stability of agricultural produce. The chapter provides a fairly detailed description of the foodgrain management systems in India, Egypt, and Israel and outlines certain unique features of the systems in a number of other countries in Southeast Asia, Africa, and Latin America.

Chapter 4 analyzes the effects of buffer stocks in absorbing variations in supply and in securing a stable flow of food to consumers by shifting consumption from a time period in which food is abundant to one in which it is scarce. The chapter outlines a series of measures for evaluating the performance of stabilization policies, the most important of which are the following:

- *Food security*—measured by the probability that the quantity available for consumption by "poor" consumers does not fall below subsistence level.
- *Price stability*—measured by the coefficient of variation of the price.
- *Security of farmers' income*—measured by the probability that farmers' income does not fall below a critical level where their livelihood and thus future prospects for food production may be seriously endangered.

The chapter then examines other performance measures of stability, as well as the measure of total economic gains or losses resulting from the policy; its effects on income distribution, on the government fiscal budget, and (when relevant) on the balance of payments.

The analysis in this chapter is carried out under a wide variety of assumptions on the storage policy, on the form of the supply function, and on the structure of the market. The main conclusion is that the specific effects of buffer stocks strongly depend on the economic environment within which they operate. The form of the supply function, the degree of serial correlation in production, the magnitude of the demand elasticities, the degree of variability in production, and the form of the stock policy all have a strong impact on the extent to which buffer stocks will stabilize the price and secure a stable flow of supply, as well as on the economic gains or losses resulting from the storage operation. In all cases, however, diminishing marginal productivity of buffer stocks is exhibited; that is, successive increases of the storage facility will lead to higher stability but at a diminishing rate. As a result, increases of stability via buffer stocks will be increasingly costly, and no reasonable amount of stocks can provide complete food security. Thus, for instance, in the base case considered in the chapter, even with a storage facility having a capacity equal to 15 percent of average annual production there will still be a probability of 8 percent of an extreme shortfall in the supply to the poor in excess of 10 percent of their normal consumption (against a probability of 17.6 percent with no stocks at all). Other policy measures would have to be put into effect if this level of food security is considered too low.

Chapter 5 examines the effects of other internal stabilization programs and of different combinations of price and stock policies. They include price support programs to farmers and subsidy programs that apply to low-income consumers only. There are two fundamental distinctions between the latter policies and a buffer stock policy. First, the stock policy applies to the general population whereas the internal price programs apply to specific target groups only. Second, the stock policy works by shifting consumption from one time period to another. The internal price programs work by shifting consumption (either directly or through the transfer of money income) from one group or sector to another within the same time period. These programs therefore require differential fiscal transfers and involve considerable changes in the income distribution. The main conclusion emerging from this chapter is that when the objectives of the policy are defined in terms of group-specific variables (such as food security), the most powerful and cost-effective policies are group-specific programs targeted on those variables (such as a subsidy program targeted on low-income consumers for attaining food security). However, these policies will have strong side effects, not all of them desirable, that must be taken into account when implementing these programs. Thus, for instance, the subsidy program will cause a substantial increase in the variability of the market price. Associated with the program therefore is an immanent trade-off between food security and price stability and hence between the well-being of the beneficiary consumers and that of the nonbeneficiary consumers and the producers.

Chapter 6 examines some of the theoretical aspects of international trade in a stochastic world where supplies and demands are unstable. The chapter demonstrates that considerable trade flows are created as a result of this instability—over and above the flows that are due to any relative advantage of the countries. A considerable portion of the world trade in agricultural products should probably be attributed to the fluctuations in supply, and even countries that are normally self-sufficient in these products must quite often resort to import in order to avoid the shortages resulting from a poor domestic harvest.

The chapter also examines the gains from trade and proves that each trading country would gain from trade even in cases where trade actually enhances rather than diminishes the instability in the country. Different stabilization policies are then considered. Of particular interest is a policy of unilateral stabilization via trade and storage that is carried out by appropriate tariffs and subsidies. Because it has the effect of exporting the internal instability to the trading countries, we call this policy "Destabilize Thy Neighbor."

Chapter 7 extends the analysis to a more generalized framework and thus more realistic economic environment. It examines the role and effects of domestic agricultural policies in an open economy and compares them with those in a closed economy. The chapter demonstrates that with free trade the role and effects of internal stabilization programs may vastly change. Thus, for instance, the subsidy program that works in a closed economy by shifting food consumption from one consumer group to another works in an open economy by allowing the additional food requirements of the beneficiary group to be imported from abroad; under foreign exchange constraint, this policy would thus have the effect of shifting imported resources from other uses (notably investments) to consumption. The chapter also demonstrates that trade liberalization acts as a substitute for buffer stocks as well as for other internal stabilization programs; the more liberal trade is, the higher the level of domestic stability and thus the smaller the effects of internal programs.

Finally, Chapter 8 analyzes several trade policies in agricultural food products under conditions of supply fluctuations in the home country and abroad. Among these policies are ad-valorem tariffs on all imports and exports, import tariffs (mostly in a generally importing country) and export taxes (mostly in a generally exporting country), other forms of trade restrictions, and variable levies. The latter policy is of particular interest since it is the centerpiece of the Common Agricultural Policy in the European Economic Community. The chapter demonstrates the trade-off between the level of domestic instability that can be maintained with this trade policy and the resulting deficit in the balance of payments.

The basic premise underlying the analysis in this book is that the objectives of agricultural policies in general and of food policies in particular are diverse and often incompatible. To varying degrees governments are concerned with securing a stable flow of supply to the population, an adequate diet for consumers at the poverty level, stable prices, and an adequate income for farmers. To cope with their food problems governments can implement many different policies, including buffer stocks, internal price and income programs, direct government procurement and distribution, various trade policies, and any combination of these. This book offers a methodological framework for evaluating the performance of the various policies. It analyzes their direct and indirect effects on the different sectors in the economy, establishes their short-term and long-term effects, and assesses their specific contribution and overall desirability in the war on hunger.

1 MANIFESTS OF HUNGER

The outcome of the war on hunger, by the year 2000 and beyond, will be determined not by forces beyond human control, but by decisions and actions well within the capability of nations and people working individually and together. —*U.S. Presidential Commission on World Hunger (1980)*

The fault, dear Brutus, is not in our stars, but in ourselves. —*Shakespeare, Julius Caesar*

THE MULTIPLE DIMENSIONS OF THE FOOD PROBLEM

In 1974, after widespread harvest failures and quadrupling oil prices had brought the international food system to the brink of chaos and millions of people in Africa and Asia to outright starvation, the thirty-six-member United Nations World Food Council vowed to create a world without hunger within a decade. By that time, they pledged, no child would go to bed hungry, no family need fear for its next day's bread, and no human being's future would be stunted by malnutrition.

Today that noble goal seems more distant than ever. Negotiations on the creation of an International Undertaking on World Food Security initiated at the 1974 U.N. World Food Conference with the aim of establishing national and regional reserves, have thus far led nowhere. Kind weather and several successive years of bumper crop harvests in the United States improved the immediate outlook for the global food system and eased the concerns about hunger. In the United States the acreage set-aside plan was reintroduced to restrict planted areas by as much as 25 percent and thus reduce the mounting surpluses.

And yet hunger still exists. Hundreds of millions struggle for their daily bread, their bodies emaciated by insufficient food and their spirits by despair. The U.N.'s Food and Agriculture Organization (FAO) estimates that one out of every eight people in the world suffers from chronic undernutrition; the World Bank estimates that over one billion people live in conditions of absolute poverty and must struggle for daily survival on incomes that cannot provide an adequate diet. Projections for the years ahead indicate that the world hunger problem is getting worse rather than better. The U.S. Presidential Commission on World Hunger warns that "A major crisis of global food supply of even more serious dimensions than the present energy crisis appears likely within the next 20 years"; others prophesy that "the biggest famine in history has just begun" (Dumont 1975).

Food security means different things to different people and is used in reference to rather different issues. Establishing a clear and unequivocal definition is important since the lack of uniformity has sometimes resulted in misunderstanding and confusion over the nature of the food problem and disagreement over how the hungry can be helped.

Food scarcity has several different manifestations. The most dramatic is when the entire food supply of a region inhabited by hundreds of thousands, sometimes millions, of people is wiped out by drought, flood, war, political strife, or other natural or man-made disasters. Far more difficult is the plight of the hundreds of millions who live in such dire poverty that they cannot secure even a minimally adequate diet. Chronic undernutrition is the most acute albeit the least visible food problem of our time. Temporary aberrations in the food delivery system occur from time to time, as a result of domestic harvest failures, price fluctuations in the domestic or world markets, or policy changes. Although such disruptions may not become calamitous and result in outright famine, they nonetheless cause deep suffering not only to the chronically undernourished but also to subsistence farmers and employees, who normally manage to provide just enough food for an adequate diet but may be brought to starvation if their purchasing power is reduced. A final aspect of the "food problem" is the increasing threat of population explosion. If the population continues to grow at its present pace then as early as fifty years from now there may be on earth, with its limited resources, too many mouths to feed.

The four aspects of the food problem are obviously intimately related and often hard to tell apart. Between the hardships experienced by large population groups in times of market disruptions and the suffering caused by a drought-induced famine, the difference is essentially a matter of degree. Poverty causes not only chronic undernutrition but is also responsible for the periodic hunger that occurs in times of market disruptions, and poverty today perpetuates and aggravates the food scarcity of tomorrow. Nonetheless, clarifying the nature of the food problem is essential for analysis but even more for designing strategies to cope with it.

Outright starvation following a natural or man-made calamity is undoubtedly the most visible and emotionally moving manifestation of the food problem. The picture of a starving child in a drought-stricken area, or the desperately weak voice of a mother overtaken by hunger and fear in a refugee camp, still shock people. The problem of starvation, however, is usually localized, and in most cases its effects can be contained or even entirely eliminated by appropriate relief measures; it would require emergency relief measures to mobilize food and other supplies and transport them speedily to the afflicted area, but the quantities needed are in most cases relatively small and make no significant demands on the donor countries or on world trade. All too often, however, the solution could have been easier and much suffering spared were it not for local government policies that unwittingly aggravate the situation instead of improving it. The following excerpt from a *Time Magazine* story entitled "The Harvest of Despair" (June 30, 1980) vividly demonstrates this point:

> In northwestern Kenya, forlorn Turkana tribesmen trek for miles through the bush to Catholic missions in Kakuma and Lodwar, where emergency food is distributed. In the strife-torn Karamoja province of northeastern Uganda, relief workers wake every morning to find the corpses of malnourished children deposited on their doorsteps. . . . The tragedy is in

part the result of drought. . . . Human failings have been even more detrimental. In Kenya, says a U.N. expert, "90% of the trouble comes from
bad marketing policies." Following a bumper crop of corn in 1978, the
Kenya government overconfidently slashed prices paid to farmers by
nearly 30% and sold more than 200,000 tons of grain on the export market. It also agreed to supply 8,000 tons of emergency food to Uganda,
where the harvest had been destroyed during the chaos of Tanzania's war
against Idi Amin. When last year's cereal crop fell short by 400,000 tons,
largely because farmers stopped planting, the country cut off the ship-
ments to Uganda after supplying only 80 tons, and was forced to buy
heavily on international grain markets after accepting a U.S. donation of
60,000 tons. In Tanzania, the lack of modern storage facilities forced the
government to export 259,000 tons of grain and other food stuffs last
year—almost enough to cover the 280,000-ton shortfall it expects in 1980.

The chronic undernutrition suffered permanently or periodically by
hundreds of millions around the world is a far more difficult problem
to resolve than catastrophic famine. According to World Bank estimates as much as 40 to 60 percent of the population in developing
countries is undernourished, and the number may increase even further in times of market disruption.[1]

The severity of dietary deficit varies widely between countries. In
Southeast Asia, for instance, the proportion of the population with
calorie deficit varies from 69 percent in India to 94 percent in Indonesia
and in Latin America it varies from 14 percent in Argentina to 40 percent in Brazil and Mexico (Reutlinger and Alderman 1980; Table 2).

In any one country the gaps between subgroups among the poor,
let alone between the rich and poor, are even more telling. Degrees of
poverty can be measured by how well individuals are capable of supporting themselves. We can thus identify a number of subsectors.[2]
The first is the group of subsistence farmers and employees in rural
and urban areas who manage in normal times to support themselves
and to provide adequate diets for their households. These families
typically spend the bulk of their income on the most basic and least
expensive food that can sustain human life, and over 50 percent of
their calorie intake comes from foodgrain. For them the market disruptions caused by shortages or by sharp rises in food prices can be
disastrous, possibly bringing them to the brink of starvation.

The second subsector among the poor consists of the chronically
undernourished. The severity of their deficit may vary with the mar-

ket's tides. The adults in these households may work when employment opportunities exist, but their incomes cannot purchase the necessary dietary requirement for all the family. Children and women are the first to suffer. It is estimated that children under five constitute over one-half of the world's malnourished population.

The third subsector consists of the chronically ill, the aged, the crippled, and the orphaned, who are incapable of earning any income to support themselves. Their fate thus totally depends on the benevolence of their government and the mercy of their neighbors.

The distinction between the poverty subsectors is necessary in order to design appropriate policies and to evaluate the likely effects of each policy on the different subsectors. To the generally self-supporting households of the first subsector, who participate in the economic development process, some of its fruits are likely to "trickle down" and help improve their living conditions. Nevertheless, the strategies of heavy investment in industry introduced in the 1950s and the 1960s to boost gross national product (GNP) may not suffice to solve their real problem. On the one hand, in most less developed countries (LDCs) strategies concentrating on aggregate growth have intensified rather than diminished the original inequities in the distribution of income and wealth. On the other hand, for people who can just afford an adequate diet in "normal" times, market disruptions can be devastating. Price hikes or supply shortages will force them to tighten their belts even when, as has been said, they have no notches left. For these people economic stability and food security must be achieved first, before self-reliance can be fostered by the lengthy process of development.

The second subsector among the poor, the inadequately nourished, remain on the fringe of economic development and share hardly at all in its fruits. They are trapped in a vicious circle of poverty marked by chronic undernutrition, poor health, unsanitary drinking water, large families, and crowded housing, which in turn increases their vulnerability to infectious diseases, hinders their motivation, and reduces their capacity for physical work, and thus dooms them ever to remain in hopeless poverty. The tragedy of these hundreds of millions of people who cannot obtain enough to eat and have no hope of becoming self-reliant is the crux of the food crisis of our time.

For this subsector, development at the aggregate level offers no relief. Even strategies of more equitable growth will not be very effective for them because, lacking the necessary means of production such as land, capital, skill, and even the sheer physical and mental capacity to work, they are unable to take part in the development process and share in its gains. "The lowest 40 percent," Robert McNamara once stated, "have neither been able to contribute significantly to national economic growth nor to share equitably in economic progress." Even increasing total food production will not save them from undernutrition if they do not have the money to buy this food.

The long-range solution requires fundamental structural changes within each country as well as on the international scene. Such changes will not occur overnight; they could well be the focus of the major political and social struggle of this generation and the next. But the poor and the hungry cannot wait that long.

The undernourished would be able to take care of their needs if they are given access to the market through appropriate price and income transfer programs. People in this subsector, the "unemployables" (Krishna 1974), will have to rely on more direct help, including such basic assistance as free meals and housing and personal health care, in order to relieve the permanent suffering to which they are otherwise doomed.

The third aspect of the food problem, which is associated with periodic shortages, arises partly from the instability inherent in agricultural production. Harvest failure due to bad weather forces subsistence farmers to cut their food consumption; the increase in price resulting from the shortfall in supply and the decrease in agricultural employment may diminish the purchasing power of the rural landless and urban employees, who may then find it no longer possible to purchase their normal food requirements, however small.

Local harvest failures are not the only source of instability. As the world trade in grain becomes increasingly integrated and the dependence of the LDCs on imports rises, instability in world prices becomes an important source of internal instability in many countries. Crop failure in one country jacks up the price in the world grain market, which, in turn, transmits the shock to all other countries. The developing countries are especially vulnerable to such disruptions. Foreign exchange constraints often force them to curtail their purchases on the world market if higher prices push their food import bills beyond their means.

Volatile world prices are only partly the result of nature's caprice, however. Far more significant are the effects of trade policies. Many countries, in the pursuit of domestic price stability, impose barriers on trade and thus contribute to the instability on the world market.[3] The best example is the Common Agricultural Policy (CAP) of the European Community, which makes extensive use of variable levies to control foreign trade and enhance internal price stability.

Another significant source of instability is domestic government policy. Even more so, *changes* in government policies, which may be introduced in an attempt to overcome food scarcity, often bring unforeseen and undesirable results. Sudden changes in price policies, subsidy levels, support prices, procurement and issue policies, or any other form of intervention all too often trigger an unexpected reaction on the part of individual producers or consumers and in the end may only aggravate the situation instead of relieving it. To mention only one example, in 1973 the Government of India assumed direct control over the entire domestic wheat market and prohibited all free trade. The objective was to secure a better distribution of wheat supply and in particular to ensure adequate food supplies in the deficit areas. In response, however, producers sharply reduced their output, and the end result was severe shortages in many states. (See Chapter 3 for more details.)

The food problem becomes especially acute in times of market disruption. For the masses of people in the LDCs whose consumption is already near or below subsistence level, even a small rise in price will effectively expose them to hunger. Partial stabilization via buffer stocks or trade may still leave them with smaller purchasing power than they need for a subsistence diet. A free market mechanism that allocates the scarce supply according to purchasing power and not according to needs offers no guarantee that any additional supplies delivered to the market in times of shortage will indeed reach those consumers who need it most. Thus, stabilization policies alone cannot solve the problem; additional distribution measures are required if access to the market is to be regulated according to need.

The traditional hedge against harvest failures is buffer stocks. When the combination of domestic production and national food stocks is not sufficient to meet a country's needs, food imported from abroad can supplement domestic supply. Compensating for domestic supply fluctuations with imports and exports has proved to be a powerful and efficient method of stabilization and has become the centerpiece of trade policy in many countries. However, the country can import enough food to compensate for internal supply shortfall only if it can mobilize the necessary foreign exchange. Having foreign exchange constraints, developing countries often face a dilemma: whether to reduce their food purchases abroad or forego other imports necessary for their long-range development. Again the free market mechanism, operating at the level of international trade, cannot guarantee that food will be sent to the countries that need it most. At the height of the 1972–1974 food crisis, grain was sold on a commercial basis to feed European cattle while food imports in many developing countries had to be trimmed because of the sharp rise in world price.

The fourth and perhaps the most ominous aspect of the food problem is the neo-Malthusian nightmare of a rapidly growing population approaching a level that the earth will not be able to feed. If present trends continue,[4] world population will double itself by the year 2020 to a total of 9 billion people. Population in the developing countries will be 7.5 billion, or 84 percent of the world population, as against 3.3 billion, or 74 percent, in 1980. With shrinking oil reserves, declining new sources of water and arable land, rising prices of fertilizers, deteriorating agricultural soil, and possibly even worsening climatic conditions for agriculture, the fears that it will become more difficult each year to increase food production rapidly enough to meet the needs of the growing population seem more real than ever before.

The key to a long-range solution of the food problem lies in stabilizing the world population. Even if there are no limits to growth, as the optimists tend to believe, and even though new technological breakthroughs in food production are certain to come, there might still be limits to the *pace* at which food production can grow. Without a drastic decline in the rate of population growth, global food supplies could suffer intolerable strains in the years ahead.

Population pressures not only limit the per capita availability of food but also create other problems that further aggravate and perpetuate malnutrition. For one, the growing competition for limited resources and the struggle of ever larger numbers of people to subsist force them to act in ways that damage the very cropland, pasture, forests, and water supplies on which they depend for their livelihood. Large areas of cropland are made unproductive by inappropriate cultivation practices,[5] overgrazing, deforestation, unsuitable irrigation and urbanization of farmland, thus reducing the world's capacity to feed itself.[6] At the same time, the massive and rapidly growing population exerts pressures on the health services, water supply systems, housing and education that the existing facilities cannot sustain, thus leading to their deterioration. The large number of children in poor families often entails discrimination against the youngest and weakest, especially the girls, in the distribution of the family food. This may damage their physical and mental potential and thus their chances of supporting themselves as they grow up. High rates of population growth thus become both the cause and the effect of poverty.

The desire for many children by poor people is mostly a response to their living conditions. Children come to be regarded as the poor peasant's working capital, bringing extra hands to help in the family chores and the hope of support in old age. Thus the poor, especially in rural areas, have as many children as they can, the more so because of the high rate of infant mortality, which forces them to reckon with the uncertainty of survival. Better nutrition and health, which would cut infant mortality and thus alter the family's expectations about survival of children, are therefore essential for bringing down the fertility rate.

Ironically, the immediate effect of better nutrition and health is likely to be population explosion. The initial result of better living conditions would be a decline in the mortality rate. At the same time improving the health and nutritional status of women would also have the sometimes undesirable effect of enhancing their return to fertility, thereby checking the hoped for decline in fertility rate. As the experience of the past thirty years has indeed proved, the introduction of advanced medicine and health services into the LDCs leads to a dramatic fall in the death rate and a sharp rise in the population growth rate. Within a period of ten years after World War II life expectancy in these countries rose by 30 to 50 percent. It takes much longer for the improved living conditions to bring about a reduction in the birth rate. The desire for many children, which stems from firmly entrenched customs and traditions, persists even though the conditions that made it necessary no longer exist.

In the race between food and mouths to feed, the key to reaching a state of balance lies in stabilizing the world population. It will undoubtedly require global efforts in education and family planning on a far more massive scale than any made until now.

The food problem has specific national and regional dimensions. The difficulties of coping with hunger in India, say, are markedly different from those in sub-Saharan Africa or Mexico or Egypt. As a result, solutions and strategies that have proved successful in one country may fail elsewhere if not adjusted to local social, psychological, political, and geographical conditions. Following is a sample of some national characteristics of the food problem. (See Chapter 3 for a more detailed review.)

India

India has long been thought of as doomed to Malthusian shortages and ever-increasing poverty and hunger. How can a country covering barely 2 percent of the world's habitable land, so the argument goes, feed a population of about 700 million, approximately 15 percent of the world's population, that may grow to 1.6 billion by the middle of the twenty-first century? And yet the dismal prophecies now appear far too pessimistic. For twenty years India had to import an average of 5 percent (and at times up to 14 percent) of the grain it needed, but since the mid–1970s the country has been entirely self-sufficient and has not only supplied all its needs but has also built large stocks and even exported some foodgrain. Over the 1970s the grain harvest grew by 20 percent, and this trend is expected to continue. Government estimates envisage grain output rising to 150 million metric tons (MMT) in 1985, compared with 131 MMT in the record 1978–79 harvest.

These quantities should suffice to feed all the people in India. And yet even today one-quarter of the population (170 million according to World Bank estimates) have a lower daily calorie intake than the minimum required for good health. Providing an adequate diet would take only about 8 to 10 MMT of grain a year, barely one-half the 1980–81 surplus. The problem then is not absolute shortage in food, but poverty. The undernourished will eat more only if they have the money to afford it, and their present income is not enough to buy the food they need.

The core of the country's poverty is in the 280 million people in rural areas, two-thirds of whom depend on farms smaller than the 2.5-acre minimum the World Bank estimates is needed to support a family at subsistence level,[7] and the rest of whom are landless workers. Although the land can feed the people it cannot give all of them work and sufficient income to subsist. Increasing competition for jobs forces the rural landless to accept minimal wages hardly sufficient for subsistence and effectively prevents any rise in their standard of living despite the general progress in the agricultural sector.[8]

Land distribution in India is highly unequal, but there is virtually no hope of a land reform substantial enough to raise the rural poor even to the level of minimal self-reliance. The large landowners are politically far too powerful to permit this to happen. On the other hand, migration to urban areas in pursuit of higher incomes and better living conditions has not siphoned enough people from the rural areas (as it has in most other developing countries) largely because of the slow rate of industrial growth. As a result the proportion of the population living in rural areas has not declined at all in twenty years, and pressures on the land and on employment opportunities in these areas have intensified.

The food problem in India is part of the much wider problem of poverty. The major barriers to its solution are social and institutional, not technical. The government of India may therefore have to opt for short-run measures that can at least make life more bearable for the poor and hungry.

Sub-Saharan Africa

Food shortages, both chronic and acute, have always existed in Africa. Over the past twenty years the problems have become even more distressing as agriculture has gradually deteriorated and food production has increasingly lagged behind population growth. Since 1970 locally grown food supplies on a per capita basis have declined by more than 10 percent, a trend likely to continue.

The situation is most desperate in the low income semiarid countries centered around the Sahel (Chad, Mali, Upper Volta, Gambia, Niger, and Mauritania), but is also spreading into northern Nigeria and Cameroon as well as to Ethiopia, Somalia, and parts of Kenya and Tanzania. Droughts and wars have brought these countries to the brink of outright starvation. The wretched plight of the millions of refugees has been perhaps the most shocking manifestation of hunger in our time. People in the affected regions were cut off completely from their food supplies and despite emergency deliveries from outside sources they fell victim to famine. Hundreds of thousands of people died in the 1972–1974 drought in the Sahel; many more would have died were it not for rapid and generous international assistance.

The African predicament is aggravated by extremely poor (or non-existent) roads and transportation, tribal and national rivalries, fragmentation of the markets, and petty and often cynical political considerations.

The agricultural policies of many African governments not only failed to improve the situation but sometimes made it even worse. They strongly favor exportable cash crops over the traditional food products grown mostly for self-consumption. Export products thus absorb the lion's share of agricultural credit, technical assistance, fertilizers, and pesticides. With regard to food production, government price and procurement policies are heavily biased against the rural sector and in favor of the urban sector. Food prices are often kept at an artifically low level; various financial and administrative means are devised to promote the production of wheat, which is consumed largely in the cities, while the production of sorghum and millet, once the customary diet of the poor peasants, is discouraged. The price of millet, for example, is fixed well below the free market price (sometimes by 50 percent). Government imports of wheat and sales at a subsidized price to domestic consumers especially in urban areas further trim the income of the peasants.

The experience of the 1970s of the sub-Saharan African countries made clear the need for a new approach, a drastic change in agricultural priorities. Particularly needed is more favorable treatment of the traditional farm sector, comprising more than 90 percent of the African peasants. Appropriate price policies, wider technical assistance, and larger regional stocks can contribute significantly to increasing food supply. More incentives for the production of sorghum and millet, which have the advantage of being highly tolerant to drought and adapted to the sandy soil of the region, can reduce fluctuations of food production. Promoting self-sufficiency in the farm and village can relieve the distress caused by the volatile African climate and politics.

Egypt

The food problem in Egypt has been precipitated by rapid population growth, near exhaustion of the agricultural production potential, and massive urbanization. The population is growing by 2.5 percent annually; 1 million people are added each year to the present population of 45 million (against 5 million at the beginning of the century). At the same time the agricultural sector has nearly reached the point where scope for further increase in agricultural output is very small and prohibitively costly; most of the agricultural land is already irrigated and very extensively cultivated. The search for new sources of income has driven millions of people to the cities, and over the years the proportion of people in the urban areas has risen from 20 percent at the beginning of the century to almost 50 percent today. As a result, Egypt has to rely increasingly on food imports to bridge the widening gap between its needs and its domestic production. Today almost half of the country's total food consumption is imported; the food import bill accounts for 20 percent of Egypt's total import expenditures and 50 percent of its total export revenues.

For Egypt, therefore, food security cannot mean self-sufficiency. Instead it means self-reliance: secured foreign exchange resources and dependable sources of imports. The government of Egypt has thus opted for a policy of changing the crop mix to more extensive cultivation of high-value crops, not necessarily food products; the main effort, however, is toward accelerated industrialization, with special emphasis on exportables, aimed at providing income and employment for the masses and securing the export revenues necessary to finance the food import bill.

In the broadest sense, the *food problem* refers to all of the dimensions and manifestations of hunger that have been considered in this section—across countries and regions, across income groups, and across time. It is in this sense that food security is defined as follows:

Food security represents the ability of a country or the world at large to supply the food needs of all its people at all times, now and in the future.

Several elements of this definition deserve attention. *Food needs* are determined by nutritional requirements and not by the effective demand or the actual purchasing power; *all its people* implies catering to the special needs of the poor. *At all times* refers to the good harvest years as well as the poor ones; *now and in the future* touches on the need for a steady growth in food production in order to keep pace with population growth. A comprehensive solution of the food problem must satisfy all of these aspects.

The requirements of food security may at first sight appear obvious. A clear distinction of the different facets of the food problem is by no means out of place, however, since much controversy on the subject arises from misunderstandings caused by a lack of precision with respect to the very definition of the problem and, even more, the remedies prescribed. Thus, for instance, many writers see the tremendous world potential for increasing food production as holding the promise for a long-range solution to the food problem; but this leaves unresolved the crucial issue of distributing the food to those who really need it. Others focus on smoothing out fluctuations in food supply or in real income via buffer stocks or buffer funds; but this is only one ingredient, and perhaps not even a major one at that, since stabilization schemes may prevent swings in food supply or price but cannot alleviate chronic undernutrition caused by poverty. Still other writers concentrate on strategies of equitable growth and on policies of income distribution. These policies attack the food problem caused by poverty but offer no relief for people in regions where the entire food supply has been wiped out by droughts, floods, or wars. In short, the multidimensionality of the food problem requires that the strategies of food security also be multidimensional. Complete food security will exist only when every aspect of the food problem has been resolved.

THE YEARS AHEAD—
IF PRESENT TRENDS CONTINUE

If present trends continue, the world in 2000 will be more crowded, more polluted, less stable ecologically, and more vulnerable to disruptions than the world we live in now. . . . For hundreds of millions of the desperately poor, the outlook for food and other necessities of life will be no better. For many it will be worse. Barring revolutionary advances in technology, life for most people on earth will be more precarious in 2000 than it is now—unless the nations of the world act decisively to alter the current trend.
—*Council on Environmental Quality*

The world food crisis since World War II has been dominated by three factors: first, an unprecedented increase in the world population, mostly in the developing countries, that added tens of millions of people annually to the hundreds of millions already suffering from undernutrition and hunger; second, a growing gap in the quantity and quality of food consumption among countries and among groups of people within countries; and third, a major change in the pattern of world trade of staple foods, marked by an increasing dependence of many LDCs on food imports. These patterns seem likely to continue into the twenty-first century, if present trends continue.[9]

World population during the past four decades has grown at a very rapid pace. More than 85 percent of this growth is in the LDCs, where population has been rising at an annual rate of 2.5 percent compared with 1 percent in the developed countries. Since 1970, however, signs of declining fertility rates have been noticed in a number of LDCs, giving rise to the hope that a movement toward more balanced growth may have started. Even taking these trends into account the world population is still expected to grow between 1980 and 2000 by more than 40 percent to a total of 6.35 billion people. These projections are presented in Table 1-1. The LDCs will account for more than 90 percent of the growth; their share in the world population rose from 66 percent in 1960 to 74 percent in 1980 and will reach 79 percent by the turn of the century.

Improved health is expected to contribute to a sharp decline (35 percent) in the death rate and an increase (10 percent) in life expectancy in the LDCs. These effects will be partially counterbalanced by a decline in the fertility rate from an average of 4.3 children per fertile woman in 1975 to 3.3 in 2000. (See Table 1-2.)

Income disparities between the rich and the poor nations are expected to widen in the next 20 years. Despite the more rapid growth projected for the LDCs, their rising populations will allow only a modest increase in the income per capita. Over the 25 years from 1975 to 2000 the LDCs are expected to grow at an annual rate of 4.5 percent, against 3.3 percent in the developed nations.[10] However,

Table 1-1. Population Projections.

	Population (millions)	Percentage of World Population	Annual Rate of Growth (%)[a]
1980			
World	4.47	. . .	1.78
More developed regions	1.17	26	0.68
Less developed regions	3.30	74	2.18
2000			
World	6.35	. . .	1.70
More developed regions	1.32	21	0.51
Less developed regions	5.03	79	2.02

[a]Growth rate of the preceding 5 years.

Source: CEQ 1980.

Table 1-2. Population Projections: Estimated Birth and Death Rates.

	Crude Birth Rate (per 1,000)		Crude Death Rate (per 1,000)		Rate of Natural Increase (%)[a]	
	1975	2000	1975	2000	1975	2000
More developed regions	16.1	15.2	9.6	10.4	0.6	0.5
Less developed regions	35.9	28.4	13.4	8.7	2.2	2.0

Source: CEQ 1980.

[a]Rate of increase in the preceding 5 years.

income per capita in the LDCs is expected to grow by 54 percent over the same period, compared with 105 percent in the industrial countries. As a result by the turn of the century GNP per capita in the LDCs will be only 5 percent of its level in the developing countries compared with 7 percent in 1975. (See Table 1-3.)

Food production is expected to be 90 percent higher in 2000 than in 1970. This assumes, rather optimistically, a growth rate over the 30-year period of about 2.2 percent, which is roughly equal to the high growth rates in the 1950s and the 1960s (including the period of the "Green Revolution"). Most of the increase in food production will come about through intensive use of technology, especially fertilizers, pesticides, and irrigation, while land under cultivation is expected to increase by only 4 percent.[11] World grain production is projected to increase by 80 percent from 1973-1975 to 2000. In the industrial countries grain production will increase by 75 percent (two-thirds of this coming from the United States), while in the LDCs it will increase by 140 percent. (See Table 1-4.)

As agriculture in many regions spreads into marginal land subject to diminishing returns and existing cropland gradually deteriorates under the pressure to increase production, the rise in agricultural productivity may slow and even show a decline in some regions (notably Africa and the Middle East).[12] Continuing hikes in oil prices will further raise the price of energy-intensive inputs such as fertilizers, pesticides, and fuels. As a result, farmers' production costs will continue the rapid rise that began in the early 1970s, and food prices, after many years of remaining steady or even showing a decline, will double (in real terms) from 1970 to 2000. This increase will be most keenly felt by the poor, whose income will not rise rapidly enough to maintain their purchasing power.

Barring some dramatic changes, average food consumption per capita from 1970 to 2000 will increase by only 15 percent. Furthermore, the average figure conceals wide differences between geographical regions, between countries, and between income groups with regard to their share in this growth. In South Asia, North Africa, and the Middle East average food consumption per capita will barely improve, and in the other African LDCs it may actually decline. (See Table 1-5.)

The rising population in the LDCs will further increase their dependence on food imports. Most of the food-deficient LDCs were self-sufficient or even net exporters only 30 years ago. In 1973-1975

Table 1-3. Per Capita GNP Projections (1975 U.S. dollars).

	1975	Average Annual Growth Rate 1975–1985 (%)	1985	Average Annual Growth Rate 1985–2000 (%)	2000
More developed countries	4,325	3.2	5,901	2.5	8,485
USSR and Eastern Europe	2,591	2.4	3,279	2.1	4,472
Market economy industrial countries	5,431	3.4	7,597	2.6	11,117
Less developed countries	382	2.8	501	2.1	587
Africa	405	2.2	505	1.4	620
Asia and Oceania	306	2.7	398	2.3	557
Latin America	1,005	2.6	1,304	1.8	1,715

Source: CEQ 1980.

Table 1-4. Projections of Grain and Total Food Production.

	Grain					Total Food
	Production 1973–1975 (MMT)	Annual Growth Rate (%)			Production 2000 (MMT)	Annual Growth Rate (%) 2000/1970
		1973–1975/ 1951–1955	1985/ 1973–1975	2000/ 1985		
World	1,203	n.a.	2.6	2.8	2,170	2.2
Industrial countries	402	2.5	2.1	1.8	710	1.2
Less developed countries	306	2.8	3.5	2.9	735	3.0

Source: CEQ 1980.

Table 1-5.   Per Capita Grain and Total Food Consumption—
Projected Changes (%).

	Grain 2000/1973-1975	Total Food 2000/1970
Industrialized countries	+35.6	+21.2
Less developed countries	+12.8	+8.6
Latin America	+16.7	+25.1
North Africa, Middle East	+6.9	+2.2
Other African LDCs	-12.3	-19.1
South Asia	+5.4	+5.8
Southeast Asia	+25.1	+14.6
East Asia	+26.7	+27.3

Source: CEQ 1980.

grain imports in these countries totaled 45 MMT and covered 13 percent of their total grain consumption. By 2000 their grain imports are expected to rise to at least 90 MMT.[13] (See Table 1-6.) The doubling of grain imports together with the doubling in food prices may strain the foreign exchange resources and the credit position of the poorer LDCs to the point of severely damaging their development plans, thus undermining the efforts to improve their food supply in the years ahead.

Despite this sobering outlook, the elimination of hunger is within the reach of mankind. The agricultural revolution of this century, marked by the introduction of more efficient crop varieties and animal strains and by the development and use of chemical fertilizers and sophisticated techniques of controlling diseases and insect pests, inspires hope and even confidence that the world is capable of producing enough food for all its inhabitants. The technologies and know-how for producing more food have already been developed and are, at least in theory, available to all. Their transfer to the LDCs, with appropriate adjustments, is likely to multiply the food potential in these countries several times over, given the wide gap in productivity, technological know-how, and advanced means of production that now exists between the developed and the developing countries. Thus, for instance, the rice yield per hectare in the LDCs is only one-quarter of the yield in the developed countries, and the productivity of the farmworker in the LDCs is on average only one-thirteenth of that of his counterpart in the developed countries. In India there is on average

Table 1-6. World Grain Trade (MMT).

	1969-1971	1973-1975	1985	2000
World export				
Developed exporters	68.3	100.6	135	180
United States	39.9	72.9	95	130
Other developed exporters	28.4	27.7	40	45
Developing exporters	11.3	13.1	25	45
Total	79.6	113.7	160	225
World importers				
Developed importers	36.2	39.0	61	98
Centrally planned imports	5.7	24.0	29	37
Developing importers	29.3	45.3	70	90

Source: CEQ 1980.

one tractor per 1,000 hectares of cropland. In the United States there are twenty-three. The Indian farmer uses only one-sixth of the fertilizers per hectare used by the American farmer. (As a result of these and many other differences, the United States is producing 2.5 times more grain than India on a smaller area and with a work force amounting to only 3 percent of the Indian rural work force.) Wide differences in productivity even between states in India itself suggest that the scope for increasing food production is far from exhausted. If, for instance, other regions of India with suitable soil and climatic conditions were to match the agricultural productivity of the Punjab, India could *double* its grain production. At the same time, demographers point out that more intensive efforts in providing family planning services would help to stabilize the world population much earlier and thus at a much more restricted population level than is presently thought possible.

The issue of ending world hunger does not hinge on the technical and physical ability to produce enough food. Instead, as the report of the U.S. Presidential Commission on World Hunger argues, the issue "comes down to a question of political choice." The report continues: "The quantities of food and money needed to wipe out hunger are presently available and the necessary human ingenuity also abounds. If the appropriate political choice is made, the world can overcome the worst aspects of hunger and malnutrition by the year 2000" (p. 58).

THE SHORT RUN AND THE LONG RUN IN
THE QUEST FOR FOOD SECURITY

Substantial agreement exists among scholars and among policymakers about the long-range strategies to cope with the food problem. These strategies can be grouped into three main categories: population control, growth, and distribution.

Population control is needed to reduce the strains on global food supply. It requires economic assistance to improve the social and economic conditions of the poor and to reduce their motivation for large families; it also needs intensive efforts to make family planning services and effective means of contraception more widely available.

Growth is the counterpart of population control in the ratio between food and mouths to feed. The World Bank (1981) estimates (see preceding section for more details) that with a higher rate of economic development, poverty and undernutrition will steadily be pushed back, but, if present trends continue, poverty will affect an ever larger number of people. By the end of this century the difference between the two scenarios may amount to as many as 250 million people living in absolute poverty.

Economic development at the aggregate level would not suffice to solve the food problem. The rapid growth that most LDCs experienced during the 1960s and 1970s did not bring the expected relief of poverty because the fruits of the growth process did not trickle down to the poor.

A United Nations document of several years ago acknowledged the failure of the aggregate growth strategies:

> National or macro-growth policies have generally failed to remove, or in some cases even to reduce, wide disparities in the level of living or quality of life. These disparities persist even in conditions of mass poverty. . . . Their intractability retards the achievement of an adequate level of living for all people, threatens national unity in some countries, and everywhere impedes the development of human resources for development. (U.N. Department of Economic and Social Affairs 1974:3)

The U.S. Presidential Commission of World Hunger reached a similar conclusion:

> Even with the highest global growth rate that can be expected, vast numbers of human beings will remain mired in absolute poverty by the year

2000. Assuming that all or nearly all of these extremely poor people will also be hungry . . . (then) even the most rapid economic growth that can reasonably be anticipated will not be enough to end hunger by the year 2000. (1980:31–32)

More direct measures are thus needed in order to overcome poverty and malnutrition and to assure that the available resources and existing food supplies will indeed reach those who need it most.

Attention must be given to promoting the growth of agriculture and especially to increasing food production. In the long run the capacity to produce enough food to feed all the people may become the biggest challenge in the battle against hunger. Technological innovations, transfer of advanced technologies into areas where productivity is still very low, and wider distribution of sophisticated means and methods of production such as fertilizers, pesticides, and agricultural machinery are all essential.

Distributive measures can be implemented at two levels. They can be confined to the additional income generated in the growth process, or they can be extended also to existing income and wealth. Conventional fiscal policies and most other distribution measures focus mostly on the distribution of new income and seek a more favorable distribution of the fruits of economic growth and a larger share for the poor. Progressive taxation, income transfers, discriminatory price policies (such as targeted subsidies or food stamps), specific programs aimed at meeting specific needs of the poor in food, health, housing are all measures aimed at enhancing the share of the poor in the nation's resources in general and in its food supply in particular. Collectively they have become known as the *basic needs approach*. Their combined effect is to regulate the market so that the poor can command a larger share of these specific resources than they can under the normal market conditions.

A simulation exercise undertaken at the World Bank demonstrates the effectiveness of distributive measures that seek more equitable growth. It estimates that even in a high-growth scenario more than 500 million people (350 million of them in the LDCs) will still be living in absolute poverty by the turn of the century. If, however, government policies manage to change the distribution of the additional income so that 40 percent of the increase in national income (instead of 25 percent as in the past) flows to the poorer 60 percent of the population, the ranks of the poorest would be diminished to less than 350 million.

The second group of distribution measures and by far the more difficult to apply concerns the reallocation of existing wealth. The most difficult measure of all within this group is agrarian reform.

The patterns of land ownership in most LDCs, where a few wealthy landlords own most of the land, are among the most important causes that deepen and perpetuate poverty. The majority of the rural population in these countries still make their living by farming land they do not own—as tenants, sharecroppers, or agricultural laborers. In Latin America and South Asia small farmers constitute about four-fifths of the agricultural population, yet they work only one-fifth and one-third of the land, respectively. These inequitable land tenure patterns severely retard agricultural production, lead to inefficient use of farm land, interfere with adoption of new technologies, and prevent the small tenants from reaping the benefits of agricultural development policies. The need for comprehensive land reform is clear and indisputable; it is needed not only to increase total food production but also to bring the small tenants to the base line of self-reliance. And yet such a reform would require so profound a transformation in the socioeconomic structure that politically it would be extremely difficult to achieve.[14]

In most countries in which a thoroughgoing land reform has taken place it has been accompanied by drastic, sometimes violent changes in the political and economic system. The examples of the Soviet Union, China, Cuba, and even South Korea, Peru, and Tanzania, raise anew the fundamental question of whether a democratic system is capable of successfully coming to grips with an issue as complex as land reform.

In contrast to the broad agreement with respect to the long-range objectives and strategies, sharp and fierce disagreements often arise with respect to the short-range. An accurate typology of the issues involved can go a long way toward clarifying the matter.

In fact there are two sides to the problem in the short-range. One is concerned with present trends as these will affect the food situation in the future; the other with current food problems and the plight of those now suffering from hunger. The former focuses on present measures to be taken as part of a long-range strategy and the latter on immediate actions aimed at relieving if not solving the suffering of today.

Disagreement over practical measures may arise because the two aspects sometimes conflict; the needs of today may have to be traded off against the needs of tomorrow. Efforts to step up food production are the focus of the long-range strategy, but they offer no comfort to people who are starving today. Welfare programs for the immediate relief of the poor and the hungry may actually impede the long-range solution, since they require resources also needed for long-range development projects.

Scholars are often (and perhaps too much) concerned with the first aspect, the short-range, as part of a continuous, long-range process; policymakers on the other hand are often overwhelmed by the magnitude of today's problems, much to the neglect of the long-range. This may account for the gap between the optimism with which academic conferences are routinely concluded and the despair that is sometimes expressed by those engaged in day-to-day policymaking. More important, it is this difference in perspective that makes many policy guidelines originating from the long-range outlook much too vague and sometimes entirely useless when it comes to practical formulation of policies from day to day. Fostering equitable growth, promoting self-reliance, raising food production, or creating purchasing power among the poor and the hungry are all essential ingredients in the long-range solution of the food problem. But when expressed in such general terms they can offer no guidance to policymakers who, in the face of severe political and economic constraints, must weigh the necessities of today against those of tomorrow, the needs of one group of people against those of another, the requirements of one geographical area against those of the others. To be useful, guidelines must not only specify the exact form and assess the effectiveness of the proposed policy instruments but must also estimate their opportunity costs in terms of objectives foregone. By how much would the development process have to be slowed if resources are directed to welfare programs? What long-range effects on agricultural production can be anticipated if today's food prices are suppressed in order to maintain a minimally adequate consumption for the poor? To be practical, moreover, these guidelines would have to be translated into specific policy recommendations such as the structure of price policies, the form of welfare and other aid programs, the pattern of trade policies.

Perhaps the most compelling reason for putting greater emphasis on the short-range is the plight of today's hungry, who might not live to see the long-range. There are other reasons as well. The poverty and hunger of today further aggravate poverty and hunger in the future. Hungry infants and young children, among whom malnutrition takes its greatest toll, are suffering mental and physical damage that will limit their ability to support themselves and thus doom them forever to the vicious circle of poverty and hunger. Second, policies that apply to the long-range will necessarily have both direct and indirect effects on the problems in the short-range and vice-versa. A familiar example, the policy of many developing countries to hold down agricultural prices in order to lower food prices in urban areas, has severe repercussions in the long-range by repressing food production, discouraging farmers from adopting new technologies, and impairing the employment opportunities and thus the income of the rural landless.

To paraphrase a Chinese expression, the long march toward a comprehensive solution of the food problem starts with the steps taken today. These steps must attend to both the short- and the long-range aspects of the problem, which are equally pressing, and with proper attention to design and planning, the steps can be mutually reinforcing.

CAN THE MARKET SYSTEM COPE?

The persistence of widespread undernutrition in a world that produces ample food for all can only be construed as a measure of the global social order's failure to satisfy human needs. —*Eric Eckholm*

More than any other social or economic phenomenon, the persistence of hunger in a world that produces ample food and the existence of chronic undernutrition at the same time as market forces allocate agricultural resources for frivolous uses raise serious, indeed passionate questions about the efficacy of the international order in general and the market system in particular. Does a system that allows the dogs and horses of the rich to "eat up the food of the children of the poor" (in the words of William Hazlitt to Malthus) indeed work in the best interest of society? Do laissez-faire capitalism and social justice represent different or even conflicting values? The presence of hundreds of millions of hungry people in a world that has attained an unprecedented level of riches and technological advancement casts a giant shadow and is held up by some people as proof that the capitalistic system, efficient though it may be, is inherently unjust.

"What constitutes the well being of a man?" Thomas Carlyle asked in the nineteenth century some 150 years ago (see Carlyle 1915); "With hunger preying on him, his contentment is likely to be small. But even with abundance, his discontent, his real misery may be great." And discontented indeed the people will be if in exchange for "abundance" they have to accept restraints on their freedom or if the basic right to food must be traded for the right to justice. No person can accept "freedom" as a substitute for food, but is it really necessary for freedom to be sacrificed in order to secure nourishment? Does it really come down to a choice between a free market and a centrally planned economy? These are the questions with which the world's economic systems must come to grips in the face of persistent hunger.

On some issues the dilemma for the market system, indeed for the democratic system as a whole, is crystal clear. If, for instance, a long-range solution of the food problem requires profound changes in land ownership, how could it be achieved without sacrificing economic freedom? Could such changes, which would inevitably alienate powerful segments of society, be carried out in a democratic state? Or must land reform necessarily be accompanied by fundamental transformations in the socioeconomic system that may even take the revolutionary path as they did in the Soviet Union, China, and Cuba?

The different experiences of India and China since the late 1940s are sometimes invoked to make a case against the ability of the market system to cope with the food problem. Both countries face massive population problems, and both have experienced similar rates of growth in their agricultural sectors. And yet hunger and malnutrition are still widely prevalent in India, while in China they have been all but eliminated. China's solution was to enforce an egalitarian distribution of land, income, and, above all, the available food supply—but it took no less than a total transformation of the economic system and an abdication of individual liberties for China to achieve this goal.

It is left for the champions of the market system to prove that a competitive market is not only the most efficient way of encouraging work, effort, and productive contribution but in the final analysis will also be to the greatest advantage of the greatest number of people, including the masses of the poor who are too powerless to claim their share, and to prove that in its dealing with the food problem the market system will be able to honor the most basic of human rights: the right to eat. The market is governed by the laws of supply and demand. It bows to those who bid the highest price and is dominated by purchasing power, effective demand, and the ability to pay. Although it does allocate resources efficiently, it is not capable of dealing with normative questions or questions of right or wrong such as: What *ought* to be each individual's share in the nation's resources? Does the distribution of resources as determined in the market accord with criteria of justice or basic needs?

Julius Nyerere, the president of Tanzania, once observed that "the market laws of supply and demand mean that the wealth of the few diverts the world's resources—including the labor and others—from meeting the real but ineffective demand of the poor into satisfying the desires of the rich. Land and labor are used to cultivate grapes instead of grain; palaces are built instead of houses for the workers and peasants" (quoted in U.S. Presidential Commission on World Hunger 1980:19). S. George presses the point home when she notes that "rich sources of protein like fishmeal which could perfectly well be used for human food are processed and exported . . . to feed America's 35 million dogs and 30 million cats" (1976:173).

It is in the nature of the market that all comers strive to improve their own lot; it is driven by self-interest, and the only relevant consideration is efficiency. The market system allocates resources in a "right" way, in the normative sense, only if one accepts the existing distribution of income and wealth as the desirable one. The competitive allocation is always "optimal" in the Pareto sense but, as Amartya Sen once remarked, the economy can be Pareto optimal and yet perfectly disgusting. Economic freedom (which libertarians like Milton Friedman would regard as a necessary condition for all freedom) and individual sovereignty are the market's fundamental principles; all individuals and businesses are assumed to have the right to act autonomously and with complete freedom of choice (barring special cases such as externalities). These principles form the foundation of the democratic system itself, and indeed a free market is essential for democracy. There are, however, fundamental differences between laissez-faire capitalism and the democratic system.

Whereas a democracy counts people, the market system weighs them by their wealth. The principle of "one person one vote" that is the basis of democracy is replaced in the market by the principle of "one dollar (or one rupee) one vote." The basic economic decisions of what to produce and for whom, made in the market via dollar voting, will therefore differ from the decisions that would be made by the state as a democratic representation of the collective will of the people and guided by the principle that all people should be treated equally.

This must create a conflict. The rule that civilization has followed for settling it is the supremacy of the state. In other words, the decisions of the state must take precedence over the decisions of the market. This can be done, however, only if constraints are placed on the market. Hence so long as income and wealth are unequally distributed there is an inherent conflict between democracy and laissez-faire capitalism. The power of the wealthy few conferred on them by their wealth would have to be held in check and their economic freedom curtailed in order to assure that the resource allocation in the market will not negate the principle of equal justice for all or the other norms that form the basis of society. (Realistically, unequal income distribution leads in turn to unequal distribution of political power, and this may vitiate the democratic principles of equal justice and equal rights. Even then the difference between the market and state would still exist.) Constraints on economic freedom are therefore not counter to the spirit of democracy but an immanent part of it.

According to the Rousseauan notion of the social contract of association (*pacte d'association*), a democratic society is formed by a free agreement to join in a common enterprise involving no abdication of any participant's rights. Such a notion must, by virtue of the unequal distribution of income and the resulting conflict, give way to the Hobbesian notion of the contract of government (*pacte de gouvernement*), which postulates an initial agreement on certain fundamental tenets to which all participants must be subject.

A democratic government is responsible for carrying out the social contract and therefore has the authority to restrict the free play of the market. Whenever necessary it must intervene in the market in order to ensure that economic decisions conform with the general will of the people, as expressed by their democratic vote. Since income and wealth are unequally distributed, the marketplace is not a resort of absolute freedom, as some libertarians would have it, but the very first place in which some measure of government authoritarianism should be exercised.

Laissez-faire capitalism has no room for considerations of right or wrong. The Darwinian struggle for the survival and well-being of self-centered individuals, which makes the market so highly efficient, allows only the fittest to outlast and cannot afford "soft" ethical or moral considerations that may require one to sacrifice one's own fitness or satisfaction. Herbert Spencer, the nineteenth-century champion of laissez-faire, carried this argument to its logical conclusion when he noted that "the command 'if any would not work neither should he eat' is simply a Christian enunciation of the law that . . . creature not energetic enough to maintain itself must die."

The market does not, however, operate in a political vacuum. It is part of a socioeconomic system whose basic elements are ethical norms that define what is right and what is wrong. Society is first and foremost a moral entity. It comprises many more elements than does a mere economic contract. In a very fundamental sense, society is the sum of its norms. What makes society possible, to echo a familiar question, are its norms. They are the bonds that hold society together and secure its cohesiveness and continuity. Although the market is driven by people's self-interest, it is subject to the constraints and guidance of a government that, as the representative of all aspects of society, must see to it that these norms will prevail.[15] Capitalism and democracy need each other, in the words of Arthur Okun, "to put some rationality into equality and some humanity into efficiency" (1975:120).

Whereas the market accepts the existing distribution of income and wealth, the democratic system may question its desirability and the government has the authority to alter it if so desired by the majority of the people. When the voices of the poor and the hungry are too weak to be heard in the marketplace, the government must represent them in the name of equal justice and equal rights on the one hand and human benevolence on the other. In short, the battle against hunger is well within the domain and the capacity of the democratic state.

Its ability to cope with hunger is above all a matter of political choice, which it is quite capable of making and carrying through. It may demand a great deal of commitment and dedication; it may also involve some constraints on economic freedom; but it does *not* necessitate a fundamental transformation of the socioeconomic system, nor require an abdication of individual liberties.

Ralf Dahrendorf distinguishes between two types of social rationality, market and plan (1968:215–31). In essence, these can be related to the two concepts of freedom that have long been debated by political scientists, namely freedom as a universal reality, distinguished by the absence of any constraint whatsoever, and freedom as a universal possibility, which is a state to be achieved.

The market rationality assumes that if the natural economic and social forces that motivate the actions of all individuals and societies are allowed to take their course undisturbed and unrestricted, they will produce the best possible solution at any given time. Plan rationality

> urges that the powers of human reason be applied to the task of designing and building the just society or, more modestly, to solving certain social problems . . . [it] consists in the consideration of every step along the way from a problem to its solution, and in the creation of suitable organizational conditions for keeping problems under control. Solutions do not come about by themselves, but only as a result of controlled and controlling action. (Dahrendorf 1968:218)

The basic element of plan rationality, indeed its raison d'être, is the set of norms that define a code of conduct and determine the strategy for the planner and thus for the economy. The basic economic decisions, namely what commodities to produce and for whom, are worked out by the planner in advance down to the last detail according to the underlying norms. Plan rationality in this "pure" form thus leaves no room for individual choice and prohibits any actions that conflict with the planner's decisions. It may require, for example, that private enterprise be abolished, private property confiscated, and individual freedom severely curtailed.

Between these two extreme forms of rationality the liberal school of thought proposes collective rationality and suggests as its model the welfare state. Collective rationality allows private enterprise and respects individual freedom but only within the boundaries of the social order. The social order itself does not demand a detailed and comprehensive plan for action as in central planning, but rather a general agreement on a set of basic values. It still requires certain constraints on individuals, however, and the government has the moral authority, the responsibility, and the power to enforce these constraints.

Plan rationality is fundamentally different from collective rationality in both approach and implementation. Plan rationality assumes direct and complete control over the entire economy and replaces the rules of the market by a system of state laws. In the actual implementation the planner usually sets detailed *quantity* goals for the individual units in the economy that conform with the goals and the norms that form the basis of the entire plan.[16]

Collective rationality, by contrast, maintains the basic structure of the market system and upholds its basic rules. The government intervenes in the market only to enforce the constraints implied by the general principles that define the social contract. In the words of Wassily Leontief, " 'sails' of profit catch the wind and move the ship of state, while the 'rudder' of planning gives the economy and society better direction" (1974:103).

A distinctive feature of collective rationality is that in its implementation the price system continues to be the basis for economic planning and the main signal according to which resources are allocated. Individuals and businesses retain their sovereignty inasmuch as they may choose their inputs and outputs, given the prices they face. Government intervention mostly takes the form of modifying the price system via tariffs, taxes, subsidies, and the like, so as to affect the choice made by the individual units and thereby also the entire resource allocation in the economy. Price policies thus become the main channel through which the government guides the economy and if necessary enforces constraints on its operation.

Two comments connect this somewhat theoretical discussion to the more mundane analysis of the balance of the book. First, land reform does not fall into the domain of policies that observe the basic rules of the market; it is perhaps the most striking example of government constraint on economic freedom, and raises difficult questions about individual rights and sometimes also about efficiency. The problematic aspects of this issue will not be discussed further here, except for noting that collective rationality does not restrict the government to operating only within the framework of the market play and that constraints such as those involved in land reform are not in violation but sometimes even an imperative of the democratic spirit when they are motivated by the interests of the majority of the people. (Of course the borderline is extremely narrow and has all too often been crossed in the name of the public interest.)

Second, for many people government intervention through the price system is associated with "horrors" of multiple pricing that in some countries reached monstrous proportions and negative marginal utility. Against these examples one can give other examples in which government intervention in the price system functioned quite smoothly and effectively. In other words, poor execution does not negate the principle. Even more important, as shown in Chapter 3, where experiences of some countries are discussed, in the vast majority

of cases in which an alternative course of action was taken, the results were much less satisfying, to say the least, and led to an ever-rising Parkinsonian spiral, with decrees issued to repair the damage of previous decrees and new bureaucracies formed to protect people against the evils of previous bureaucracies. The search for the most suitable policy cannot realistically be expected to end with the best of all options, the *optimum optimorum*. Given the multitude of economic, social and political constraints, it is often, as somebody has once put it, a choice between the very bad and the worse.

FOOD POLICIES IN A MARKET ECONOMY

In his 1976 Elmhirst lecture, Theodore W. Schultz concluded that the performance of the agricultural sectors of the countries of the world has been decisively determined by the actions of their governments through their respective economic policies. Yet, observed Schultz, when governments do intervene, they seem to have a penchant for doing more harm than good. (See Schultz 1977.) A U.S. Department of Agriculture survey (USDA 1974) of fifty developing countries seems to confirm this somber observation. It reveals that forty-six of the fifty countries have policies that discourage expansion of the agricultural sector. These policies include controls on the selling price of producers or on the retail price to consumers, noncompetitive procurement, export controls or taxes, exchange rate controls, government imports for sale at a subsidized price, and restrictions on domestic movements of agricultural products. In India, for example, the price of rice has been consistently held below the world price, thus depressing production and discouraging the adoption of high-yielding varieties. Another example is the rice premium that for almost two decades was the centerpiece of the food policy in Thailand. This levy on rice exports depressed the domestic price of rice, thus benefiting urban consumers even though their average income was higher than that of the farmers. D. Gale Johnson has estimated that between 1966 and 1970 the levy had the effect of decreasing rice production by 1.5 million tons (or about 15 percent of actual production during the period) and reducing foreign exchange earnings by an average of $250 million a year (1977:19). In Tanzania the official price of coffee was set at only one-sixth of its price in its neighbor Kenya. As a result, nearly 30 percent of the crop was smuggled by

coffee growers to Kenya; many peasants reverted to producing food, mostly for self-consumption, and parts of the country slipped back into basic barter economy.

Food policies in a market economy can be grouped into five main categories:

1.   Price policies
2.   Supplementary feeding programs
3.   Distribution policies (including agrarian reform)
4.   Agricultural and rural development programs
5.   Aggregate growth policies

The second category includes welfare-like programs that offer the most immediate relief of undernutrition and specific food deficiencies. These pivotal short-term relief measures work directly on the affected population and can thus achieve meaningful results even in the absence of more fundamental measures. They are also relatively easy to implement from a political point of view and can attract foreign aid in money and personnel. Obviously, these measures cannot solve the fundamental food problem and can only help in the transition period until other more radical measures can take effect.

Agrarian reform is by far the most difficult and, in the view of some, also the most important policy measure toward a long-range solution of the food problem in many countries. It is an uphill battle against very powerful segments of society, however, and in any event it may take a very long time before its effects are felt.

A word of caution about land reform may be in order. While many share the view, as expressed for instance by Claire Whittemore (1981:12), that "unjust land tenure system and the political, economic and social policies which enable them to prevail are the chief causes of hunger and poverty in the Third World today," the experience in a number of countries suggests that land reform is by no means a guarantee for a successful solution. In Peru, for instance, a radical land reform took place shortly after the military takeover in 1968, transforming most of the country's large ranches into peasant cooperatives. The peasants were ill-prepared for the transition, so that bad management and lack of capital hurt their productivity and forced them to eat valuable livestock and seed grains. Between 1970 and 1980 per capita agricultural production fell by nearly 40 percent, resulting in widespread food shortages and leading to meat rationing.

In Tanzania, 11 million peasants were moved during 1974–75 into 8,300 *ujamaa* villages or agricultural collectives, this land reform sometimes forcibly uprooting people from their ancestral homes. The result was a disastrous decline in agricultural output from which the country has recovered only after several years.

Price policies are the main policy instruments being applied in the market economies to cope with the food problem. They are the core of both short-range and long-range solutions. In some countries price policies with regard to food products are the most important policy decisions affecting the lives of the majority of the people. Price policies with regard to food products are the central subject of this book.

To be sure, this category contains a wide range of policies, and the emphasis on "price" may be somewhat misleading. Included are food stock policies to stabilize food prices; subsidies to the entire population or to specific target groups, via food stamps or other financial arrangements or directly through a public distribution system; various support programs to farmers, such as floor price, income maintenance, input subsidies, credit provisions, but also direct government procurement programs; and various trade policies, exchange controls, variable levies, and so on that may be either an integral part of the government food policy or indirectly influence the agricultural sector.

In these broad terms, price policies are interwoven with the other categories of government food policy. Agricultural and rural development, for instance, would be accelerated if the farmers, especially the small farmers, could be induced to adopt new technologies, if agricultural inputs such as fertilizers were financially within their reach, and if they could afford investment in irrigation facilities and other improvements. All these categories depend very heavily on the government price and credit policies. Farmers will lack adequate incentives to take advantage of improved farming methods if the government pricing policy is to hold down the price of food crops, if they have no access to credit, if price fluctuations endanger the return on their investments, and so on. Even the pace of technological innovation is affected by government pricing policies. In the final analysis, price rather than necessity or moral obligation is the mother of progress.

Pricing policies are also an important vehicle for redistribution. Their direct effect is on the distribution of the available food supply;

it is only through the resulting income effect that they will influence the income distribution as well. The major reason for the government to be actively involved, through its pricing and other policies, in the allocation of food among consumers is the need to secure a more favorable distribution of the available food supply and a larger share for the poor, which cannot await the long-range policies of income and wealth distribution to have their effect. The government can and indeed should intervene at least to contain if not entirely ward off undernutrition, even before dealing with the poverty problem and working out a comprehensive solution to the food problem. In the words of the U.S. Presidential Commission of World Hunger, "people who are poor need not be hungry as well." The commission concluded that "food subsidy programs seem to represent the best path for providing massive temporary aid for hungry people in or near urban areas." They noted, however, that although these programs have proved to be effective, "the drain on the public treasury can be very high, administrative difficulties are usually severe, and there is a serious danger of undercutting prices that local farmers should receive for their own harvests" (1980:40ff).

Price policies are also crucial in determining the composition of production and consumption. On the production side, price policies in many LDCs have been responsible for the move toward cash crops and away from traditional nonmarketable crops such as millet, a move that proved to be highly undesirable, even disastrous, for the farmers. On the consumption side, price policies can play an important role in changing the consumption habits of the very rich and the very poor, a change that some hold to be essential for solving the food problem. The arguments against "calorie-wasting" food consumption habits of the rich have a great deal of passion though not always the same degree of merit. The direct consumption of grain, characteristic of low-income diets, so the argument goes, provides a much more efficient source of calories than grain-fed animal products. On average five to six units of grain go to produce one unit of beef. Yet, cereals and beef provide weight for weight roughly the same number of calories, while the net protein utilization in beef is only 50 percent higher (USDA 1974:14). It is indeed a fact that the large share of meat, milk, poultry, and eggs in the diet of people in the industrial countries diverts large quantities of grain from human beings to animals. Only part of the animal feed supplied is foodgrain, however, while another part, grazing, has no substitute in human food. At present, however, nearly one-third of the world grain production is used for animal feed, and appropriate price policies to change the consumption habits of the people in the developed countries may release some grain for human consumption. This was vividly demonstrated in the crisis of 1974–75, in which prices rose sharply and demand declined by nearly 45 MMT. Significantly, 80 percent of this decline in grain consumption occurred in the United States as wheat and other grains were diverted from domestic livestock feeding into exports (for more details see Crosson and Fredrick (1977)).

Changing consumption patterns among the poor is equally important. Thus, for instance, soybeans can play a significant role in overcoming protein-deficient malnutrition, especially in Southeast Asia, provided that the people can be induced to include them in their diet. They contain 40 percent protein and 20 percent oils and are rich in calories, minerals, and vitamins and could be an excellent substitute for fish and meat. Although eating habits are notoriously difficult to change, experience shows that appropriate price policies can be amazingly persuasive.

The scope for substitution in production and consumption proves that for all practical purposes the potential for increasing food production is limitless and the Malthusian race between food and mouths to feed should never be lost. The full measure of this potential must take into account not only the growth in arable land and productivity but also the possibility of using appropriate price policies to divert land and other resources to the production of food.

Even in the efforts at population control price policies can play a part. As an illustration of the ingenuity that abounds in the market system, I would like to quote from an admittedly far-fetched suggestion made by Kenneth Boulding, who proposed a system of marketable licenses to have children:

> Each girl on approaching maturity would be presented with a certificate which will entitle its owner to have, say, 2.2 children or whatever number would ensure [a zero population growth]. The unit of these certificates might be 'decichild,' and accumulation of ten of these units would permit a woman in maturity to have one legal child. We would then set up a market in these units in which the rich and the philoprogenitive would purchase them from the poor, the nuns, the maiden aunts and so on. (1965:135–136)[17]

Somewhat less surrealistic would be a plan of marketable marriage licensing. According to this scheme, each couple would need a license to get married. However, instead of imposing a rigid minimum age constraint, as is presently done in a number of countries (China being the most noteworthy example), the scheme would impose progressively higher license fees at younger ages. This would allow more freedom of choice while at the same time enforcing the necessary social controls. The progressive fees may also cause differential reproduction rates of the different income groups, with the more affluent having the higher rate. As always, the most difficult question, which I leave out at this stage, concerns the sanctions to be taken against those who violate the arrangement.

THE CHALLENGE AHEAD

The food problem, more than any other social or economic phenomenon, has put the global order on trial. Along with demands for a radical change and a New International Economic Order, there are also expressions of despair or cold realism claiming that the problem is already out of control. Some self-styled realists even invoke the analogy of the "triage"—a metaphor borrowed from the battlefield, where the wounded are divided into three categories: those who will recover even without treatment; those who will die irrespective of treatment, and those who will live only if they receive treatment. Given the scarcity of resources, the argument goes, all efforts should be devoted to those in the third category. The lifeboat version of this approach would regard food aid to nations in the second category, the hopeless, not only as wasteful but also as unethical and even suicidal. On the one hand such aid would have to be at the expense of nations in the third category, the survivors; on the other hand the food provided will merely subsidize further destructive population growth. On these grounds Garret Hardin (1981), to mention one example, is calling for what he calls a "toughlove" solution (a euphemism for "shape up or ship out") and against any form of aid to "hopeless" nations since by accelerating their population growth (a euphemism for saving the lives of the hungry) such aid will in the end bring about an even greater catastrophe. In his opinion, while the poor nations are fast outstripping their lands' capacities, the developed nations should give precedence to their own survival and prosperity.

In one important respect this cynical view has some validity. In the 1950s and 1960s, with the emergence of the Third World as a global power and the outbreak of the food problem, it was believed that eliminating hunger and giving the LDCs a greater share in the world wealth were also in the interest of the developed nations. President Harry S. Truman expressed this view when he said that "the poverty of the people in the less developed nations is a handicap and a threat both to these nations and to the more prosperous nations." The poorer nations in their quest for a solution of their most pressing problems, so the argument goes, may use force and endanger the entire global order. The ruling elite, both among and within nations, it was said, must thus relinquish some of its power and wealth to the poor or risk losing everything in the imminent and uncompromising war waged by the poor for survival.

Today it is increasingly evident that these fears were exaggerated. At the international level the LDCs,[18] independently or jointly, cannot possibly threaten a global order that is dominated by superpowers and guarded by ever more expensive and more sophisticated weapons. At the national level the state of mind imposed by a hand-to-mouth existence rules out any possibility of a grass-roots movement among the poorest of the poor. The desperate struggle for mere survival is highly devisive and leaves no room for the development of political consciousness.

"Beware of the children of the poor," says an old Hebrew expression, "because from them the law will come." For Karl Marx they are the seeds of a revolution that will change the existing order. For Ralf Dahrendorf the dialectic of power and resistance is the motive force of history. The sad truth, however, is that the children of the undernourished cannot bring about any change, being too physically drained to resist the ruling power or to revolt against it. Hunger and poverty have appropriated their aspirations and hopes, and, as Samuel Johnson has said, when there is no hope there is no endeavor. A cynical conclusion of this state of events is that the belief that prudence on the part of the affluent will motivate them to aid the poor in the name of their own self-interests is unfounded. There is no internal force, be it political, economic, or military, that can help the poor to keep their place in the lifeboat or threaten the place of those who stay afloat.

But is it true that it is against the interest of the affluent to help the poor? Or that aid will do more harm than good? The fact of the matter is that the basic premises of the lifeboat approach are totally false. First, there is enough food in the world to feed all the people, now and in the foreseeable future. Food aid to one country need not therefore be at another country's expense. Second, the crux of the food problem is not that there are poor nations whose difficulties are insurmountable but that there are poor people in *all* nations, including the rich countries, who live in such poverty that they cannot afford even the minimum diet. Even today, one out of every three people suffering from undernutrition lives in the middle- and high-income countries. The poor need help in order to break from the trap of hunger and poverty and reach a base line from which they will be able to become self-reliant. Without such help and having no real voice and hardly any weight in policy decisions, there is very little that they can do to "shape-up" or help themselves.

There is an even more alarming quandary about this approach. It suggests, perhaps for the first time in the history of modern civilization, that mankind should give up all hope of mastering its own fate and should not even strive to control nature with the aim of determining its future.

In order to highlight the dilemma, let us consider the case of Bangladesh, perhaps the poorest of all nations. In 1980 the population of this country totaled nearly 100 million people and more than 2 million are added each year. There is no doubt that even under the most extensive effort of agricultural development, the land of that country will not be able to feed all its inhabitants and keep pace with the population growth. One way or another, adjustments to the constrained capacity of food production will have to be made. The question, however, is whether these adjustments will take place through mass starvation and low life expectancy due to diseases and infant mortality caused by malnutrition. Or will it be possible to spare these sufferings through family planning, other forms of population control, development of alternative sources of income, etc.? In other words, will the people of Bangladesh, together with other nations whose aid will be necessary, be capable of taking all measures to make these adjustments in an orderly manner and determine their course of life before allowing the forces of nature to take their brutal course?

The demand for food is not merely a request for charity. More even than a claim for justice it is a claim for hope—hope for the poor that their misery will end and hope for all mankind that it is capable of commanding its future and coping with the challenges ahead.

NOTES

1. Reutlinger and Alderman (1980) estimate that the calorie intake of more than 800 million people or 60 percent of the population in the LDCs

is below the requirement level established by the FAO and the WHO (World Health Organization). They also estimate that the calorie intake of some 600 million people or close to 50 percent of the population in the LDCs is below 90 percent of the FAO/WHO requirement level. See also Reutlinger and Selowsky 1976; Knudsen and Scandizzo 1979.

2. The division of the poverty sector into groups for analytical purposes has already been suggested before. Raj Krishna (1974:3), for instance, concluded: "Fundamentally, of course, it is poverty that must be eliminated. But the poverty of the employed, the unemployed, the self employed, and the unemployable require different treatment." William C. Thiesenhusen (1981) writes: "For the LDCs the income pyramid is almost invariably characterized by a sector of poverty making up perhaps 40 percent of the population. This has always included a sub-sector whose poverty tested the ingenuity and good will of society because it could be alleviated by job creation, distribution of productive resources, and collective action. For another sub-sector, the basic requirements of a minimum living standard could be met only by income transfers. Yet the most imaginative use of these measures has always left another sub-sector whose poverty has been utterly unresponsive to any technique yet devised by any capitalist society."

3. D. Gale Johnson (1976) argues that if trade could move freely across national borders, production shortages in one area could be covered more easily by suppliers from other areas than by buffer stocks.

4. And this is assuming rather optimistically that by the year 2000 the population growth rate will have declined from the present annual rate of about 2.0 percent to a rate of 1.7 percent.

5. For example, land is allowed less fallow time to regenerate its nutrients and moisture. Land on higher hillside areas that is brought under cultivation suffers more from water and wind erosion. See CEQ 1980 for more details on the dangers to the environment.

6. Present global losses to desertification, which is one result of these practices, are estimated at around 6 million hectares a year.

7. By 1971 more than 50 percent of India's farms, covering less than 10 percent of the agricultural land, were below the 2.5-acre subsistance level.

8. Government estimates indicate that the distribution of income and assets in rural areas has become *less* equitable over the years.

9. Sources for this review are Council on Environmental Quality (CEQ) 1980; Enzer, Drobnick, and Alter 1978; Wortman and Cummings 1978; Chou, Harmon, and Wittwer 1977; Crosson and Frederick 1977; USDA 1979; FAO 1976; International Food Research Institute 1977; World Bank 1979, 1980, 1981. Most of the figures are taken from the first of these sources.

10.   It should be noted that later projections by the World Bank and the
      Organization for Economic Cooperation and Development (OECD)
      are considerably less optimistic than these, which are taken from CEQ
      1980. The World Bank's *World Development Report* of 1981 predicts
      that in the absence of considerable policy changes, the middle-income
      countries will grow at 4.3 percent annually and the low-income coun-
      tries at only 3 percent. The difference between this dismal outlook and
      the other may amount to as many as 220 million more people living in
      absolute poverty.

11.   All of the increase in arable land will take place in the LDCs, where it
      is projected to increase by 10 percent, while arable land in the indus-
      trial countries may even decline slightly.

12.   Another result of these trends may be greater risks of massive crop
      failures and higher vulnerability to weather fluctuations.

13.   This projection assumes no change in the proportion of imports in
      their total consumption. The FAO came out with a more pessimistic
      projection, estimating a rise in the share of imports to as much as 26
      percent and an increase of up to 170 MMT in the food gap by 2000.

14.   In India, for instance, land reform appears formally in the rule book
      and every state puts a ceiling on the size of farms. In practice, how-
      ever, only a handful of state governments have seriously tried to en-
      force these ceilings, while most have been reluctant to take steps that
      might alienate the politically powerful farmers. Frequently these
      farmers circumvent the law by registering land in the names of rela-
      tives, tenants, and others.

15.   I am well aware of the simplification inherent in this utopian por-
      trayal of a representative government, if not its outright naivete. Al-
      though this is a side issue in the main discussion, I feel obliged to
      balance the picture somewhat by quoting Thrasymachus's argument
      with Socrates: "In every case the laws are made by the ruling party in
      its own interest. By making these laws they define as 'right' for their
      subjects whatever is for their own interest, and they call anyone who
      breaks them a 'wrongdoer' and punish him accordingly" (Plato 1966:
      18). The specific subject of eradicating hunger and poverty falls well
      within the interests of the ruling party as the following quotation
      from a Bolivian newspaper, highly typical of Latin American politics,
      colorfully illustrates: "Either the Indians are integrated into the
      present system or else they will massacre our children."

16.   Of course plan rationality in this pure form does not exist in reality,
      and around the world we find different mixtures of these forms.

17.   Boulding noted also that "this plan would have the additional ad-
      vantage of developing a long-run tendency toward equality of income,

for the rich would have many children and become poor and the poor would have few children and become rich."

18. Obviously not all the 240 countries who are presently classified as "developing" would welcome a radical change in the global order. The LDCs include the Organization of Petroleum Exporting Countries (OPEC), the "middle-income" countries like Brazil (with a $1,750 per capita annual income), and the "least developed," or the "Fourth World" countries, a group of about thirty-five countries having a population of 1.1 billion and a per capita income of less than $300 per year.

2 THE THEORY OF COMMODITY PRICE STABILIZATION AND BUFFER STOCKS OPERATION

Despite the importance of the subject and the wide attention it has drawn in the last decade by policymakers, operations researchers, and economists, the theoretical framework most commonly used to analyze the effects of commodity price stabilization remains intriguingly simplistic. Most of the theoretical and empirical work on the subject is still carried out within the analytical model advanced by Waugh (1944), Oi (1961), and Massell (1969). Despite its theoretical neatness and appeal, this model is unsatisfactory for a number of reasons. First, the measure of welfare gains from stabilization via the economic surplus concept is seriously deficient, is only partly relevant for evaluating stabilization policies, and disregards a number of very important aspects of these policies. One example is the reduction in risk due to the policy and its effect on the decisions of producers and consumers. Another example is the multiple dimensionality of stabilization goals; countries are concerned not only with price stabilization but also with the availability of adequate supply especially to the vulnerable sections of the population, with the solvency of the farm sectors, and more. Second, underlying the basic Waugh-Oi-Massell model are several simplifying but highly unrealistic assumptions that greatly restrict the generality of its conclusion. Efforts to generalize the basic model and relax some of these assumptions such as linearity and the form of the supply function have resulted in far more ambiguous results than those indicated by Massell. Third, this model examines the case of "pure" price stabilization, namely a policy that is self-financed, does not involve any fiscal transfers, manifests the net social gains due solely to changing the intertemporal flow of supply, and causes only minimal disruptions of normal market clearing functions. Buffer stocks thus become the main if not the only instrument of stabilization. This approach is not very useful for practical decisionmaking since in reality price stabilization is sought by a wide variety of "mixed" instruments directed to several different and sometimes conflicting objectives.

Of all the foregoing qualifications the last mentioned is perhaps the most important and explains why the conclusions that came out of the present study are qualitatively different from those obtained in other studies. Postponed to later chapters, however, is the analysis of mixed stabilization strategies; the focus of this chapter is on the foundations of the theory of commodity price stabilization and the operation of buffer stocks. The starting point in this analysis is the basic model originated and developed by Waugh, Oi, and Massell.

Waugh was the first to establish the proposition that consumers, having a downward-sloping demand curve, gain from price fluctuations that result from stochastic disturbances in supply. Such consumers will therefore be worse off if the price is stabilized. Later, Oi demonstrated that producers, having an upward-sloping supply curve, will gain from price fluctuations that result from stochastic disturbances in demand. Again, producers will be worse off in this case if the price is stabilized. It remained for Massell to show that if one integrates the arguments of both Waugh and Oi into a single framework, price fluctuations will always result in welfare losses when both consumers and producers are taken into account. This will occur regardless of the source of the fluctuations and even though one of the groups may actually lose. The supposed welfare gains from price *instability,* which Waugh and Oi have shown, are nothing but an artifice, and the sum of producers' and consumers' surpluses will always be higher when the price is stabilized, indicating that price stabilization is indeed desirable.

THE BASIC MODEL

The basic features of the Waugh-Oi-Massell analytical framework are as follows: It assumes linear demand and supply schedules, instantaneous reaction of supply and demand to changes in market prices, additive stochastic disturbances, and price stabilization at the mean of the prices that would have prevailed in an unstabilized market. In their analyses Waugh, Oi, and Massell considered the case of "perfect" stabilization, in which the authorities at all times maintain sufficient stock to offset fully any random disturbance in private demand or supply and thus maintain a stable price. Finally, the criterion by which the desirability of price stabilization is evaluated in Massell's work is the resulting change in net social welfare, which combines the expected consumers' surplus and the expected producers' surplus.

The present context, concerned with agricultural primary products, necessitates departing slightly from the basic Waugh-Oi-Massell framework by assuming first that supply is determined by the *expected* rather than the actual price. This assumption is more appropriate for agricultural products, where most if not all of the production costs are incurred before the market price is known. Expectations are thus assumed to be rational, and the price predicted by producers equals the mean price, which is also the price generated by the economic system, except for the random term. A second departure is to ignore stochastic shifts in demand and concentrate on supply fluctuations only.

The basic model consists of linear demand and supply equations of the following form:

$$S(P_t) = a + b\bar{P} + u_t \tag{2-1}$$

$$D(P_t) = c - d P_t \tag{2-2}$$

where $S(P_t)$ and $D(P_t)$ denote market supply and demand, respectively; P_t denotes the short-run market clearing price and $\bar{P}$ denotes the long-run average market clearing price. $\bar{P}$ will also be the stable price, the price at which the storage authority buys or sells the commodity. The stochastic disturbances in supply U_t are symmetrically distributed with zero mean, finite variance σ^2, and no serial correlation. The parameters a, b, c, and d, are deterministic constants.

In the absence of price stabilization, the market clearing price P_t is determined by the equilibrium condition $S(P_t) = D(P_t)$ and is given by

$$P_t = \frac{c-a}{d} - \frac{d}{d}\,\bar{P} - \frac{u_t}{d}$$

$$= \bar{P} - \frac{u_t}{d} \tag{2-3}$$

A price stabilization scheme with buffer stocks requires the storage authority to buffer any random disturbance in supply by buying and selling the commodity at the price $\bar{P}$. Over the long run the buffer stock will be self-liquidating in the sense that its expected value is zero. However, at any point of time the authorities are assumed to hold sufficient stocks to meet any shortfall in supply.

Producers' gains from price stabilization are simply the resulting change in their income, given by

$$G_P^s = \int_{P_t}^{\bar{P}} S(P) \, dP' \quad , \tag{2-4}$$

where the superscript s denotes a policy of perfect stabilization. Substituting the linear supply function (2-1) and the short-run equilibrium price equation (2-3), we get

$$G_P^s = S(P_t) \cdot (\bar{P} - P_t)$$
$$= (a + b\bar{P} + u_t)\left(\frac{u_t}{d}\right). \tag{2-5}$$

The expected gains are obtained by taking the expected value of (2-5), yielding

$$E(G_P^s) = \frac{\sigma^2}{d} > 0 \tag{2-6}$$

Hence, producers will always gain from price stabilization when the source of the random disturbances is fluctuations in supply.

Consumers' gains are measured by the change in consumers' surplus and given by

$$G_c^s = \int_{\bar{P}}^{P_t} D(P') \, dP' \quad . \tag{2-7}$$

Substituting the linear demand function (2-2) and the price equation (2-3), we get

$$G_C^s = -\frac{1}{2}[D(\bar{P}) + D(P_t)](\bar{P} - P_t)$$

$$= -\frac{1}{2}[(c - d\bar{P}) \cdot 2 + u]\left(\frac{u}{d}\right). \tag{2-8}$$

Consumers' expected gains are therefore given by

$$E(G_C^s) = -\frac{1}{2}\frac{\sigma^2}{d} < 0. \tag{2-9}$$

Hence, consumers always lose from price stabilization when the source of the random disturbances is fluctuation in supply.

Measuring total welfare by the sum of producers' and consumers' surplus, we get

$$E(G_E^s) = E(G_p^s) + E(G_c^s)$$

$$= \frac{1}{2}\frac{\sigma^2}{d} > 0. \tag{2-10}$$

Thus, the economy at large always gains from price stabilization, with the gainers being able in principle to compensate the losers.

The results obtained in Eqs. (2-6), (2-9), and (2-10) specify most of Massell's conclusions. These results can be illustrated as in Figure 2-1, where the assumption is made that output can assume one of two values Q_1 or Q_2, each with a probability of 1/2. When output is Q_1 and the price is stabilized at its mean $\bar{P}$, the storage authority must release the amount $(Q - Q_1)$ into the market. As a result, consumers gain the amount designated by the area $(A + B)$ in Figure 2-1, and producers lose the amount designated by the area A. When output is Q_2 and the price is stabilized at its mean, the storage authority must buy the amount $(Q_2 - \bar{Q})$ in the market. As a result, consumers lose the amount designated by the area $(C + D)$ and producers gain the amount designated by the area $(C + D + E)$. On average, producers therefore gain because $(C + D + E) > A$, whereas consumers lose because $(C + D) > (A + B)$. The economy at large always gains.

Figure 2-1.   Economic Gains from Complete Price Stabilization.

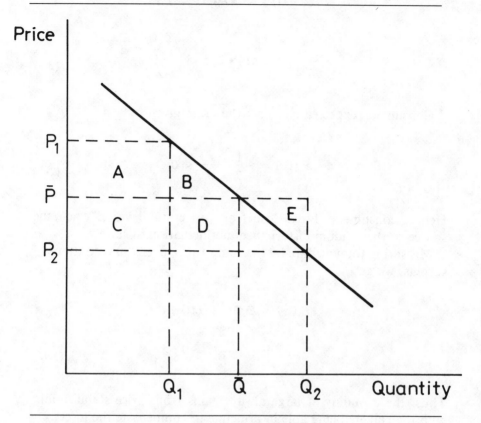

PARTIAL STABILIZATION SCHEMES

A major criticism of the basic Waugh-Oi-Massell model is that it assumes perfect and costless price stabilization since it is based on contrasting the case of no stabilization with the case in which prices are completely stabilized. It therefore assumes that the storage authorities are able to put into storage or release from storage as much of the commodity as is necessary to offset any random fluctuation in supply so that the price can always remain perfectly stable. However, this means that the authorities must then hold very large (theoretically, infinite) buffer stocks and very large vacant storage capacity for an indefinite period of time. Obviously, such a scheme would be prohibitively costly and thus unfeasible.

In practice, the authorities must be engaged in only partial stabilization and tolerate some degree of price instability. Massell (1970) began to consider a scheme of partial stabilization in which the storage authorities are engaged in offsetting only a (fixed) proportion of the random fluctuations in supply. This buffer policy, later considered also by Just (1975) and Turnovsky (1978b), among others, has the effect of modifying the demand curve by purchasing and selling quantities to make up the difference in actual and modified demand. It is illustrated diagrammatically in Figure 2-2. When the quantity produced is Q_2, the price is determined by the modified demand curve $D(Pm)$ at Pm_2, and the quantity X_2 is put into storage. Consumers lose the amount designated by the shaded area C, and producers gain the amount designated by the area $(C + D)$. When the quantity produced is Q_1 the price is determined at Pm_1 and the quantity X_1 is

Figure 2-2.   Economic Gains from Partial Price Stabilization.

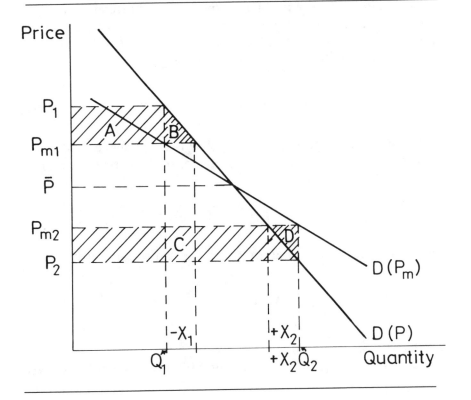

released from storage. Consumers gain the amount designated by the area $(A + B)$, while producers lose the amount designated by the area A.

Assume the authorities make no error in predicting the mean price $\overline{P}$ (see Turnovsky 1978a for an analysis of the case in which allowance is made for such an error). Then the modified demand curve $D(Pm)$ indeed crosses the original demand curve $D(P)$ at $\overline{P}$, and the amount put into or taken out of storage is determined in accordance with the following adjustment rule:

$$X_t = m(\overline{P} - Pm_t). \qquad (2\text{-}11)$$

This linear adjustment rule ensures that a fixed proportion of the excess of any given crop over a normal crop is saved for times of shortage.

$X_t > 0$ implies that the authorities are buying; $X_t < 0$ implies that they are selling. As before, over the long run the buffer stock will be self-liquidating. The parameter m specifies the difference between the modified and the original demand curves and thus determines the intensity of the intervention. When the demand curve is the one given in (2–2), the modified demand curve will be given by

$$D(Pm_t) = (c + m\overline{P}) - (d + m)P_t. \qquad (2\text{-}12)$$

Another way of presenting this policy is as a scheme that evenly reduces price fluctuations by a fixed factor α. This stabilization rule is given by

$$Pm_t = P_t + \alpha(\overline{P} - P_t).$$

In terms of the notations given earlier one can readily verify that

$$Pm_t = P_t + \left(\frac{m}{d + m}\right) \cdot (\overline{P} - P_t),$$

so that $\alpha = m/(d + m)$.

The short-run equilibrium condition with this buffer policy is given by

$$D(Pm_t) = D(P_t) + X_t = S(P_t),$$

from which we can determine the clearing market price

$$Pm_t = \bar{P} - \frac{u_t}{d + m} .$$

(2-13)

Producers' gains from this policy are given by

$$G_p^m = S(Pm_t) \cdot (Pm_t - P_t)$$

$$= (a + b\bar{P} + u_t)\left[\left(\bar{P} - \frac{u}{d + m}\right) - \left(\bar{P} - \frac{u}{d}\right)\right] .$$

(2-14)

Their expected gains are therefore given by

$$E(G_p^m) = \frac{m}{d(d + m)} \quad \sigma^2 > 0 .$$

(2-15)

Hence, producers will always gain from the linear partial stabilization scheme if the sources of the fluctuations are random disturbances in supply.

Consumers' gains are given by

$$G_c^m = \frac{1}{2}[D(P\mu_t) + D(P_t)] (Pm_t - P_t) .$$

(2-16)

Hence, consumers' expected gains are given by

$$E(G_c^m) = -\frac{1}{2} \cdot \frac{2md + m^2}{d(d + m)} \quad \sigma^2 < 0 .$$

(2-17)

And, hence, consumers will always lose from this partial stabilization scheme if the sources of the random disturbances are fluctuations in supply.

The combined consumers' and producers' welfare gains are therefore given by

$$E(G_c^m) + E(G_p^m) = \frac{1}{2}\left[\frac{m^2 \cdot \sigma^2}{d(d + m)^2}\right] > 0 .$$

(2-18)

Hence, the total gains to the private sector are always positive. Now, however, the financial costs of the scheme, which in this case are represented by the net value of the purchases, must also be taken into account. The net gains of the storage authority are given by

$$G_g^m = -Pm_t \bullet X_t .$$ (2-19)

The expected net gains of the storage authorities are therefore given by

$$E(G_g^m) = \frac{m \, \sigma^2}{(d + m)^2} .$$ (2-20)

Hence, the storage authorities will make profits from stabilization. It should be noted, however, that this calculation still ignores handling costs and amortization of the storage facility as well as the financial costs of maintaining the desired quantity of the commodity in storage until it is necessary. The next chapter shows that when these costs are included in the calculations the results are qualitatively different.

The overall economic gains are given by the combined welfare gains of the private sector and the net financial gains of the storage authority. Hence,

$$E(G_E^m) = \frac{1}{2} \frac{m \, \sigma^2}{d(d + m)^2} \, (m + 2d) > 0 .$$ (2-21)

The economy therefore gains from price stabilization, and these gains rise with m up to the level where $m = d$, that is up to the level of complete stabilization. It is interesting to note that the gains from the storage operation will also rise with m up to the level of complete stabilization. However, most of the reservations mentioned earlier in this chapter about the assumptions underlying Waugh-Oi-Massell's model and especially the calculation of the financial costs of the storage operation are relevant to this scheme as well.

Although the linear adjustment rule allows a rather thoroughgoing analysis, other schemes of partial stabilization become considerably more complicated to analyze within the theoretical framework of Waugh, Oi, and Massell. The main reason is that the operation of buffer stocks has the effect of altering the probability distribution of the market price in a nonsymmetric way. The linear adjustment rule, by contrast, has the advantage of condensing the spread of the probability distribution of the price while preserving its shape and its mean.[1] This, however, is no longer the case with other partial stabilization schemes.

In practice, however, the most common scheme of partial price stabilization is that of the price band. In this scheme, the storage authority allows the price to fluctuate freely within the range $P_2 \leq P_t \leq P_1$, where P_1 and P_2 are the upper and lower limits of the price band. If supply falls to the extent that the market price may rise above the upper band P_1, the storage authority will release a sufficient amount to prevent the price from rising above P_1. If supply is so plentiful that the price may fall below the lower band P_2, the authority will put the excess into storage to prevent the price from falling below P_2. The extent to which the storage authority is actually successful in maintaining the price within the band depends on the quantity available in storage from the previous year and the remaining vacant capacity.

From the point of view of the producer, this storage policy has the effect of changing the demand curve so that it includes also the demand of the storage authority. The effective demand curve is thus of the form of the curve $D'D'$ in Figure 2-3, where DD is the consumers' demand curve. Suppose that supply is normally distributed around the mean $\overline{Q}$. If the demand curve is linear, the derived distribution of prices will also be normal around the mean $\overline{P}$. With price-band storage policy the demand curve becomes $D'D'$ and the price distribution changes, as illustrated in Figure 2-3. Obviously, the exact form of the distribution depends on the amount of stock (denoted by S in Figure 2-3) and the vacant capacity (denoted by V). Hence this policy not only compresses the distribution but also changes the mean, which now becomes a function of the price band, of the amount in storage, and of the vacant capacity. This point will be treated later.

SUPPLY RESPONSE

A number of recent studies have emphasized the fact that the welfare gains from stabilization as measured in the Waugh–Oi–Massell model are only the net gains from the *transfer of income* associated with the scheme. (This argument is made most strongly by Newbery and Stiglitz 1979, 1981.) That the economy at large "gains" from stabilization—when the gains are as measured in the conventional model—is only an indication that those to whom money income has been trans-

Figure 2-3.   Effective Demand and Price Distribution with Buffer Stocks.

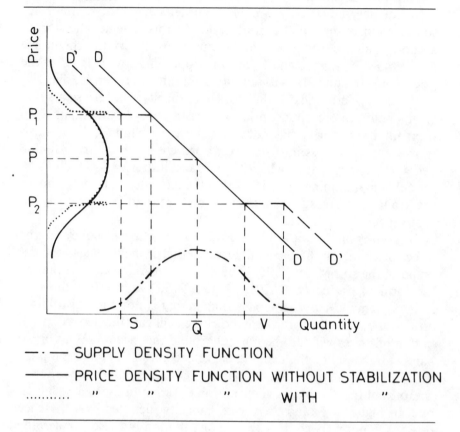

— · — SUPPLY DENSITY FUNCTION

———— PRICE DENSITY FUNCTION WITHOUT STABILIZATION

··········   "   "   "   WITH   "

ferred as an effect of the stabilization scheme are "willing to pay" more than those from whom money income has been taken. These distributional gains are, however, only part of the gains of stabilization. To these must be added the efficiency gains, which result from the reduction in risk.

The risk associated with price variability affects producers in several ways. It leads to a lower rate of capital accumulation by destroying the continuity and stability so necessary for investment. It leads to a choice of more flexible techniques and thus to inefficient allocation of resources and higher variable costs. It affects the choice of product mix (or crop mix) and induces producers to reduce their output of products with volatile prices. It affects negatively the number of producers and the amount of resources (including land) allocated for production.

The consequences of price uncertainty have been well demonstrated in numerous studies, both theoretical and empirical, on the behavior of risk-averse producers. As Sandmo (1971), Leland (1972), and others have demonstrated, a major implication of producers' risk aversion is that the expected utility of profit will be at a maximum when the marginal cost of planned output is *less* than the expected price; thus, output under uncertainty will be smaller. A strong case for price stabilization thus exists in situations where producers are risk averse. A reduction in risk by stabilizing the price is likely to lead to a more efficient allocation of resources, a choice of more efficient techniques, and an allocation of more resources for production and hence more output and lower price. The resulting welfare gains to producers as well as to consumers are referred to as the efficiency gains. Neglecting these gains in the conventional model may result in an underestimation of the total gains from stabilization and hence a possible distortion in the final conclusion as to whether stabilization is desirable.

In order to allow for the efficiency gains, several studies have evaluated the benefits to consumers and producers in terms of the expected utility rather than in terms of consumers' and producers' surplus (see, for example, Hanoch 1974; Feder, Just, and Schmitz 1977; Eaton 1979; Turnovsky, Shalit, and Schmitz 1980; and Shalit 1980). The common conclusion of these studies is that in general, stabilization will result in higher expected utility of risk-averse consumers and producers and is thus desirable. Other studies have retained the basic analytical framework but generalized the concepts of consumers' and producers' surplus to the case with risk in order to provide a money measure to the efficiency gains (see, for example, Bigman and Leite 1978; Just 1978; Lutz 1978; and Scandizzo, Hazell, and Anderson 1980).

To provide a measure of the efficiency gains, consider a single risk-averse producer operating in a competitive market and facing a random product price with known mean $\bar{P}$ and standard deviation σ_{p^2}. (This illustration is after Just 1978, where the special case considered here as well as the more general case is examined.) The producer makes short-term decisions by maximizing a mean-variance expected utility function:

$$E\left[U\left(\bar{P},\, \sigma_p,\, w\right)\right] = E(\pi) - k \cdot \sqrt{\mathrm{Var}\,(\pi)}$$

$$= \bar{P} \cdot Q - w'X - k \cdot Q \cdot \sigma_p \, , \qquad (2\text{-}22)$$

where U is utility; π is quasi-rent (profits plus fixed costs); Q is the quantity produced; w and X are vectors of input prices and input quantities, respectively; and k is a parameter specifying the degree of risk aversion.

When the producer faces a stable price P_s, the maximand (2–22) becomes

$$E[U(P_s, w, 0)] = E(\pi)$$

$$= P_s Q - wX . \qquad (2\text{–}23)$$

This would also be the maximand for the risk-neutral producer facing a random price P with a mean of P_s. From (2–22) and (2–23) we can see that at each level of output, the stable price P_s (and also the expected price facing the risk-neutral producer) is related to the expected price $\overline{P}$ facing the risk-averse producer, according to the relation

$$P_s = \overline{P} - k \cdot \sigma_p . \qquad (2\text{–}24)$$

The supply schedule of the risk-averse producer as a function of expected price thus lies above the supply schedule of the producer facing nonstochastic price, by an amount equal to ($k\,\sigma_p$). This amount can be thought of as an insurance premium that the risk-averse producer is willing to pay for each unit of output in order to avoid the risk.

Another way of analyzing the supply response to risk reduction is via "safety-first" criteria. (This analysis is after Bigman and Leite 1978.) These are criteria suggested by Roy (1952), Telser (1955–56), Kataoka (1963), and Baumol (1963) for a firm operating under uncertainty. According to the Kataoka–Baumol criterion, the firm maximizes profits that it can obtain with a certain (prespecified) degree of reliability (say, $[1 - \alpha]$). The firm thus maximizes the α-fractile of the profit distribution. The production decisions are therefore made according to the rule

$$\text{Max } Z$$

$$\text{Subject to: } P_r(\pi \le Z) < \alpha \quad,$$

where P_r is a probability statement, Z is the "subsistence" or "disaster" level of returns, and α is the (subjectively) required level of reliability that disaster will not occur. Assuming that the probability distribution of π can be fully described by the parameters of the first two moments, we can make the transformation

$$P_r(\pi - Z) = F[(Z - \pi) / \sigma_p] \ ,$$

where F is the distribution function of π. From this expression we can develop an expression for Z, given by

$$Z < \bar{\pi} + F^{-1}(\alpha) \cdot \sigma \ .$$

This is exactly Baumol's confidence criterion. For a symmetric distribution, $F^{-1}(1/2) = 0$; risk aversion is manifested when the degree of reliability required is such that $\alpha < 1/2$, in which case $F^{-1}(\alpha) < 0$.

The problem of the firm maximizing its reliable profits and facing a random price with a known mean $\bar{P}$ and standard deviation σ_p can thus be formalized as

$$\text{Max } P_z \cdot Q - C(Q)$$
$$\text{Subject to: } P_r(P \leq P_z) < \alpha \, ,$$

where $C(Q)$ is the cost function. Let $F[P_z - P)/\sigma_p] = \alpha$, and define $k = -F^{-1}(\alpha)$. The maximization problem can then be written as

$$\underset{Q}{\text{Max}} \quad (\bar{P} - k\sigma) \cdot Q - C(Q) \ . \tag{2-26}$$

This problem yields the first-order conditions[2]

$$\bar{P} - k\sigma_p = C'(Q) \, , \tag{2-27}$$

where $C'(Q)$ is the marginal cost. The magnitude $k\sigma_p$ in this context is the safety margin required by the firm when prices are random.

From (2-27) we can see that while the supply schedule of the firm facing stable prices is given by its marginal cost curve $C'(Q)$, the supply schedule of the firm facing stochastic prices is given by $C'(Q) + k\sigma$. Hence the two ways of analyzing the supply response produce the same conclusion with regard to its form, granted that disturbances are additive.

Hueth, Just, and Schmitz (1980) have shown that the change in producers' surplus (or Mishan's (1977) equivalent measure of quasi-rent) is also an exact measure of both the compensating and equivalent variations that are the true measures of the welfare change. Hence, a money measure of the efficiency gains in expected utility resulting from stabilization is given by the difference between the area above the supply curve with risk—considered as a function of the expected price—and below the mean price, and the area above the supply curve without risk and the stable price. Consider now Figure 2–4. If the mean price persists, these gains would be given by the area $(E + B + C)$. However, as producers respond to the reduction in risk, supply increases and the price falls to P_s. As a result, producers' net gains are only $(E - A)$, indicating that they may also lose in the process. Consumers, however, always gain from the reduction

Figure 2-4.   Economic Gains from Price Stabilization with Supply Response.

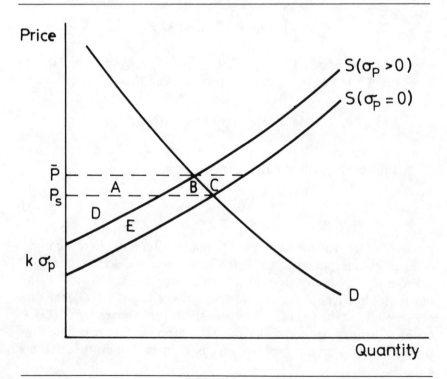

in the mean price; their expected gains are given by the area $(A + B)$. Thus, the total net efficiency gains to the private sector (consumers and producers) resulting from price stabilization are given by the area $(E + B)$.

Two complications that result from the supply response need to be taken into account. First, the storage authority must now continuously adjust its policy. If, for instance, the authority attempts to stabilize the price at or around the mean price prevailing before the stabilization program, thus failing to take into account the supply response to the reduction in risk, it will face a steady accumulation of stocks and thus suffer increasing losses. These losses will eventually force the storage authority to stabilize the price at or around a lower level. Perfect adjustment of its policy to the supply response would require of the storage authority complete information on the exact parameters of the model, including those specifying the degree of risk aversion. Obviously, such complete information cannot be assumed, and without it the storage authority may suffer losses in the transition period before a new equilibrium price and a new policy are reached.

A second complication is related to the degree to which farmers are assumed to be rational in their decision. In the formulation of the model in Eqs. (2-1) and (2-2), farmers are assumed to be rational in that they predict the equilibrium price that is also the mean price. If supply responds to the reduction in risk, however, the average quantity increases and the price declines. Rationality in this dynamic context requires that farmers have not only "perfect foresight," which amounts to an exact knowledge of the form of the supply response of *all* farmers at *all* times, but also an exact knowledge of the future policies of the storage authority.

Suppose, though, that while farmers have rational expectations concerning the distribution of prices in steady-state equilibria, it takes them some time to adjust their expectations when the economic system shifts to a new equilibrium. In the interim there may be systematic misconceptions, resulting in welfare losses. If farmers believe that the storage authority will continue to determine the same price band as before, but the storage authority in fact adjusts its policy to take account of the supply response, then farmers may be expecting a higher price than the one that will ultimately prevail. This misconception will lead to an overallocation of resources and thus to welfare losses.

OTHER EXTENSIONS OF THE BASIC MODEL

The limitations inherent in the Waugh-Oi-Massell basic analytical framework have been increasingly recognized, and many of the conclusions pertaining to the distribution of welfare gains from stabilization have been shown to be specific to the assumptions made in the basic model and cannot be extended to more general cases. As the model is generalized to consider nonlinearities, heteroscedasticity, different expectational forms, and so on, the qualitative welfare implications of price stabilization are drastically changing. In this section some of these extensions are examined and the main theoretical findings in the literature briefly reviewed.

Nonlinearities

It has long been evident that the welfare impact of price stabilization is sensitive to the functional form assumed for demand and supply and that with sufficient convexity or concavity of the underlying functions some of Massell's propositions are no longer valid. Turnovsky (1974), who pioneered a methodology for examining the role of nonlinearities, concluded that while stabilization still leads to an overall welfare gain (unless either demand or supply are perfectly elastic), the distribution of these gains between producers and consumers is indeterminate and depends on the corresponding elasticities. Just et al. (1978) extended Turnovsky's methodology to the framework of international trade and demonstrated that the shapes of supply curves are critical in determining qualitative effects of stabilization. For instance, they show that, for the range of elasticity estimates coming from most econometric studies of coarse grain supply and demand, a switch in specification from linearity to log-linearity can be sufficient for a reversal in who gains and who loses from price stabilization.

To see the effect of nonlinearities, consider Figure 2–5. When the schedule is the linear curve DD, producers' losses when the price drops with stabilization from P_1 to $\bar{P}$ are given by the area A. Earlier we noted that this loss is more than outweighed by the gains when the price rises with stabilization, as given by the area $(C + D + E)$, so that on average producers will gain from price stabilization. However, when the demand curve is "kinked" linear with its left portion

Figure 2-5. Economic Gains from Price Stabilization with Non-linear Demand.

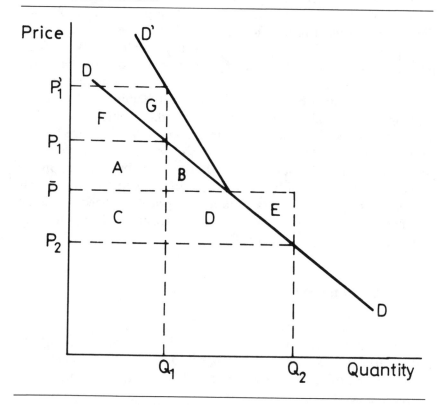

being less elastic, the conclusions may be reversed. If the demand curve is DD', the nonstabilized price will be P_1' instead of P_1, and producers will lose the total of $(A + F + G)$. In that case it is no longer certain that their gains when the price rises from P_2 to $\bar{P}$ will indeed outweigh their losses when the price drops from P_1' to $\bar{P}$. As one can readily see, there are certain values of demand elasticity for which producers will in fact lose from stabilization whereas consumers will be the ones who gain.

The Form of Disturbances

The Waugh-Oi-Massell model assumes additive disturbances, implying that the random fluctuations consist of parallel shifts in the demand and supply curves. For most agricultural products, however, multiplicative disturbances seem more appropriate. This, for instance, is the form appropriate in Nerlov's type of production function, where *planned* production is a function of the acreage utilized and the average yield per acre. *Actual* production may deviate from planned production as a result of random deviations of the actual yield per acre from the average yield. Turnovsky (1976) has demonstrated that the distributional conclusions are highly sensitive to the form in which random disturbances enter the problem. As an example Turnovsky has shown that in the multiplicative case the desirability of price stabilization "*does not depend on the source of price instability,* as it does in the additive case, but only upon the shapes of the deterministic components of the demand and supply curves. If one group benefits from having price stabilized, it will do so whether the random price arises from stochastic disturbances in demand or in supply" (1978b:127).

Expectations Formation

The basic model assumes that firms make their decisions on the basis of actual selling price and adjust instantaneously to any change in price. Earlier it was noted that the model can easily be extended to include the case of rational expectations. The rationality hypothesis is formally described by

$$P_t^{\text{exp}} = E_{t-1}(P_t), \qquad (2\text{-}28)$$

where E_{t-1} denotes expectations at time $(t - 1)$ conditional on the information available at that time. Expectations are rational in the sense of Muth (1961) if the price generated by the system is equal to the price predicted by the individual agents. If the only information available is the probability distribution of the price, then $P_t^{\text{exp}} = \bar{P}$, which is the case considered earlier in Eq. (2-1).

In empirical studies, however, another expectational form is widely used: adaptive expectations. These forms and also all the other autoregressive forecasting procedures have a serious limitation in that they do not incorporate all the available information in deriving the forecast. The adaptive expectations hypothesis is formally described by

$$P_{t-1}^{\exp} - P_t^{\exp} = \xi (P_{t-1} - P_{t-1}^{\exp}) \; ; \, 0 \leq \xi \leq 1 \, . \qquad (2\text{-}29)$$

In words, Eq. (2-29) states that the change in expectations equals some fraction ξ of the previous period's forecasting error. Under this scheme Turnovsky (1974) could only state that nothing conclusive can be inferred in regard to distribution of the gains from stabilization until the various parameters of the model are specified: "As in Massell's model, stabilizing for supply fluctuations will improve the welfare of producers and deteriorate that of consumers. On the other hand, stabilizing for demand fluctuations can have very different welfare effects from those implied by the previous model" (1974: 711).

Quantity Stabilization

Sabotnik and Houck (1976) have considered a scheme of stabilizing consumption and production as opposed to the more conventional price stabilization scheme. Using a framework very similar to the one in (2-1) and (2-2), they show that demand stabilization is the least beneficial in its welfare implication. The gains from supply stabilization can, however, be at least as great as those from price stabilization under certain values of the corresponding demand and supply elasticities, but the ranking of supply and price stabilization can be reversed under different values of these parameters.

Among the various extensions of the basic model, the most important is an analysis of the gains from price stabilization in an international context, pioneered by Hueth and Schmitz (1972) (see Chapters 6 and 7). Other extensions include an analysis of stabilization in a multicommodity context and an analysis of different intervention rules. Still others follow a different approach altogether, evaluating the benefits to consumers and producers in terms of a utility function rather than in terms of consumers' and producers' surplus. In yet a different direction, a number of recent studies have followed Samuelson's seminal work (1972a) and examined the benefits from stabilization using a general equilibrium model, which allows for the repercussions in other markets of stabilizing the price of a given commodity and the resulting feedbacks on that market.

The most important conclusion emerging from all the extensions of the basic model is that although price stabilization will indeed improve the welfare of the general population, the distribution of these gains between the various groups of the population is highly sensitive to the exact specification of the model. In other words, whether or not certain groups or sectors will gain from stabilization is a question that can only be answered on a case-by-case basis. In the following chapters we analyze in detail a specific country case and examine how the specification of the model and the magnitude of the parameters affect the desirability of price stabilization and the distribution of the welfare gains among the various population groups.

CRITICISM OF THE BASIC MODEL

Despite considerable efforts to generalize the basic model that Waugh introduced some thirty-five years ago, the scope of this analytical framework still remains very restricted and not very useful for actual decisionmaking. Criticism of the model covers two major aspects. Some critics still cast doubt on some of the underlying assumptions and on the methodology. Others raise serious questions as to whether this model is at all relevant for assessing the desirability of government intervention.

The Measure of Welfare Gains

Welfare gains or losses from price stabilization are measured in the model in terms of the economic surpluses. The limitations of this measure have been widely discussed and its use heavily criticized in the economic literature ever since it was introduced by Marshall in 1890. Samuelson for one (1947:194–95) argues that consumers' surplus is a worse than useless concept because it is confusing (see also Burns 1973; Mishan 1977; Silberberg 1972; and Little 1957:180, to cite only a few). Cochrane finds this concept "both slippery and of limited use" (1980:508). A number of recent papers have concluded, however, that in most cases the observed consumers' and producers' surpluses are reasonable approximations of the unobservable compensating and equivalent variations, which are the correct theoretical measures of the welfare gains (see, for example, Willig 1976; Just and Hueth 1979; Bigman and Shalit 1980; Hueth, Just, and Schmitz 1982). Thus, for instance, while it was generally believed that in order for the Marshallian measure of consumers' surplus to give a meaningful measure of welfare the income must be negligible, Willig (1976) shows that even for relatively high values of the income elasticity of demand the error of approximation is quite small. Hueth, Just, and Schmitz show that the change in producers' surplus (or Mishan's equivalent measure of quasi-rent) is an exact measure of both the compensating and equivalent variations of the producer. Nevertheless, Cochrane argues that "consumer surplus will not properly measure the change in utility to consumers, particularly poor consumers, for a significant change in the price of food because the income effect of such a price change becomes large relative to the incomes of those consumers; hence, the price change induces a significant change in the marginal utility of money for those consumers" (1980: 508).

One more aspect is important in the context of agricultural primary products, especially in developing countries. The theoretical literature assumes consumers and producers to be two distinct entities, calculating welfare gains or losses for each of the two groups separately. Often a large segment of the consumers are peasants who also produce these products, and their overall welfare gains from a change in their output prices can no longer be given as the simple summation of their gains (or losses) as producers and their gains (or losses) as consumers.

Bigman and Shalit (1980) show that whether or not the economic surplus concept is still useful in a cost/benefit analysis for this type of consumer-producer depends crucially on the share of total output that is directly consumed by the producer—that is, producer's excess marketed supply in proportion to producer's total supply. In these cases the error of approximation of the Marshallian economic surplus can be very large.

Income vs. Price Stabilization

The argument in favor of price stabilization emphasizes the reduction in risk and the resulting efficiency gains. However, producers are concerned with price stabilization only to the extent that it stabilizes their income. And not only is the income variability considerably different from price variability, but in some special cases stabilization of price actually enhances income variability.

Consider, for instance, the case of linear demand and supply functions as in the basic model. Income Y is given by

$$Y = PQ = \left(\bar{P} - \frac{u}{d}\right)(a + b\bar{P} + u).$$

Hence

$$\text{Var}(Y) = E[PQ - E(PQ)]^2$$

$$= \frac{\sigma^2}{d^2}[a + (b - d)\bar{P}]^2$$

$$= \text{Var}(P) \cdot [a + (b - d)\bar{P}]^2.$$

When prices are stabilized at their mean, income is given by

$$Y = \bar{P} \cdot Q = \bar{P}(a + b\bar{P} + u),$$

and

$$\text{Var}(\bar{Y}) = \bar{P}^2 \sigma^2.$$

Comparing the variability of income in these two cases, one can verify that

$$\text{Var}(\bar{Y}) < \text{Var}(Y)$$

if and only if, at the mean,

$$\eta > \tfrac{1}{2}$$

where η is the price elasticity of demand. For some primary agricultural products this condition indeed holds, so that price stabilization does indeed lower also the variability of income. For other products, especially staple foods, this condition may not hold and for them it is possible to have the price stabilized and yet the income becoming more volatile.

Buffer Stocks Operation

The conventional analysis compares the case of no stabilization with the case in which prices are completely stabilized. Stabilization is assumed to be self-financing and self-liquidating. It has already been noted here that setting up buffer stock large enough to ensure that a fixed price is always maintained will be infinitely costly and thus not feasible. But even when partial stabilization is considered, the costs of handling the stocks and maintaining the storage facility cannot be ignored as they have been in most theoretical studies.[3] Moreover, even when the stabilization scheme is designed to be self-financing, buffer stocks can be started only in periods of ample supply and low prices, and thus some initial government funding will still be necessary. Only later can the storage authority earn enough money from sales of the stored commodity to finance its operations. Thus, when all costs of starting and maintaining buffer stocks are taken into account, the present value of the income from the storage operations will be considerably smaller than envisaged by the simple model, whereas the present value of the expenditure will be considerably larger. In other words, taking the time dimension and the "cost of waiting" into account will lead to results substantially different from those obtained in the conventional model.

Privately Held Stocks

The stabilizing effect of public storage may be severely undermined as a result of the reaction of private holders of stocks. Obviously, public stocks replace private stocks, at least to some degree. By reducing the fluctuations in price and thus reducing the difference between "low" prices when the commodity is bought and "high" prices when it is sold, the public stock cuts the profits of private stockholders, reducing their motivation to hold further stock. Helmberger and Weaver (1977) have strongly criticized the conventional models for disregarding the interaction between private and public storage and have argued that the distribution of welfare gains from price stabilization may be very different when these interactions are adequately considered.

The Dynamics of the Model

Although the model analyzes a series of events over time, it is not truly dynamic in the sense of carrying over the consequences from one period to the next. Instead, the model is quasi-static in the sense that it can be viewed as a single one-period game repeated an infinite number of times.

That the model is not truly dynamic is manifested in a number of ways, some of them mentioned earlier. Most important, neither the amount carried over in storage from one period to the next nor the vacant storage capacity has any influence on the activities in the subsequent period. In fact, these quantities *do* have an effect. By carrying over stocks from one period to the next the storage operation creates a strong link between consecutive periods. Thus, for instance, the storage operation introduces serial correlation in prices, which exists even if there is no such correlation in production. This is so because the price depends now on the entire quantity supplied during the year, including the quantity released from storage. But the quantity available in storage was accumulated in the previous year and is thus correlated with the previous year's price. When, in addition, expectations are adaptive, the storage operation will also generate serial correlation in production through its effect on prices, even though there is no such correlation in the random disturbances.

Moreover, even when expectations are "rational," buffer stocks will have an effect on production decisions and through them on the entire dynamics of the system. To see this, recall that the rationality hypothesis defined in Eq. (2-29) is specified in terms of expectations conditional on *all* the information available. Obviously, this information must include the quantity available in storage as well as the vacant capacity. If, for instance, producers know that a large quantity is carried over in stocks from the previous year, they must also realize that the storage authority is better able to prevent the price from rising above the prespecified upper band price than when such stocks are not available. In that case, the price expected in the next period, conditional on the amount available in storage, is higher than the expected price when this condition is not taken into account.

To examine the effect of existing stocks and storage capacity on the expected price, consider Figures 2-6 and 2-7. Figure 2-6 shows the expected price calculated as a function of the storage capacity and the amount in storage.[4] When there is no storage facility the price is distributed normally with a mean of 100 and a coefficient of variation of 7 percent. With an increase in the storage capacity, the expected price declines monotonically if the storage facility is full and

Figure 2-6.   Expected Price at Different Storage Capacities.

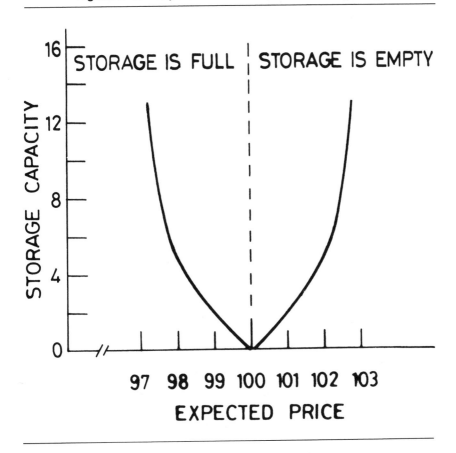

rises monotonically if the storage facility is empty. When the storage capacity is 15 percent of the average level of production, for instance, the expected market price with a storage facility can be some 3 percent higher or lower than the expected market price without a storage facility, according to whether the facility is empty or full. In Figure 2-7 the expected price of a storage facility with a capacity of 12 percent of mean production is calculated as a function of the amount in storage and the remaining storage capacity. We can also see that the expected price with a storage facility deviates more from the expected price without a storage facility as the standard deviation increases.

Figure 2-7. Expected Price of a 12 MMT Storage Facility as a Function of the Vacant Capacity.

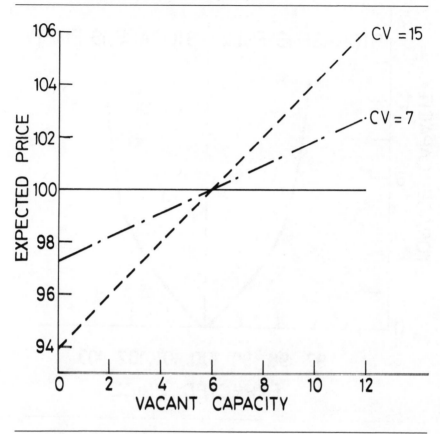

SOME SIMULATION EXPERIMENTS

To examine the quantitative aspects of some of the factors mentioned in the theoretical review a simulation model was constructed and orders of magnitude estimated for the welfare gains from complete price stabilization (in keeping with the theoretical model of Waugh, Oi, and Massell). Of particular interest are two factors; one the effects of producers' price expectations on the magnitude of the welfare gains from price stabilization, the other the effect of supply response and the efficiency gains.

The structure of the model is essentially the one described in Eqs. (2-1) and (2-2). Specifically, producers are assumed to plan their production on the basis of the expected price. Several functional forms of the supply function were considered, each associated with a different expectation formation:

- *Rational expectations.* Producers expect the mean price, assumed to be known, to be the best predicter of next year's price.
- *Adaptively rational expectations.* Producers predict next year's price on the basis of past prices. The supply function thus has the form

$$S_t = a + b \, E(P_t) + u_t \, ,$$

where

$$E(P_t) = \frac{1}{n} \sum_{j=1}^{n} P_{t-j} \, .$$

- *Adaptive expectations.* This year's price is taken to be the best predicter of next year's price.

The simulation experiments were conducted by drawing a large number of random events, such as weather, describing possible disturbances in supply. On the basis of the assumed structure of demand and supply, the market clearing price producers' revenue and consumers' surplus were calculated for each random event. From the large sample of random events the frequency distributions of these measures were generated and their characteristic parameters calculated. The numerical results presented below are based on 9,000 iterations (random events) drawn from an approximately normal distribution. The coefficient of variation in supply was assumed to be 7 percent; the price elasticity of demand at the mean point was assumed to be 0.5 and the price elasticity of supply at that point was assumed to be 0.25. The analysis was carried out both for the case in which there is no serial correlation and for the case in which serial correlation is exhibited between consecutive observations.

Table 2-1 summarizes the main results of these simulation experiments. A number of observations stand out. First, the magnitude of the welfare gains from complete price stabilization is very miniscule

Table 2-1. Stability and Welfare Gains from Complete Price Stabilization under Different Expectational Forms.

Forms of Price Expectations	Instability Indicators[a]				Rate of Economic Gains (+) or Losses (−) from Complete Price Stabilization		
	(1)	(2)	(3)	(4)	Consumers[b]	Producers[c]	Total[b]
				No Serial Correlation			
Rational expectations	13.95	7.7	7.6	11.0	− 0.35	+ 0.91	+ 0.56
Adaptively rational expectations	14.16	7.9	7.7	11.1	− 0.40	+ 0.96	+ 0.56
Adaptive expectations	16.0	10.5	10.6	14.3	− 0.25	+ 1.09	+ 0.84
			With Serial Correlation ($R^2 = 0.3$)				
Rational expectations	14.0	7.3	7.8	10.8	− 0.27	+ 0.88	+ 0.61
Adaptively rational expectations	13.0	6.1	6.4	9.1	− 0.27	+ 0.78	+ 0.51
Adaptive expectations	12.2	4.9	5.1	7.8	+ 0.04	+ 0.56	0.60

[a](1) Coefficient of variation of price; (2) Probability that price falls below 20 percent of the stable level; (3) Probability that supply falls below 10 percent of the stable level; (4) Probability that farmers' income falls below 10 percent of the stable level.

[b]As a percentage of consumers' expenditures in a normal (stable) year.

[c]As a percentage of producers' income in a normal (stable) year.

in proportion to consumers' total expenditures or farmers' total income in an average year and is of the order of magnitude of 0.5 of 1 percent. Second, when there is no serial correlation, the mean price is the "best" predicter in the sense that "rational expectations" lead to the least instability of the price, of the quantity supplied and of farmers' income compared with the other expectational forms. For the same reason, complete stabilization is more beneficial (and more expensive) under "adaptive expectations," which lead to the largest instability. These results are reversed, however, in the presence of serial correlation. In that case the naive notion, adaptive expectations, has a higher predictive power than either one of the rational predicters. Thus, for instance, the coefficient of variation of the price is 14 percent under rational expectations but only 12.2 percent under adaptive expectations. The same holds for all other instability indicators. Third, the presence of serial correlation does not change the order of magnitude of the welfare gains from price stabilization. However, when expectations are adaptive then with serial correlation it is possible that not only producers gain from price stabilization but also consumers, contrary to what Massell's theoretical analysis predicts.

To explore the quantitative aspects of the efficiency gains a supply function of the following form was considered:

$$S_t = a + bE(P_t) - c\hat{\sigma}_t + u_t$$

where $\hat{\sigma}_t$ is the producers' prediction of price standard deviation, which stands as a proxy for the risk. Producers are assumed to be adaptively rational in estimating both the price and the variance in the sense that they perform their predictions on the basis of past observations. Specifically it is assumed that

$$E(P_t) = \frac{1}{n} \sum_{j=1}^{n} P_{t-j} \, ,$$

$$\hat{\sigma}_t^2 = \frac{1}{n} \sum_{j=1}^{n} [P_{t-j} - E(P_t)]^2 \ .$$

In the simulation experiments, these estimates were made on the basis of the past five observations. The risk coefficient c was assumed to be 0.5.

Table 2-2 summarizes the main results of these experiments. The most noteworthy result is the very large difference between the relative importance of the efficiency gains and that of the distribution gains. For the economy as a whole, the distribution gains constitute only 7 percent of the total gains from price stabilization whereas 93 percent were the efficiency gains. Obviously these results depend on the values of the parameters assumed for the model and particularly on the value of c. However, empirical studies that employed a similar functional form of the supply function indicate that the value of 0.5 assumed for c in our experiments is by no means exaggerated. (Many studies suggest that the value of this parameter is around 1.)

Consumers gain from price stabilization as a result of the increase in production and hence the decrease in price that follows the elimination of the risk. Producers' losses result from the decrease in price but their losses are offset in part by the general increase in production. Moreover, at least part of the supposed gains of producers under price instability must be considered as an insurance premium paid to provide some protection against the fluctuations of the price. As a consequence their losses due to stabilization are in effect smaller than indicated by these results. (For a more detailed analysis of this issue in a different framework, see Shalit 1980.)

In conclusion, the simulation experiments indicate that the efficiency gains are far more important for consumers and producers

Table 2-2. Distribution and Efficiency Gains from Complete Price Stabilization with Supply Response.

| | Economic Gains (+) or Losses (−) | | |
	Consumers[a]	Producers[b]	Total[a]
Distribution gains	− 0.4	+ 1.0	+ 0.6
Efficiency gains	+ 12.5	− 4.7	+ 7.8
Total gains	+ 12.1	− 3.7	+ 8.4
	With Serial Correlation ($R^2 = 0.3$)		
Distribution gains	− 0.27	+ 0.78	+ 0.51
Efficiency gains	+ 10.27	− 3.88	+ 6.39
Total gains	+ 10.00	− 3.10	+ 6.90

[a]As percentage of consumers' annual expenditures in a stable year.

[b]As percentage of producers' annual income in a stable year.

than the distribution gains. The neglect of these gains in the conventional models may have led to a severe understatement of the welfare gains from price stabilization.

IS THIS MODEL RELEVANT?

Despite its wide use in the theoretical economic literature, the Waugh-Oi-Massell model in all of its versions has rarely been applied in the formulation of practical guidelines for either national or international buffer stock policies. Four decades after the model was introduced, the question still remains: is this model appropriate for assessing the desirability of price stabilization? Is this the correct analytical framework for determining the need for buffer stocks? Is it relevant at all? Above all, the approach underlying this analytical framework reflects the persistent striving of welfare economists to find a single index with which to determine whether society is better off or worse off as a result of a given policy action. Despite the controversy, the concept of economic surplus is still regarded as the most useful index for that purpose in many practical cost/benefit analyses. Thus the extension offered by Waugh, Oi, and Massell of applying this concept in analyzing the desirability of price stabilization appeared to be a logical and very natural step. Yet in several respects their analytical framework is far too simplistic to be of any help in actual policymaking, and for some uses it must be considered entirely inappropriate.

As mentioned earlier, the usual form of the model fails to take into account the most important aspect of price stabilization, namely the reduction in risk and the resulting consequences for consumers and producers. If this aspect is ignored, then all that the model does is estimate the welfare gains or losses associated with the transfer of income from one group to another as a *byproduct* of shifting consumption from one time period to another. Concentrating on the distributional gains to the exclusion of the efficiency gains may result in severely underestimating the overall gains from stabilization and thus impair the usefulness of the model.

Moreover, and most important in regard to agricultural primary products (for which the model was originally designed and is most commonly applied), the model fails to take into account several crucial considerations underlying all stabilization schemes. In his pioneering contribution Waugh was careful to note that "this theorem (namely, that consumers may lose from price stabilization) is true only if the consumer can adjust his expenditure among the *n* periods" (1944:613). This, of course, is not the case with respect to staple food, for which the consumer can adjust expenditure only if sufficient private hoarding is possible (the costs of which are not taken into account) so that the consumer will be able to meet any future supply shortages that, it is implicitly assumed, he or she can perfectly foresee. In a more realistic world there is no way for us to measure the total of welfare losses caused in times of supply shortfalls and high prices, because there is no way for us to measure the damage caused by malnutrition or the loss of human life caused by starvation. Nor is conventional cost/benefit analysis capable of assessing the long-run effects of large downswings in farm product prices that can leave many producers financially ruined. The welfare gains from price instability promised by Waugh to consumers "over the long run" provide no comfort for those who are unable to obtain enough food for their mere survival at times of high prices and thus are forced into a state of starvation. Nor do the welfare gains from price instability promised by Oi to producers "over the long run" provide solace for those producers who, in the face of an imperfect capital market, are unable to cash in on these gains, and thus never reach the "long run" because they may go bankrupt when prices are plummeting.

To inject a dose of reality into this discussion, let us consider the results of a study undertaken by the United Nations Food and Agricultural Organization (FAO) among a group of ninety-three member countries, twenty-three developed and seventy developing countries. Countries were asked to state and rank their basic objectives in formulating national cereal stock policies. A sample of the responses is given in Table 2-3. The study concludes that most countries considered maintaining a continuous flow of supply at reasonable prices, offsetting fluctuations, and meeting shortfalls in production as the primary objectives of their stock policies. A number of countries specifically emphasized the needs of the vulnerable sections of the population. Half of the countries included among their primary objectives the establishment of emergency food reserves, either to meet extreme crop failures (mostly African countries) or to meet national security requirements (mostly the developed nations). Price stabilization was included by all countries as a primary objective. Several countries stated that they employ stock policies to encourage cereal

Table 2-3.   National Cereal Stock Policies.

Developing countries	General Aims
Algeria	Ensure domestic supply
	Stabilize prices
Bangladesh	Support price stabilization
	Meet emergencies, natural calamities, crop failures
Cameroon	Maintain supply to consumers
	Stabilize prices
	Meet emergencies
Chile	Maintain regular supplies to domestic markets
	Control prices
	Meet emergencies
Guatemala	Ensure domestic supply at reasonable prices
	Meet emergencies
India	Import interseasonal stability to internal supplies and prices
	Ensure adequate supplies at reasonable prices, especially to vulnerable sections of the population
Kenya	Maintain regular flow of supplies to domestic consumers
	Support price stabilization programs
	Meet emergencies
Mauritania	Ensure supplies to internal market
	Meet emergencies
	Stabilize prices
Mexico	Maintain supply to consumers at reasonable prices
	Cover emergencies
	Stabilize prices
Nigeria	Maintain domestic consumption
	Ensure food availability in times of disaster
	Stabilize prices
Pakistan	Maintain regular flow of supplies for domestic consumers at reasonable prices
	Meet emergencies
Philippines	Maintain regular flow of cereal supply for domestic consumption
	Stabilize prices
	Meet crop failures and emergencies

Table 2-3.   *(continued)*

Sri Lánka	Ensure equitable distribution of basic food-stuffs at reasonable prices
	Meet emergencies
Turkey	Meet emergencies
	Stabilize prices
	Strengthen government machinery of control over grain market
Uganda	Meet emergencies
	Support price stabilization
	Food aid
Zambia	Meet domestic consumption requirements
	Encourage domestic production of grain

Developed countries

Australia	Stable and remunerative prices to producers
	Maintain continuity of supply to regular customers
	Meet emergencies
Canada	Ensure that domestic requirements are covered
	Enable servicing of regular commercial markets
	Ensure strategic requirements and emergencies
	Enable the meeting of potential additional market opportunities
Finland	Ensure the needs of domestic consumption and food aid programs
	Stabilize prices
Japan	Maintain regular flow of supplies to domestic consumers
	Meet emergencies
Sweden	Maintain a regular flow of supplies to domestic markets
	Meet emergencies (including national security)
United States	Assume adequate supplies to consumers at reasonable prices
	Maintain producers' income at reasonable level
	Meet export obligations

Source: FAO 1977.

production, mostly through local purchases of grain for reserves at prices that provide an incentive to producers.

What are we to conclude from all this? The most obvious conclusion is that stabilization policies involve several diverse and sometimes conflicting objectives, not all of which can be found in the realm of pure welfare economics. There is no single measure such as "overall welfare gains" that can adequately represent the motivation of governments to be actively engaged in stabilization policies. Countries are concerned with price stabilization; they want to assume that a sufficient supply is always available at "reasonable" prices so that everyone, especially the poor, can obtain the basic nutritional requirements; they want to assure the solvency of the farm sector. Policymakers are not seeking a single index that can show the extent to which these concerns are justified. Welfare gains or losses that result from stabilization policies should not in themselves be taken as an indication of whether or not the policies are desirable. Instead, welfare losses should be regarded as an insurance premium paid by the economy in order to achieve a certain degree of price stabilization.

The model should not be scrapped entirely as some have suggested (for instance, Hathaway 1976 and Cochrane 1980). The baby should not be thrown out with the bath water. Besides knowing how successful certain policies are in achieving their specified stabilization goals, economists and policymakers need to know the overall cost to the economy at large of achieving these goals. It is for this purpose that the analytical framework advanced by Waugh, Oi, and Massell is useful and indeed necessary.

NOTES

1. With the linear adjustment rule the variance of the market price is given by $\underline{\sigma}^2/(d + m)^2$ and it therefore decreases monotonically with m.

2. When disturbances are multiplicative the first-order conditions for maximum are

$$\bar{P}(1 - k\sigma_p) = C'(Q).$$

In that case the *slope* of the supply curve of a risk-averse producer increases with an increase in price variability. The safety margins are then larger the larger is the quantity produced.

3. In some studies these costs are taken into acount in a very crude way, as by being made proportional to the standard deviation.
4. The details of the calculations are as follows: Let $P = D(Q)$ be the demand function; P_1 and P_2 are the upper and lower trigger prices for the storage operation (see Figure 2–3) and Q_1 and Q_2 are the corresponding quantities: V is the vacant storage capacity and S is the quantity of the commodity in storage. Given the frequency distribution of production and a price-band storage policy, the expected price is determined by

$$E(P) = \int_0^{Q_2 + V} D(Q)\, f(Q)\, dQ + P_2 \int_{Q_2 + V}^{Q_2} f(Q)\, dQ + \int_{Q_2}^{Q_1} D(Q)\, f(Q)\, dQ$$

$$+ P_1 \int_{Q_1}^{Q_1 + S} f(Q)\, dQ + \int_{Q_1 + S}^{\infty} D(Q)\, f(Q)\, dQ .$$

In the simulation experiments presented in Figures 2–6 and 2–7 a linear demand function with an elasticity of 1 at the mean point $\bar{Q} = 100$, $\bar{P} = 100$ is assumed.

3 HOW COUNTRIES ARE COPING

Various policies are used in developing countries to cope with the problems of food security and price stabilization. The elaborate and very comprehensive foodgrain management system in India, reviewed here, is of particular interest not only because of the magnitude of the problem in that country but also because it has become a model that many countries are trying to follow. The brief descriptions that follow of the foodgrain policies in Pakistan, Bangladesh, Sri Lanka, and the ASEAN region (Indonesia, Malaysia, the Philippines, Singapore, and Thailand) highlight their similarities to India's foodgrain policy as well as the differences that result from adjusting the system to their specific needs.

East Africa faces a problem completely different from that of Asia, yet its foodgrain management system shows a number of intriguing similarities to the system in many of the Asian nations. One source of difficulty in Africa is the fragmentation of the foodgrain markets, a phenomenon arising out of socioeconomic factors such as tribal rivalry on the one hand and logistic impediments such as poor transportation infrastructure on the other. The efforts of some governments in the East African countries to create an integrated system has usually resulted in a strong bias against the rural sector, which has increased rather than diminished the country's vulnerability to hunger.

Egypt, which by the standards of many countries does not suffer from deprivation of food, faces a completely different problem. More than half of its foodgrain supply—almost all of the wheat and a substantial proportion of the other foods—is imported. Food security in Egypt thus depends on the availability of imported foodgrains and hence on the availability of foreign exchange and of secured sources of supply.

The chapter then briefly reviews certain elements of the food policies in Columbia, Mexico, and Brazil, concluding with a description of the system in Israel. Although Israel is free from many of the problems facing the other developing countries, one element in the Israeli experience deserves special attention: the functioning of the system under the pressures of rapid inflation.

It is not the object of this chapter to provide an in-depth review of the problems facing each of the countries, nor is appraisal of the functioning of the various systems attempted. The purpose instead is to describe the various policy instruments applied in these countries and to examine the conditions and principles that underlie the design of these policies.

INDIA

The Bengal famine of 1943, which took the lives of more than two million people, marked a turning point in the scope and form of the foodgrain policy in India. Until the late 1930s the country was essentially self-sufficient; before that it was even an exporter of foodgrain. However, rapid population growth turned India into a net importer of foodgrain and heightened its vulnerability to the unstable weather conditions characteristic of the subcontinent. In the aftermath of the Bengal famine a comprehensive all-India system was established to manage the foodgrain market. Interdistrict movement of grain was restricted; special policy committees were set up to determine floor prices for foodgrain; the central government procured grain from surplus areas for distribution in deficit areas; the state government distributed and rationed foodgrain in urban areas; statutory price controls and licensing of traders were enforced; the central government assumed direct control over imports.

The current foodgrain policy in India owes a good deal to the legacy of British rule. Perhaps its most basic feature, that difficult food situations must be managed by government administration, grew out of the preindependence system. The postindependence foodgrain policy has become considerably more elaborate and comprehensive over the years. As a result, government decisions in regard to the procurement and distribution of foodgrain have become an extremely important variable in the day-to-day lives of most of the people.

The system has evolved against a background of a number of factors: capricious and unpredictable climatic conditions that cause considerable instability in production; poor domestic distribution between surplus and deficit areas; a rapidly growing population that, at the present rate, doubles itself every twenty-eight years; swiftly expanding urban centers, crowded with multitudes of migrants from rural areas; and periodically gaps between domestic production and consumption, which necessitates more imports to make up the difference.

The general goal of the system is to safeguard, in the words of an oft-repeated election slogan, "equitable distribution of foodgrain at reasonable prices." Specifically, government objectives include:

- Steady growth of consumption. The supply of foodgrain should increase at a rate higher than the rate of growth of the population, so as to permit a steady growth in per capita consumption and thus overcome existing dietary deficiencies. Fluctuations in supply should be reduced; localized or widespread famine and undernutrition should be avoided.
- Fair price distribution. Remunerative prices to farmers should be maintained; farmers should be provided with incentives to adopt improved technology; prices should be stabilized; low prices should be secured for the vulnerable sections of the population; negative effects on the general cost of living and wages should be prevented.
- Self-sufficiency. Dependence on imports should be gradually eliminated.

To achieve these objectives and to cope with the difficulties arising from the strenuous conditions existing in India, the central government and the state governments have developed an extremely elaborate system of grain marketing. Its basic premise is that a free market economy cannot be relied on to secure an equitable distribution and to attain these objectives. The free market for foodgrain is regarded as highly imperfect and unstable, dominated by large monopoly elements and thus incapable of handling the foodgrain distribution in a way that suits the national interest. The faith in the free market system is so small and the striving for a socialist pattern of society so widespread that socialization of the entire trade in grain is considered by many a necessary step if the government is to achieve its objectives. Over the years since independence the government has made continual efforts to increase its share in the foodgrain trade and to gain a position of strength in the market so as to be able to regulate the price. In 1973 the government even made an attempt to nationalize the entire wholesale trade in wheat, but had to retreat as the plan proved to be a complete failure. Still, public procurement has risen steadily and by the late 1970s was more than 10 percent of total output (sometimes as high as 20 percent), so that its share in the marketed surplus was over 30 percent.

The achievement of equitable distribution of foodgrain at reasonable prices has been sought by the government through a policy of partial control of trading in cereals by means of instruments such as internal procurement, public distribution, imports, multiple pricing, restrictions on interstate private trading, regulation of bank advances against foodgrain, and a ban on all forms of forward trading. A brief review of the major instruments follows.

Internal Procurement

The central government, on the recommendation of the Agricultural Prices Commission, fixes procurement prices of wheat, paddy rice, and other cereals, and determines targets of procurement for each state. The procurement price is announced on the eve of the marketing season and is chiefly determined on the basis of the expected volume of the crop, the expected level of market prices, the target quantity planned for procurement, and the likely effects on the market price. Earlier in the year, before the sowing season starts, the government announces the minimum support prices. The basic consideration in determining these prices is that they should cover the cost of cultivation and leave an adequate margin of profit. The minimum prices are largely meaningless since market prices at harvest time are invariably higher than the minimum prices, and over the years the procurement price has become the effective minimum price.

The announcement of the procurement prices along with the quantitative goals is considered to be a major item of government economic policy. Intensive lobbying and even demonstrations are used by farmers' groups and other interested parties to influence the decisions.

The actual procurement of grain is done by the departments of civil supply in the various states. The method of procurement varies from state to state and from one type of foodgrain to another. The problem facing the authorities is how to procure a sufficient quantity of foodgrain at reasonable prices without jeopardizing the farmers' incentive to produce more.

The most effective and least complicated method of procurement is by purchase in the open market. This, however, may require the state to pay prices considerably higher than the announced procurement price and thus disrupt the central government's effort to secure low prices for the public distribution system. The zone system, which existed until 1977, was designed to aid the procurement drive by forcing the accumulation of grain in the surplus districts or states, thereby causing the price in these zones to drop and approach the announced procurement price. The system restricted interzonal private trading and required road checks, policing of borders, and civil control of smuggling. Its primary objective was to ensure the transfer of foodgrain to the public distribution system in the deficit areas, especially when supply was tight. It was thus tuned more to the needs of low-income consumers who depend on the public distribution system, and less to the needs of the rest of the population in the deficit areas.

A procurement method frequently used for rice and occasionally for wheat is a levy on the middlemen or the processors. Thus, for instance, millers are required to sell a proportion (and sometimes all) of the rice they process to the government at the procurement price. Compliance with this requirement is often a condition of retaining the license to operate.

Another method is a direct levy on producers, which requires them to sell to the government a certain amount of their yield at the procurement price. The levy is usually progressively graded, with complete exemption for smaller farmers and differing assessments for produce from irrigated and unirrigated land. This method is not used, however, in the states that provide most of the surplus.

Different combinations of these administrative practices are used in the country. Even within a single state, more than one method is often used. The resulting complex of rules and procedures requires a great deal of interpretation and adjustment, as shown in the following illustration.

The Rice Procurement System in the State of Orissa.   (This illustration draws on J. Wall (1978: Annex II)). The government of Orissa typically procures 5 to 6 percent of the state's total production, which amounts to about 20 percent of the quantity entering the market. The procurement operation is directed by the government of Orissa's Food and Civil Supplies Department and uses a variety of agents, including the Food Corporation of India, the civil administration (district collector) Revenue Department, cooperative structures and private millers.

Before the procurement drive begins each year, the chief minister, food minister, and secretary of the Food and Supply Department discuss with representatives of the central government (Agricultural Prices Commission and Ministry of Food, Agriculture, and Irrigation) the conditions in the state, prices to be set, and target quantities to be procured. An all-India procurement price for rice and a target quantity for Orissa are eventually fixed, and the state is then free to implement the policy to the best of its ability.

The commonest procurement system in Orissa is monopoly procurement. In theory this system should prevent anyone from buying, selling, or storing paddy (unprocessed rice) in wholesale quantities except on government account. This would make the government of Orissa a monopoly procurer of paddy and rice. In practice, however, these regulations have never been enforced, and the share of government procurement in the total marketing of paddy and rice has never exceeded 25 percent.

The way the system actually works is through a levy on large rice millers. Surplus areas in the state are cordoned off and the shipment of paddy and rice from these areas is prohibited. Millers in the surplus areas are licensed to procure paddy from farmers on the government's account, mill it into rice, and then deliver the rice to a storage facility belonging to the government of Orissa or to an official distribution agent. The government pays the millers a flat price calculated on the basis of the official procurement price of paddy, adjusted to allow for an average output of rice from the paddy plus an allowance for operating expenses. Large millers must comply with the regulations in order to hold a license to operate. Small millers are allowed to operate only as custom hullers but not on their own account. With the lack of effective enforcement, however, small millers do in fact operate in part on their own account. The very large number of small mills makes it extremely difficult for the government of Orissa to control the entire procurement drive or even a major part of it. This is also an important factor motivating the small millers to continue operating despite their use of outmoded technology.

To compete with the small millers the large ones have to offer farmers a price for their paddy higher than the official procurement price. Even though they must officially procure paddy only on government account and must turn over the milled rice to the government at a price based on the official procurement price, they are able to offer a higher price to the farmers for several reasons. First, they are more efficient at procuring, handling, storing, and milling rice than the government assumes in its calculations. For instance, the calculation allows for a 65 percent output of rice from paddy; the rice millers can achieve 70 percent or more, leaving them with extra rice that can be sold in the open market. Second, they are freely permitted to sell the byproducts of rice milling, such as the rice bran. Third, and perhaps most important, large millers do in fact operate illegally on their own account. They buy paddy, mill it, and sell the rice in the open market, and the government is unable to control these illicit operations effectively. Moreover, the government deliberately refrains from exerting its control and allows the millers, sometimes openly, to sell part of their milled rice in the open market (up to 50 percent or more). This is done in order to enable the large millers to pay the farmers higher prices for their paddy and still deliver some rice to the government. The government is perfectly aware that if the regulations were strictly enforced, especially when the market price of paddy far exceeds the procurement price, mills would have to stop operating and would thus deliver no rice to the government.

In 1974–75, monopoly procurement was replaced by a new system involving a levy on millers. The new regulations allowed millers to sell legally 25 percent of the milled rice in the open market and deliver only 75 percent of their output to the government. This not only legalized part of their illegal activities but also made it easier for them to expand them. Whereas under monopoly procurement millers could openly sell only very small quantities of rice, under the millers' levy system they could legitimately deal in large quantities on their own account and could therefore deal in even larger quantities illegitimately.

In the same marketing year, 1974–75, a producers' levy was also introduced. Farmers with less than four acres of irrigated land or eight acres of unirrigated land were exempted. Thereafter the levy rose progressively from one to three quintals per acre, depending on the area and type of land. The revenue department prepared assessment lists based on land records and sent notices to farmers informing them where, when, and in what quantities they were to deliver their levied paddy. They were to be paid the official procurement price of paddy plus incidental charges on delivery. Collection agents, either cooperatives or private individuals, were appointed to receive the paddy, pay the farmers, and deliver the paddy to government milling or storage agents. District collectors were to oversee the operation of the levy.

The producers' levy has not worked well. Land records were in bad shape, and this has led to many disputes and appeals; the government was not adequately prepared to administer the new system; unusually large differences between the official procurement price and the market price, as a result of very small yields, have led to serious and at times violent confrontations between government officials and farmers; the legislation has been appealed against in Orissa's High Court, rejected, and appealed again in the Supreme Court of India. As a result, only very small quantities have been procured through the producers' levy in the first few years after its introduction.

Public Distribution

A portion of the grain procured by the states is retained for their own public distribution system. The rest is sold to the central government; this, plus the imported grain and the net quantity released from government storage, is allocated to states for sale through public distribution shops. The allocation is made so as to supplement food supply in deficit states and to ensure a low price for the foodgrains distributed through these shops. Political factors may also play a role in determining the allocation.

The foodgrain procured by the state or purchased from the central government is channeled through the state's public distribution system to retail "fair-price" shops that sell to the public. The price at which grain is sold in fair-price shops is the issue price fixed by the government each year. It is set so as to cover the cost of procuring the grain plus handling expenses (but not including administration expenses, which may be substantial) while at the same time taking into account the price of imported grain.

In many states the sale of foodgrain in the fair-price shops is formally rationed; only eligible households holding special ration cards can buy and even then no more than the amount specified in the cards. In all states, however, there is also informal rationing. This is partly done by locating the fair-price shops in low-income neighborhoods. The long lines in front of the shops and the quality of the grain offered for sale may also deter less needy customers and thus also serve a rationing function. However, quite often house servants go to the ration shops for these consumers.

To date there are more than a quarter-million fair-price shops, located mostly in large urban centers. A large part of the distributed foodgrain goes to two metropolitan centers, Bombay and Calcutta. In contrast, smaller urban areas and rural areas do not benefit at all from the public distribution system, even though in these areas there are people living in the most abject poverty. In addition, leakages and abuse of the system are often reported, especially when there is a substantial difference between the market price and the issue price.

Imports

The central government has a monopoly on all foreign trade in foodgrains. Almost all of the grain imported is wheat. Imports amount to about 40 percent of the quantity supplied by the public distribution system, though on occasion the government will substantially increase its imports of foodgrain to meet existing shortages or to supplement its buffer stocks, as illustrated in Table 3-1 for the crisis period 1970–1976.

Performance of the System

An overall evaluation of the performance of India's foodgrain management system is not only very difficult but is also unlikely to lead to any unequivocal conclusions. Because the system is highly complex, its repercussions are felt throughout the economy either directly or indirectly, so that its overall effects are almost impossible

Table 3-1. Public Distribution: Resources and Uses
(Million Metric Tons).

Year	Internal Procurement	Imports	Issues	Change in Government Stocks
1970	6.7	3.6	8.8	+0.9
1971	8.9	2.1	7.8	+2.6
1972	7.7	0.5	11.4	−4.5
1973	8.4	3.6	11.4	−0.5
1974	5.6	4.8	10.8	−0.4
1975	9.4	7.4	11.3	+5.4
1976	12.7	6.5	9.2	+10.7

Source: Wall (1978).

to measure. Moreover, the various goals pursued are often inconsistent and even conflicting.

In one important aspect the system has fulfilled its function. Ever since the Bengal famine of 1943, the government of India has always managed to mobilize sufficient supplies of foodgrain to avoid another widespread catastrophic famine. Still, as late as 1974, a World Bank memo records

> undereating on the part of many, outright hunger among considerable numbers, reported death from starvation or prolonged malnutrition in numbers both overstated and understated, depending on the source of information, occasional suicides, desertion of children, greater crowding of cities, and sale of land by small holders to meet immediate food needs. (Ladejinsky 1974)

A detailed evaluation of the foodgrain management system is beyond the scope of this book. (See, for instance, Krishna 1977; Krishna and Paychanduri 1980; Scandizzo and Swami 1981; Wall 1978.) Offered here instead are some comments on the economic rationale of several elements of the system and the main policy instruments, with analytical and quantitative analyses of these instruments postponed to later chapters.

The public distribution system in India functions essentially as a redistribution mechanism that works by transferring income from producers and nonbeneficiary consumers to those consumers who receive the distributed foodgrain. For instance, procurement below the market price is essentially a form of taxation on agricultural income.

In addition, internal procurement reduces the quantity available for the free market, thereby raising the market price to the cost of those consumers who buy there.

As a form of tax-cum-subsidy mechanism the foodgrain management system has a number of drawbacks. First, the internal procurement system is a regressive form of taxation because the small farmer who lacks storage capacity is generally forced to sell his surplus at harvest time at the lower procurement price, while the larger and richer farmer with a large storage capacity and access to cheap credit can sell a substantial part of his output later at a much higher price. (On the other hand this policy has very little effect on small producers who produce largely for self-consumption.)

The degree to which the public distribution system actually reaches its target group, the low-income consumers, has often been seriously questioned. Foodgrain is distributed to an overwhelming extent in large urban areas, whereas consumers in most rural and small urban areas do not benefit at all. In addition, the system is often abused, and formal rationing has not always proved effective. Nevertheless, the informal together with the formal rationing does increase the likelihood that a large portion of the grain offered in fair-price shops does in fact reach the low-income consumers.

Another drawback of the foodgrain management system fixing the procurement price at below the market price must result in an excess demand for foodgrain that can be curbed only by distribution controls and/or rationing. Thus, rationing and distribution controls are concomitants of price control, and the price control can only be as effective as the associated distribution controls. In the case of India, widespread evasion, illicit trading, and massive adjustments to the rules make it very difficult for the government to procure the target amounts when the procurement price is set far below the market price. At the same time a rise in the procurement price may create expectations of a higher market price during the harvest, leading to hoarding, and thus bringing about a further rise in price.

Replacing the procurement system with open market purchases by the government has often been proposed but rejected on the grounds that such purchases would raise the market prices and thus necessitate heavy subsidies when the grain was distributed to the public. At the same time, however, the huge administrative costs required by the present system, and the opportunities it offers for widespread evasion and corruption, which have an immeasurably negative effect on all walks of life in India, should be taken into account. Incompetence and corruption in the lower ranks of both the central government's and the states' administration play a pivotal role in the process and have led to a situation in which, in the words of Minhas, the system "has not only become stagnant, it has also acquired a degree of illegitimacy which is becoming socially intolerable" (1976:240).

Strong dissatisfaction with the system led the government of India to experiment with a policy of complete takeover of the wholesale wheat trade in 1973. Despite all the legal and administrative preparatory efforts, the plan failed badly and had to be hastily withdrawn. Procurement of wheat under the government takeover fell far short of the statewide operational targets and was much lower even than that of the previous year. This, combined with the very low level of stocks and the high world prices of foodgrains, produced an unbearable strain on the working of the public distribution system and brought the experiment to an early end.

The search for a better system of foodgrain management in India has not yet ended. Monopoly procurement or complete takeover of the wholesale trade is still on the law books of several states. It seems, however, that the free market system has not as yet been given a fair chance, and other forms of intervention, which would permit the market to operate freely and without heavy administrative controls but would regulate its operation in the desired direction, have still to be tried.

PAKISTAN

Pakistan has an extensive system of licensed ration shops, in which among the ordinary retail goods, rationed wheat flour and refined sugar are sold at a fixed mark-up. Rationed quantities are dispensed per capita, without reference to any measure of need or wealth. The government procures the wheat at competitive prices from domestic producers and, when necessary, from abroad. Ration wheat, thought to be of lower quality than open market wheat, provides the poorest 5 percent of the population with more than 50 percent of their caloric intake and 66 percent of their protein. Two aspects of the food production and distribution system in Pakistan will be discussed in this review. One is Pakistan's trade policy toward agricultural products;

the other is yet another example of the impediments imposed on the system by a bureaucratic maze.

Pakistan's price and distribution policy is heavily biased against the rural sector and in favor of the urban sector. This is most clearly demonstrated in its trade policy. Until 1972 multiple exchange rates were practiced and agricultural exports received the lowest exchange rate. In addition, the export of most foodstuffs other than rice was banned. The objective of this policy was to hold down domestic prices to urban consumers and thus facilitate the processes of urbanization and industrialization. After a devaluation of the rupee in 1972 the practices of multiple exchange rates were abolished, but the bias against the agricultural sector has since then been manifested in substantial export taxes. This policy has had the effect of transferring income, through the price system, from rural to urban consumers and to the government.

To some extent this effect is offset by the government's subsidies to agricultural inputs. However, these subsidies benefit mainly the larger and wealthier farmers, who get most of the institutional credit for agriculture and who buy most of the subsidized fertilizers, tubewells, and farm machinery. The small grower is not only deprived of the benefits from the subsidies but also pays the taxes out of which the subsidies are funded.

The bureaucratic maze and the inefficiency involved in the public procurement and distribution systems are by no means unique to Pakistan; indeed the situation there is probably no worse than in neighboring countries. It is important to emphasize, however, that corruption and incompetence, especially at the lower level of the government bureaucracy, may impose considerable burdens on the system and interfere in its operation, as the following example illustrates. In mid-1976, the nationalization of rice and flour milling led to a considerable increase in the hardships of corruption and bribery. Rice brought by the farmers to the government rice mill would be rejected (similar phenomena were noted for other crops, especially cotton). The farmers would be told to take their rice home and dry it for another week or that it was too dirty or not acceptable for other reasons. To take the rice back would have caused serious hardship to the farmers, many of whom had brought their rice by bullock cart. With a bribe to the mill purchaser the rice suddenly became acceptable.

A common explanation for petty corruption during the nationalization period was that salaries were too low and the penalties too small to act as a deterrent to government employees. Private millers and other dealers know perfectly well that dishonesty will cost them their customers and future income. Government employees are free from any such considerations.

BANGLADESH

Bangladesh has a long history of food problems, which reached crisis proportion in the 1970s. An inherent distrust of the private sector and its ability to meet the special needs of the poor and malnourished, coupled with a strong preference for visible administrative measures in periods of crisis, have led to a system that is largely dominated by the government. Although the system has a great deal in common with the system in India, one aspect deserves special attention.

In recent years government price policies and the public distribution system have put special emphasis on the consumption characteristics of basic staple foods. Wheat, for instance, is considered an inferior commodity in this region and is relatively more important as a food supply to the poor. The government has made special efforts to increase the domestic supply of wheat through concessional imports and by encouraging more productive wheat technology. In 1978 an experimental program was set up for the distribution of sorghum through selected ration shops in urban and rural areas. Its aim was to direct part of the public food distribution toward the poor and malnourished by introducing this very poorly regarded (or low status) but nutritionally valuable food. The results indicated that the use of such "self-targeting" goods has considerable potential for affecting malnutrition and the distribution of income.

SRI LANKA

A very large part of the paddy marketed in Sri Lanka is handled through the public sector procurement and rationing operations. At times more than 75 percent of all the rice consumed in the country passes through the public system, and food subsidies have averaged approximately 20 percent of the gross national product over the past fifteen years. Rice is procured from the farmers at a guaranteed price and distributed at a subsidized price through the ration system. Wheat is not rationed and is sold through the usual retail outlets.

Each year the government announces the procurement price, which then in effect becomes the market price, and the paddy can therefore be procured freely without any need of procurement quotas. The government has pursued a policy of maintaining low rice prices through a Guaranteed Price Scheme (GPS) and encouraging production mainly through irrigation, land settlement, and the subsidization of inputs. The GPS is administered by the Paddy Marketing Board, and procurement is carried out by its agents throughout the country. Once the Paddy Marketing Board receives the paddy, it makes arrangements to have it milled and transported to the district warehouse of the Food Commissioner's Department. From there the rice is distributed to approximately 10,000 authorized distributors around the country, most of which are retail cooperatives.

All the rice entering the public distribution system is formally rationed, using special ration cards. Until 1978, however, almost the entire population of Sri Lanka received an allotment of rice at the subsidized price. After 1967 a portion of the allotment was made available free of charge. In 1978 the newly elected government completely abandoned the rationing scheme for a food stamp scheme that covers only 50 percent of the population. Stamps are redeemable for any of ten different sorts of food and the unused stamps can be deposited in post office savings banks. The change in the system has lowered the subsidy costs by more than 40 percent.

Before 1972, when world prices of wheat, rice, and sugar were low, most of the costs of operating the food subsidy scheme were covered by the sale of the imported sugar and wheat at prices higher than the import price. Since then world prices of these products have risen sharply and the government, attempting to prevent a parallel domestic price rise, has had to carry an increasing fiscal burden.

In 1973 an attempt was made to enforce government monopoly procurement by prohibiting the transport of paddy by private persons. Farmers, however, were reluctant to sell to the government at the announced prices, which were very low especially when compared with the rising import prices. As a result the proportion of production entering the public system declined drastically. After two unsuccessful years the government withdrew in 1975 from the monopoly procurement plan.

THE ASEAN REGION:
INDONESIA, MALAYSIA, THE PHILIPPINES,
SINGAPORE, AND THAILAND

The five countries comprising the Association for South East Asian Nations (ASEAN) are almost exclusively dependent on rice. Thailand is the only one of these countries that is a net exporter of rice, while the others are net importers. The small quantities of rice traded in the world market, less than 5 percent of world production, and the high degree of instability in world prices have motivated the importing countries in the region to adopt policies that lessen their dependence on foreign trade and to aim for self-sufficiency. This is generally pursued through instruments having only medium or long term impact, like production drives or heavy investment in irrigation. In the short run, however, their strategy is totally inconsistent with self-sufficiency, and their main policy instrument for coping with harvest fluctuations is compensating changes in the level of imports.

The extent of market intervention by the governments of the ASEAN countries varies from country to country, the main differences being in the extent of reliance on the free market mechanism and the use of the price system in the exercise of controls. Government intervention has been most extensive in Indonesia, while Thailand's policies still leave considerable scope for private traders, although even there government policies are a major factor in price determination.

A common feature of the policies in all these countries is a gradual replacement of the middleman, particularly in price stabilization, foreign trade, and stock operations, by various public and government measures. Thus, for instance, the Rice and Corn Administration in the Philippines and the National Logistics Agency (Bulog) in Indonesia have assumed all the tasks of rice procurement and imports.

In the 1970s, with the sharp rise in world prices of foodgrains, there was a shift toward policies more favorable to producers' interests. In Indonesia, for example, a program of supporting farm prices was more aggressively promoted. Financial resources were made available to Bulog for procuring larger amounts of domestic rice to shore up the support price. In Malaysia support prices were announced for domestically produced rice and backed by a government procurement program. The procured stocks were disposed of through a system requiring all rice importers to buy domestic rice from the government stockpile in a specified proportion to the amount they wished to import. This caused the price of imported rice to rise, thus effectively taxing the imported rice in order to subsidize the domestic product. In 1973 this policy was changed. The Paddy and Rice Marketing Board was given an import monopoly and was charged with maintaining a domestic stockpile of rice to ensure security of supplies.

Thailand, because of her unique position as a rice exporter, has a totally different history, with the private sector being given more scope than in other countries. The primary, indeed, the sole impact of the rice policy is felt at the export level, as the government manipulates its foreign trade volume to ensure sufficient domestic supplies. This is carried out mainly via the price system through measures such as export tax but is supplemented at times by direct quantitative restrictions on exports. In general, however, the government makes efforts to minimize its intervention. Thus, for instance, although about one-half of the rice exported from Thailand is on a government-to-government basis, the government procures this rice in the open market. By using the export tax policy fairly extensively to stabilize the domestic price, Thailand has introduced a destabilizing element into the world market, exporting its domestic fluctuations to the importing countries. Because of Thailand's significant role in the world rice market, the result has been much higher instability in that market.

Although the long-term objective of the importing countries in the ASEAN region is to achieve self-sufficiency in rice, recourse to foreign trade for supplementing domestic production is a regular phenomenon. Fluctuations in domestic production are usually countered by opposite movements at the import level, the objective being to stabilize the price at a predetermined target. However, lack of information about the expected levels of supply and required consumption often results in errors in the calculation of the required level of imports. Furthermore, the international rice market has proved to be a very volatile and unreliable source. The overall result is that government efforts to attain food security and price stabilization through adjustments in the volume of imports are often frustrated, leading to a higher instead of a lower degree of domestic price instability.

EAST AFRICA

Foodgrain markets in East Africa are typically fragmented, with an urban sector supplied through an official distribution system that is usually monopolized by the government, and scattered rural and urban markets supplied through the unofficial system. The sources of supply for the official system, which accounts for only a small fraction of total food transactions, are the state-controlled large-scale production units such as the state farms in Tanzania and Ethiopia, certain quantities procured from the traditional farm producers, imports, and government stocks.

For a number of reasons distribution through the official, government-operated channels is directed mostly to urban centers. First, food availability and stable prices are considered vital for political reasons. Second, the local handling of rural distribution is very difficult to administer. Third, inadequate transport and storage handling facilities create serious logistic difficulties in arranging effective distribution to rural areas. Fourth, the higher prices of the foodgrain that passes through the official distribution system would necessitate large subsidy payments if an extensive rural distribution was undertaken.

In times of shortage the public distribution system often dries up. This happens because its sources of supply switch as far as possible to the unofficial market, which at that time is paying considerably higher prices. Also, the demand for food grain through the official channels increases substantially, especially with the rise in price in the unofficial distribution channels. In addition, the official price applies only for part of the season; after the main harvest period farmers can sell stored crops at higher prices, sometimes more than double the official price. Thus the actual price facing most consumers and producers may differ substantially from the official prices and may also vary from one area to another.

Because very little of the public distribution system trickles into rural areas, food security in these areas is largely a question of rural self-sufficiency. This requires the designing of appropriate policies. Thus, for instance, consortia for crops have been promoted in Tanzania because they are more reliable, even though monoculture is more efficient. In several countries the promotion of drought-resistant crops such as millet and sorghum in order to achieve self-sufficiency at the village level requires a special subsidy program to support these crops during the good years because their market value is then very small.

EGYPT

Rapid population growth (currently at an annual rate of 2.5 percent) on the one hand and a very slow increase in food production on the other have forced Egypt to rely increasingly on food imports to bridge the gap between food consumption and domestic production. Not only has the population increased eight times, from 5 million at the turn of the century to almost 40 million at the end of the 1970s, but the urbanization process has intensified. In 1897, 81 percent of the total population was rural; by 1976 this rate had dropped to 56 percent. The vast majority of the population is still concentrated along the Nile and its delta, and in the 80-year period since 1897 the amount of agricultural land has increased only marginally (from 5.1 million feddans in 1897 to about 6.0 million feddans in 1976).

Development over the last twenty-five years, especially in industry, with the resulting increase in average income, has permitted a slow but steady increase in the per capita consumption and calorie intake at an average annual rate of more than 1 percent. Cereal consumption, which constitutes more than 50 percent of total food consumption, has also risen steadily. These trends resulted in a growing food deficit, which had to be met by imports, and by the end of the 1970s more than half of Egypt's total food consumption was imported. The import bill in grain and flour amounts to some 20 percent of total import expenditures and more than 50 percent of total export revenues. Moreover, because Egypt's cultivable land area is limited and most of it is already irrigated, yields are already quite high; significant production increases will therefore be difficult to achieve, and the need for increasingly large imports will continue into the foreseeable future.

The government of Egypt is very extensively involved in the foodgrain markets, in some operations having complete monopoly and in others having direct control. The overall goals of the government food policies are:

- To stabilize the price at a sufficiently low level to allow the entire population, and particularly the urban poor, to consume at least the necessary amount of food;
- To allow a steady increase in per capita consumption;
- To achieve self-sufficiency in all staple food products except for wheat and to reduce the burden on the balance of payments and the fiscal budget.

Government long-run strategy toward achieving these goals consists of expanding agricultural land through land reclamation; improving land productivity; changing the crop mix toward more extensive cultivation of high-value crops, not necessarily food products; increasing the overall export proceeds; securing dependable sources of imports; and ensuring the desired distribution of food, so that all income groups can receive at least the minimum subsistence quantity.

The growing deficit between food consumption and domestic food production, the increasing burden on the fiscal budget of the various food subsidies, and the extreme political sensitivity of these issues exert considerable strain on the system, sometimes resulting in widespread riots, and the government has frequently been forced to shift from one set of policies to another in order to accommodate the most immediately pressing needs. At various periods these policies have included support prices, producer subsidization, public distribution and consumer subsidization, and various trade policies.

Support prices. Egyptian farmers are required to sell specified quotas (sometimes reaching one-half of their production) of paddy rice at a fixed price to the government. Quotas for wheat were waived in 1970, and corn for human consumption is traded freely, mostly in rural areas, without support or guaranteed or fixed prices. The price fixed by the government for wheat and rice is usually lower than the prevailing market price in the rural areas but is regarded as the secured support price.

Producer subsidization. Cereal production is subsidized in various ways. Irrigation water is supplied free to the farm (but the farmer has to pay for irrigation pumps to lift the water from the canals to his field). Drainage of excess water is free; construction and maintenance of a network of irrigation canals and drainage ditches are the responsibility of the government. Seeds for certain crops are sold at reduced prices. Diesel oil, the primary fuel used to operate tractors and water pumps, is sold to farmers below cost. Fertilizers are subsidized by the government, but growers are allowed only specified quantities of fertilizer per unit area, depending on the crop and on the general fertility of the land in the district. Interest rates on agricultural loans are often subsidized. Customs duties on imports of agricultural machinery have been suspended.

Public distribution and consumer subsidization. Most cereals are heavily subsidized by the government in order to secure low prices for staple food. To subsidize wheat and wheat flour alone, more than

$850 million was allocated in the budget of 1979.

Subsidization occurs at various points in the distribution process. Flour mills, for instance, pay the same fixed price for imported and domestic wheat. In 1979 this price was only 55 percent of the price paid for wheat procured internally and less than 35 percent of the average CIF price for imported wheat. The wheat procured and imported is milled mainly in government mills at a subsidized rate. The product of domestic milling is balady flour, which is sold to bakeries at a subsidized price. As a result of all these subsidies balady bread is sold to consumers at a price one-fifth its actual cost. Similarly, bakeries pay only 45 percent of the CIF price for imported wheat flour, which is used to produce European bread, and the products of the imported flour are further subsidized.

Rice is both subsidized and rationed. However, the rationing applies to the entire population, with each person receiving an allotment of between 0.75 to 5 kilograms, which can be bought only at the government food stores. Corn, which is the main food in the rural areas, is not usually subsidized. The price of domestic corn, which is mostly used for on-farm human consumption, is determined freely in the local market, while the price of imported corn, used mainly for animal and poultry feeding, is fixed by the government regardless of the actual import price.

Trade policies.   Most cereals are imported by the Ministry of Supply. Private traders are allowed to import flour and rice but are subject to direct government controls. Exports of rice are controlled by the government through specialized state-owned firms.

Much of Egypt's trade moves through bilateral arrangements made with the objective of assuring a source of supply for needed commodities. Agreements for the purchase of wheat and wheat flour are negotiated separately and are signed at least a year in advance. To prevent fluctuations in the world price of certain imported commodities from being transmitted to the domestic market, a special price stabilization fund is used. It works by subsidizing the exchange rate applied to these products.

MEXICO

The price policies of the government of Mexico represent one of the largest scale attempts at price intervention in the developing world.

In this brief review only the basic principles of the system are presented. The government intervenes in the market through a special agency in charge of price regulation and control, CONSUPO. The main activities of this agency are setting and maintaining guaranteed prices at the farm gate (involving substantial food storage activities) and distributing staple foods at discount prices to low-income families through its subsidiary agency DICONSA.

The original goal of CONSUPO was to protect small farmers from the grain traders who used their monopsonistic position to buy grain, especially corn, cheaply from the producers and sell it for much higher prices (sometimes several times higher) in the city. Today the government intervenes in agricultural prices through its direct and very active involvement in the domestic and foreign trade of grain, and by setting guaranteed prices.[1] CONSUPO is often accused of concentrating its activity on wheat, a crop produced mostly on large farms and consumed in the form of bread by the higher income consumers. It plays a much smaller role in the marketing of corn, which predominates in the food budget of the poor and is produced mostly in small farms and communal farm villages.

The retail branch of the agency, DICONSA, aims at providing cheap food for the low income population, mainly in urban areas. By 1974 the agency operated 2,700 outlets, of which only 670 were in rural areas. Although the overall subsidy is fairly small, the sales concentrate on products traditionally preferred by the poor. This tendency to target both the subsidies and the sales in the public distribution system on a recommended basic basket of food commodities has increased considerably in recent years.

COLOMBIA

In the mid-1970s the government of Colombia started a food stamp program targeted on low-income families. In 1980 more than 100,000 households encompassing 600,000 people received food free of charge under the program. The total budget for food subsidies in 1980 was less than 0.5 percent of the total current spending of the central government. The program augments the income of eligible families by about 10 percent and their calorie and protein intake by roughly the same proportion.

The program operates on three levels: first, it is aimed at families with pregnant or nursing mothers and small children; second, it is targeted on the population in the poorer regions of the country; and third, it is restricted to a selected group of food products. The food stamp program in Colombia provides a useful small-scale example of a food subsidy scheme that works effectively within the framework of a market-oriented system.

BRAZIL

Brazil has a policy of minimum prices linked to selected agricultural products. Four commodities—cotton lint, rice, corn, and soybeans—account for 90 percent of the funds allocated to the program. The minimum prices are generally announced before the planting season and are normally set below the expected price at harvest time. Producers, cooperatives, and private handlers may participate in the program, either by selling their products directly to the government at the minimum price or by obtaining loans for storage based on the minimum price. The basic objectives of the program are to stimulate production of the supported commodities and to reduce annual and seasonal price variations.

Through government acquisitions and government loans, the program provides a twofold guarantee that the market prices will not fall below the minimum price. Under the acquisition program the government can purchase, at the minimum price, all of the commodity that is offered for sale and store it. These stocks, which the government considers to be buffer stocks, can be sold on the internal market or released for export when prices are more favorable.

Government loans are of two types. The first includes an option to sell the product to the government. The commodity is handled as if a direct sale to the government under the acquisition program is intended. However, instead of direct payment the owner of the commodity receives a loan based on 100 percent of the minimum price and repayable over a maximum period (180 days in the case of corn). If the market price rises during the period of the loan, the owner may sell the commodity in the free market and repay the loan plus interest and storage costs. If the price remains low, however, the owner "sells" the product to the government merely by not paying off the loan. In this case, the owner pays no interest or storage costs.

The second type of loan is for up to 80 percent of the minimum price and requires the owner to store the product on the farm. In this case the government will not purchase the commodity in the event of low prices, and the principal plus interest must be repaid by the end of the loan period.

The government attempts to determine the minimum price between the expected market price and the production costs. Thus minimum prices may vary between different geoeconomic zones, primarily reflecting differences in production and transportation costs. In more remote regions the purchase of some commodities, such as rice and corn, represents a substantial proportion of total production. Government expenses on the program account for 6 to 8 percent of the federal budget.

ISRAEL

Most of Israel's grain is imported. Domestic production of wheat, the major cereal, ranges between 15 and 35 percent of consumption, and practically all the animal and poultry feedgrains are imported. The import of grain is mostly a government monopoly, and is carried out by an autonomous agency connected to the Ministry of Commerce and Industry. The ministry prepares and continuously updates monthly forecasts of the quantities needed for consumption and storage over the following twelve months. Its representatives abroad purchase the grain in the world market (mostly in the United States and Canada) according to these forecasts. The ministry arranges to have the grain transported to Israel and distributed to wholesale traders (feedgrains) or to local mills (wheat). The ministry is also in charge of most of the storage of the grain.

To secure the sources of supply, most of the grain purchases in the world market are made in the futures market, generally between four and seven months in advance. The wheat produced domestically is procured by the Ministry of Agriculture at prices announced before the sowing season. These prices are determined according to the prevailing world prices of wheat in the futures market. Because of the rapid rate of inflation in Israel since the mid-1970s and the associated continuous devaluation of the domestic currency, the price of wheat for domestic producers is quoted in U.S. dollars so that they will not have to assume the exchange risk. Nonetheless, domestic production of wheat is very unstable, partly because of the unstable weather conditions and partly because of wide variations in the opportunity costs of growing wheat (in terms of the expected profits from alternative produce).

Since 1978 all subsidies on grain products and other staple foods, with the exception of bread, have been discontinued. Bread continues to be subsidized heavily and is sold at less than one-half its real cost (and sometimes even less than one-third). The subsidized bread is not rationed and is distributed through the regular retail outlets.

Nevertheless, the rapid inflation in Israel on the one hand and the special method by which grain prices are determined on the other have created a form of de facto subsidy, which at times can be quite substantial. Since this phenomenon is characteristic not only of Israel but also of many other developing nations it will be discussed in some detail.

In October 1977 Israel changed its exchange rate system and floated its currency. With the rapid inflationary process, the exchange rate also declined rapidly against the other currencies at a rate of up to 5 or 6 and sometimes even 10 percent per month. To prevent a continuous rise in the grain price in terms of the Israeli currency, the Ministry of Commerce determines and updates the price of grain to domestic users only once every several months.[2] The purpose of the updating is to adjust the domestic price of the mostly imported grains to the changes in the exchange rate. Otherwise, the growing gap between the actual price of grains fixed by the ministry and the real price, given by the dollar price times the actual exchange rate, would result in an ever-growing subsidy. To prevent this de facto subsidy, the method of adjusting the price of grain to domestic users is as follows: if the planned time interval between consecutive adjustments is four months, then the price for the four-month period is calculated on the basis of the average exchange rate expected for that period. Thus, while at the beginning of the period the price in domestic currency is based on an exchange rate that is higher than the current rate, at the end of the period it will be based on a lower exchange rate than the one current at that time. If no subsidies are to be granted, the entire import activity should be self-financed so that the ministry's revenues from selling the grain to domestic users should cover its purchase costs as determined by the current exchange rate.

The main argument in favor of this method over its simpler alternative of pricing the grain according to the actual exchange rate at the time of sale, and thus continuously adjusting the price upward, is that such continuous and automatic adjustment would introduce an additional element of instability into the already unstable economy. Another argument is that control over the prices of these imported commodities gives the government an extra degree of freedom and one more instrument for influencing the general cost of living. However, in light of the declared intention to grant no subsidies for grain and for only a few of its final products, this method suffers from a number of deficiencies. Because the price is determined by the authorities there is a great temptation to postpone adjustment if the time is deemed unsuitable for political or other reasons, as indeed has been the case during the past four years. This leads to some undesirable results. Extra subsidy payments are needed for the period beyond the date previously planned for the adjustment (since this date is the basis for the calculation of the average exchange rate and thus also of the price). The extra subsidy means a larger government budgetary deficit, which in due course leads to the pumping of more money into the economy and higher inflationary pressures. Moreover, in times of high inflation and thus also of continuous decline in the exchange rate, maintaining the price at a constant level in nominal terms must require *ever-increasing* subsidy.

Another undesirable result is that any postponement must mean, in the existing climate of inflation, a substantially larger upward hike in price when the adjustment is finally made. The result is a far stronger shock to the economy. As an illustration, in April 1980 the price of bread was more than doubled after being constant for a long period (thus bringing the effective subsidy to more than 75 percent of the cost). The increase caused considerable labor unrest, and the opposition party in Parliament raised the issue for a vote of no confidence. During that same week the price of milk was raised by some 15 percent. This rise was barely mentioned in the press, although over the previous six months the price of milk had risen by far more than the price of bread. The reason: milk prices (which are also determined by the Ministry of Commerce) were raised frequently but at relatively small rates and thus became a "no-news" item.

A large increase in the price of bread (and possibly also of other "sensitive" products) need not in itself contribute much to the general cost of living because its weight in the index is very small. The overall inflationary impact of such a price rise may, however, far exceed the direct effect because it tends to generate strong inflationary expectations, labor unrest, and sometimes even new demands for wage increases.

Figure 3-1 demonstrates the consequences of this policy in terms

Figure 3-1.   The Share of Subsidy in the Costs of Bread Relative to the Share of Market Price.

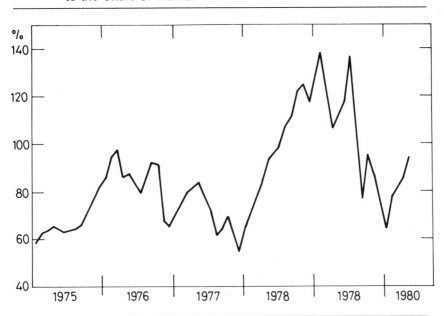

of the subsidy rate. In 1975 the subsidy rate, the subsidy per unit of bread relative to the price consumers pay, was about 55 percent. This rate rose moderately as a result of inflation and the corresponding adjustments in 1976–77. The average subsidy rate during those two years was, however, 70 percent. In 1978, as inflation rose from an annual rate of 35 percent to more than 100 percent, the subsidy rate rose sharply to over 140 percent. Thus at times consumers paid only one-quarter of the cost of bread, and the unplanned subsidy payments more than tripled.

In conclusion we can see that inflation imposes a considerable burden on the government's grain management system. If the conventional methods of intervention through the price system are not adjusted to the conditions of rapidly rising prices, they may change their original form, leading to unexpected subsidy levels and creating a burden on the fiscal budget utterly different from the one originally planned.

CONCLUDING REMARKS

Foodgrain management systems in many developing countries show a common pattern in one important aspect: While the government assumes many functions of the market system, it nevertheless allows other functions to remain in the hands of the private sector. Imports and exports are generally handled as a government monopoly or at least under its direct control; buffer stocks are often held by a government agency or financed by special government funds; internal trade at the wholesale level is under direct government control or even entirely monopolized by the government. Still, unlike centrally planned economies, production is mostly in the hands of the farmers,[3] who are given considerable freedom to choose their crop mix, technology, the extent of the area to be cultivated and, most important, the marketed surplus—the amount to be sold in excess of their own consumption. Internal trading at the retail level is also largely in private hands.

Government involvement in distribution can be very substantial, however, and government agencies in many countries operate special retail outlets that sell staple foods. The objectives of such direct involvement are to achieve a more equitable distribution of food among consumer groups and, in particular, to ensure that enough food is available to the vulnerable sections of the population who might find themselves deprived under a private distribution system. Government intervention may take several forms and operate at different stages of the production-distribution chain. In some countries the price of foodgrains or foodgrain products is subsidized either at the final distribution stage or at an intermediate stage of the production process, while unrationed distribution is allowed through the usual retail outlets. In other countries the government operates its own network of retail outlets for the sale of staple foods at prices lower than the market price, usually under some form of rationing. A notable example is the network of fair-price shops in India, but similar arrangements exist not only in other Asian countries but also in some countries in Africa and Latin America. Even in these countries most of the retail trading is still either through barter or in the hands of the private sector.

An important aspect of coexistence of a public distribution system side by side with a private production-distribution system, in which the two operate in parallel and sometimes even in cooperation with each other, is that the price system is still the major signal that guides the economy. Producers' prices of outputs and inputs are still the main determinants of the level of production, choice of cropping mix, choice of technology, and the decision on the marketed surplus; consumers' prices are still the main determinants of the levels of consumption, choice of the consumption basket, and the way in which the foodgrains are distributed between the poor and the rich, between rural and urban consumers, and between different regions in the country. The price system is moreover the main medium through which the government can intervene in the foodgrain market with the objective of guiding it to specific goals.

The instruments governments use to intervene in the price system include subsidies to consumers, price support to producers on their final products or subsidies on their inputs. When these seem insufficient to ensure attainment of their goals, many governments tend in addition to impose distribution controls. These may take the form of procurement quotas imposed on producers or on the middlemen, rationing the supply to consumers, and so on.

The need of governments in many developing countries to apply an assortment of price controls along with distribution controls arises mainly from the often inconsistent and even conflicting objectives inherent in their foodgrain policies. On the production side governments attempt to stabilize the price at the highest possible level in order to secure at least remunerative prices and to provide incentives to farmers to increase production and adopt more advanced technologies. On the consumption side governments try to stabilize the price at the lowest possible level in order to assure that all consumers, and especially the poor, can afford at least the minimum nutritional requirement.

Many governments make fairly extensive use of commodity pricing and distribution to accomplish nonagricultural objectives such as income redistribution, due to the limited ability of their bureaucracies to administer, dispense, and collect more desirable income transfers. Furthermore, governments may find themselves under strong financial constraint to undertake programs involving costs beyond their fiscal means or to incur foreign exchange expenses the economy cannot afford.

The multiplicity of objectives makes it sometimes necessary or politically expedient to depart from a single system of pricing that applies uniformly to all groups and sectors in favor of *multiple* pricing that, by definition, discriminates between the poor and the rich, between consumers and producers, between regions and between crops. One noteworthy example is the tendency in many developing countries to discriminate against agriculture and rural consumers and in favor of industry and urban consumers. Pricing of agricultural products are often held below economic level for the sake of encouraging industrial development via low-priced food for the urban consumers. A system of multiple pricing, however, involves difficult logistic problems, mainly to do with administering the distribution and preventing the product from infiltrating to ineligible groups. If the country lacks the administrative means to monitor a system of multiple and discriminatory prices, it may find the performance of the system much less satisfactory than expected.

The multiplicity of government policies is also the product of inappropriate planning. All too often governments do not take into full account the economywide effects of each policy or program; nor do they attempt to design an overall policy that best suits the conditions existing in the country and the objectives the government seeks to achieve. Instead, policymaking is largely piecemeal, each program being designed to solve one specific problem or to achieve a single objective without taking into account the direct and indirect effects on the other segments of the economy and on the other objectives. Under such circumstances governments often impose distribution controls with the sole purpose of correcting the damage caused by other controls. Procurement quotas, rationing, and zoning are notable examples of such "corrective" measures. Distribution controls augment the role of government administration in general and of the public distribution system in particular. In the most extreme case distributive controls may take the form of complete government monopoly.

A major role for the government in market operations has its roots in the ideology prevailing in many developing nations, which tend to view the "capitalistic" free market system with suspicion and skepticism, and lean more toward direct government involvement and a greater degree of central planning. This lack of trust is often rooted in past experience (usually preindependence) with a system dominated by monopolistic foreign powers, which are regarded as having exploited the country and its people.

Regrettably, the extremely complex system of price controls, multiple pricing, and distribution controls that has evolved in many developing countries does not appear to work well. Although in most countries the system must be given credit at least for avoiding widespread famine, in some countries it has been accompanied by an increasing dependence on foreign aid and on diminishing foreign reserves. Moreover, inadequate and piecemeal planning, coupled with incompetence and corruption, especially at the lower ranks of the administration, have created a hopeless bureaucratic maze, which, even when it has succeeded in achieving some of the objectives, has done so in a very inefficient and costly way.

Perhaps the most important requirement in designing or improving the price and distribution system for food and other products is a broader view of the interrelations between various objectives and between different policies, the degree to which these policies can complement or substitute each other, and their direct and indirect effects on the various segments of the economy. It is only by adopting a broad perspective that a system of policies can be selected that will best answer the given set of objectives.

NOTES

1. Price setting by the government may have its drawbacks, as the following episode illustrates. For several years before 1973 the price of beans was fixed in nominal terms and thus showed a considerable decline relative to the prices of other crops. As a result farmers shifted out of bean production, and there was large speculative hoarding by private traders. Within a period of two years, in 1973 and 1974, CONSUPO more than tripled the price. Traders started selling their speculative stocks, mostly to the agency. These sales increased as rumors spread that CONSUPO might lower the price again, which caused substantial losses to the agency, eventually forcing it to lower the price. Farmers were also hurt, and those who had resumed production of beans following the price rise were forced out again as the price fell.

2. The same is true for many other imported staple food products as well as for imported oil (and thus also electricity and public transport).

3. Production on government land and under direct government supervision, where this exists, is still on a relatively small scale.

4 THE ROLE AND EFFECTS OF BUFFER STOCKS

And there was no bread in all the land; for the famine was very sore so that the land of Egypt and the land of Canaan languished by reason of the famine.
—*Genesis 41*

Such were the conditions in Egypt and its neighboring countries during the first of the seven lean years. Pharaoh, the king of Egypt, was fortunate enough to have had both warning of what was in store and the good advice of Joseph, who counseled conservation during the fat years in order to avoid famine during the lean.[1]

Unfortunately, today we can no longer count on such accurate forecasting as that provided by Joseph. Even more troubling is the fact that exporters and importers, poor countries and rich, cannot come to any agreement on how to share the burden of building and operating an international system of food stocks. As a result the multilateral negotiations on this undertaking, which have already gone on for many years, cannot be brought to a conclusion, and the creation of international buffer stocks to alleviate food scarcity in times of need has yet to be accomplished.

Until the crisis of the early 1970s there was no serious problem. During the 1950s and 1960s the international prices of grain were almost perfectly stable and there was no shortage in supply. This was largely due to an accumulation of huge amounts of stocks, not as a result of any deliberate stabilizing policy, but rather as a byproduct of purely domestic policies in Canada and the United States. Price support targets that were established to protect the farm sector brought in a much larger supply than the domestic market demanded at that price. Programs of food aid, export subsidies, constraints of various kinds on the level of production, and the extent of cultivated land helped to some degree to reduce the huge surpluses. Still, large quantities were consigned to storage each year, thus ensuring stable prices.

The glut ended in 1972 after a series of severe crop failures in several key countries. A good deal of the existing stocks were disposed of during that crisis and since then the world has entered an era of price gyrations, volatile supply, and more acute food problems.

These developments have reawakened an interest in grain reserves on the part of decisionmakers and scholars, which is manifested at three levels. Efforts have greatly intensified to create a system of internationally operated buffer stocks or internationally coordinated national stocks along with other forms of food aid. Many countries have built their own systems of buffer stocks in order to protect themselves against growing instability in the world market and have increased their efforts to reach a greater degree of self-sufficiency. And the literature on commodity stabilization and buffer stocks operation has quickly proliferated.

In this chapter the role and effects of buffer stocks are analyzed at the level of an individual country. The simple model used is quite similar to that of Massell. The effects of buffer stocks are quantified in terms of several performance measures rather than economic efficiency alone as in Massell's model. This enables us to examine the different and diverse objectives of the stocks policy and to detect possible conflicts between them. Analyzed and compared are several intervention rules as determined by the prices that trigger purchases or sales of grain by the storage authority and by different storage capacities. Then different forms of the supply function are considered; these in turn reflect different forms of price expectations by producers. Finally, the efficiency gains resulting from producers' response to the reduction in risk are estimated. The entire analysis is carried out under alternative assumptions about the structure of the market, allowing for the effects of serial correlation, different levels of demand elasticities, and other effects.

The model is different from conventional models in that it considers the case in which the trigger prices for the storage operation are determined each year on the basis of the conditions existing in that year rather than being fixed a priori for the duration of the storage operation. The latter assumption is not only typical of many commodity agreements but also characterizes the vast majority of the theoretical analyses. This analysis demonstrates, however, that the "fixed" band rule introduces a certain rigidity into the storage operation, which reduces its efficiency. More flexible rules may thus enhance the effectiveness of buffer stocks.

The main tool of this analysis is a simulation model. The relevant performance measures are estimated, and their frequency distributions generated on the basis of the assumed market structure and the policy rules. Obviously, analysis based on simulation experiments is limited in that it depends on the specific values of the predetermined parameters, and its conclusions need not therefore be universally valid. However, this limitation applies to the theoretical analyses as well. Chapter 2 showed that once the simple structure of Waugh–Oi–Massell is generalized to include, for instance, nonlinearities or any other modification, even that simple analytical model can no longer yield results that are universally valid. On the other hand, the simulation analysis permits a much more profound and thoroughgoing analysis, as will be shown in this chapter and even more in subsequent chapters. To determine the robustness of the conclusions and the range of parameter values within which they are valid, detailed sensitivity analyses are carried out and note taken of the direction in which the results may change to the extent that they depend on the specific values of the parameters.

The plan of the chapter is as follows: the measures for evaluating the performance of the stock policies are reviewed, the structure of the model is presented in detail, and the data and parameters underlying the illustrative results presented in the subsequent sections are given. Then different aspects of the simulation results are reviewed, and finally the main conclusions are summarized.

THE MEASURES FOR
EVALUATING GAINS FROM STORAGE

The general goals of a buffer stock system can be grouped into three categories: food security, stability, and economic welfare. Each of these can be quantified by several performance measures. The level of food security can be evaluated by determining the average quantity available for consumption by the entire population. Given the calorie and protein content of the various food products this measure estimates the average calorie and protein intake for that country. Perhaps a more meaningful measure is the average quantity available for each consumer group, because the problem of food scarcity is usually a problem of only certain sectors of the population, notably the low-income consumers. The average level calculated for the entire population fails to convey the necessary information about the calorie and protein deficiencies among the groups more vulnerable to malnutrition. However, even the calculation of averages for each consumer group may fail to convey the true dimensions of the food problem. This is because these values provide information about an average or a normal year, whereas the food problem becomes especially acute in years when production falls below the average.

To determine in what years famine is likely to occur, the frequency of extreme events must be known. Frequency can be measured from the spread of the appropriate distributions, as from the two considered here, one the ordinary coefficient of variation (CV), the other the probability that the variable under consideration does not exceed a certain critical level, that is, the cumulative probability in one tail of the distribution only. Difficulties may arise with the standard measure of the coefficient of variation when the variables considered are not normally distributed and even more so when their distribution is non-symmetric. In these cases the coefficient of variation does not provide the same information as it does in a symmetric distribution. As is well known, in nonsymmetric distributions the two parameters, mean and standard deviation, are no longer sufficient to characterize the distribution; information about the skewedness of the distribution is also needed. Information on the cumulative probability at a given tail would thus complement other data about the structure of the distribution. Moreover, in several cases this item of information would be the *only* relevant one. For instance, for the goal of food security, the main performance measure is the probability that the amount of food-grain available for consumption by low-income urban consumers does not fall below subsistence level. This measure defines the *reliability* of the system. The four performance measures for the food security goal are as follows:

- Instability of food supply to urban poor, CV;
- Instability of food supply to rural consumers, CV;

- Probability that total supply falls below critical level;
- Probability that supply to urban poor falls below critical level.

The last two measures define the level of food *insecurity*.

The stability goal is measured by the effects on the market price, on total supply, and on farmers' income. The six performance measures for this goal include:

- Variability of the market price, CV;
- Instability of total food supply, CV;
- Instability of farmers' income, CV;
- Probability that market price falls below critical floor;
- Probability that market price exceeds critical ceiling;
- Probability that farmers' income falls below critical level.

The goal of economic welfare indicates the combined effect of the policy on the welfare of producers and of various consumer groups, as well as the effect on the government fiscal budget. The change in consumers' welfare is measured by the expected change in their economic surplus and is calculated for each consumer group separately. The change in producers' welfare is measured by the expected change in their income when supply is fixed in the short run (in a given year the supply curve is completely inelastic) and by expected change in their economic surplus when supply is price responsive. Government gains or losses are in this case (when no other policy is in effect) the net financial expenses involved in operating the storage facility. There are seven performance measures:

- Welfare gains to urban poor;
- Welfare gains to urban affluent;
- Welfare gains to rural consumers;
- Total consumers' gains (= (1) + (2) + (3));
- Total producers' gains;
- Total government finances (which include capital costs of the storage facility);
- Total economic gains (= (4) + (5) + (6)).

When supply responds to risk reduction the total welfare gains will include the distribution gains together with the efficiency gains. The main performance measures that indicate efficiency gains only, that is, the net effect of risk reduction, are:

- Change in the mean market price;
- Change in the mean quantity produced;
- Change in mean farmers' income;
- Total net efficiency gains.

Finally, we consider some measures that evaluate the financial performance of the storage operation:

- Operating costs;
- Capital costs;
- Total storage costs (= (1) + (2));
- Probability that operating costs exceeds critical level;
- Net economic gains from storage (including capital expenses);
- Rate of utilization of storage.

In subsequent chapters as other policies are considered, additional performance measures will, of course, be added. The starting point, however, will always be the performance measures just presented.

THE MODEL

The simulation model describes a discrete decision process taking place over time. The state of the model at the beginning of the tth period is described by a vector of *state variables*, denoted by Y_{t-1} to signify that they have already been determined in the previous period. The elements of Y_{t-1} are the values assumed by variables such as the demand parameters and the area planted.

During the tth period, random events occur. The most obvious examples in the present context are weather events. These random events are denoted by the vector Z_t, and their probability distribution is assumed to be known.

The authorities determine their actions on the basis of the initial state and the current random events. These decisions are denoted by the vector of decision variables X_t and are determined according to a set of decision rules D_t. That is,

$$X_t = D_t(Y_{t-1}, Z_t).   \tag{4-1}$$

Examples of such decisions involve changes in the level of stocks or price support to farmers. In the first example the decision determines the trigger price for the storage operation.

Depending on the initial state of the model, the random event, and the set of decisions, the state of the economy at time t can be determined. That is,

$$Y_t = F_t (Y_{t-1}, Z_t, X_t)$$

$$= F_t [Y_{t-1}, Z_t, D_t (Y_{t-1}, Z_t)] . \qquad (4\text{--}2)$$

A deterministic and known relation F_t is assumed to exist between the state variables Y_t on the one hand, and the random events Z_t, the decisions X_t, and the state variables Y_{t-1} in the preceding period on the other hand. The function F_t may also incorporate technological progress, population growth, and other time-dependent processes.

In Eq. (4–2) we can see that as a result of its recurrent nature the state variables at any time t may be written as functions of the initial conditions Y_0, the set of decision rules D_t, and the random events $Z_1, \ldots, Z_t$. Given an objective function that depends on the entire sequence of state variables, the decision problem becomes one of finding a set of decision rules $D_1, \ldots, D_{T-1}$, which for given initial conditions Y_0 and a given sequence $t = 1, 2, \ldots, T$ will yield the highest ranking outcome attainable according to the order determined by the objective function.

The simulation method employed in our analysis consists of three steps:

- Applying Monte Carlo simulations for yielding the random events according to the prespecified probability distribution;
- Calculating the state variables for each trial, or each independent random event, according to the decision rules specified in the model and according to the initial conditions;
- Repeating the process a large number of times and averaging the results, thus calculating the value of the objective function.

Stochastic simulations can therefore be regarded as a method for transforming the probability distributions of the random variables Z_t into probability distributions of the state variables. The objective function is then determined on the basis of the characteristics of these distributions.

The model is a partial equilibrium model of a storable agricultural product (henceforth, *grain*). Random disturbances in supply are the only sources of price fluctuations in the domestic market. (This is so because disturbances originating in foreign markets have no effect on the domestic market since we consider at this stage the case of a "closed" economy.)

Among the main components of the model are a country market model that estimates market price and distribution of available supply among consumer groups according to the specific demand parameters, the quantity produced, and the policy rules, and a system of decision rules that represent government policies in the market. For each level of grain production the model estimates the market price, the quantity consumed, the level of stocks, and the economic and financial gains to the various sectors on the basis of the country's market model and the prespecified policies. Monte Carlo simulation experiments generate these estimates for a large number of production levels and the results are then aggregated into frequency distributions. The following subsections describe the main building blocks of the model.

Country's Demand. Consumers in the country are divided into three groups: low-income urban consumers; middle- to high-income urban consumers, and rural consumers. A separate demand function is specified for each group, and total demand of the country is the sum of the demands of the three population groups. The division of consumers into income groups allows us to examine the effects of various events or different government policies on each of the groups separately. It also allows consideration of policies directed to only one of the groups.

Country's Production. Production in the country is assumed to fluctuate randomly around the long-run equilibrium level.[2] A number of different functional forms of the supply function have been considered. They include:

Rational expectations, specified by the equation

$$Q_t = a + b\overline{P} + u_t, \tag{4-3}$$

where u_t is random disturbance, which may or may not be serially correlated (see below), and $\overline{P}$ is the long-run equilibrium price.

Fully rational expectations, specified by the equation

$$Q_t = a + b\overline{\overline{P}} + u_t, \tag{4-4}$$

where $\overline{\overline{P}}$ is the objective mean of the price distribution *after* taking into account the potential effects of the storage operation, that is, the effects of the quantity available in storage and the remaining storage capacity on the expected price, as explained and illustrated in Chapter 2.

Adaptively rational expectations, given by the equation

$$Q_t = a + b\hat{P}_t + u_t,$$

where

$$\hat{P}_t = \frac{1}{n} \sum_{j=1}^{n} P_{t-j}. \tag{4-5}$$

In this case producers do not have perfect foresight about the long-run mean production and price, but rather estimate the average price on the basis of the previous n observations.

Adaptive expectations, given by the equation

$$Q_t = a + bP_{t-1} + u_t. \tag{4-6}$$

Adaptively rational expectations with supply response, given by equation

$$Q_t = a + b\hat{P}_t - c\,\hat{\sigma}_t + u_t,$$

where

$$\hat{\sigma}_t^2 = \frac{1}{n} \sum_{j=1}^{n} (P_{t-j} - P_t)^2. \tag{4-7}$$

In this case producers learn adaptively not only the mean price but also the standard deviation. If as a result of a certain policy the standard deviation is reduced, producers will respond favorably by increasing their planned production.

The random disturbance u_t in all of the foregoing supply functions is assumed to be normally distributed. If serial correlation exists in the country's production, the disturbances u_t will have the form

$$u_t = \rho\, u_{t-1} + \sqrt{1-\rho^2} \bullet \epsilon_t, \tag{4-8}$$

where ϵ_t is a normally distributed random disturbance and ρ is the coefficient of serial correlation.

Buffer Stocks Operation.   The storage policy is specified in terms of a predetermined price band[3] and the overall capacity of the storage facility. The intervention rule postulates that the storage authorities allow prices to float freely inside a certain predetermined price band and intervene in the market only if prices move outside the band. However, the storage authorities can stabilize the price within that band only if there are sufficient stocks to meet possible shortfalls in production or sufficient vacant capacity to store possible excesses.

The price band itself is determined in relation to the long-run equilibrium price.[4]. Here we consider two alternative assumptions. First, assume the authorities to have perfect foresight and hence to determine the price band in relation to the true long-run equilibrium price. Alternatively, assume that the authorities do not have such perfect foresight and that they estimate the equilibrium price on the basis of past observations. (See also Hwa and Kulatilaka 1979 for a similar approach.) In the latter case, the price band is affected not only by the form of the supply function but also by the nature of the intervention.

Considered were two types of price (or quantity) trigger bands. One is the standard intervention rule, which specifies a symmetric band

Figure 4-1. Storage Operation: Grain Put into Storage.

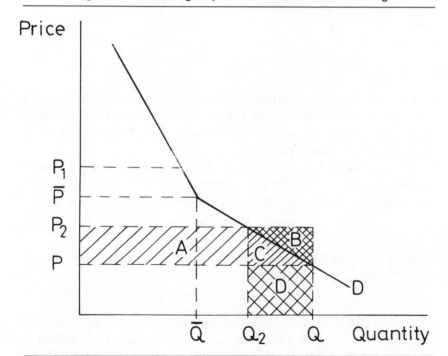

Figure 4-2. Storage Operation: Grain Released from Storage.

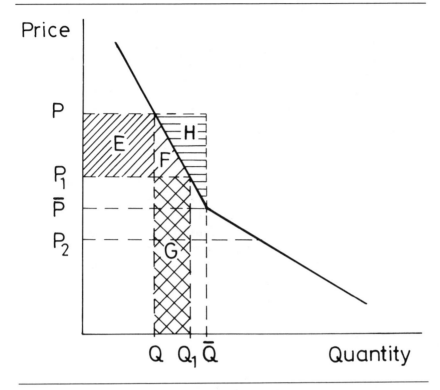

centered on the long-run equilibrium price. The other is an insurance oriented intervention rule, which gives priority to the food security objectives. It requires that grain be purchased for storage as soon as the price falls below the long-run equilibrium level but allows the sales of grain out of storage only if the price rises above a certain critical level. This rule thus specifies an asymmetric band in order to increase the probability that enough grain will be in storage in times of serious production shortfalls.

Gains and Losses from Storage Operation.   Figures 4–1 and 4–2 illustrate in detail the storage intervention rules and the calculation of gains and losses. In these figures P_1 and P_2 define the upper and lower limits, respectively, of the trigger price band. $\bar{P}$ is the long-run equilibrium price, which corresponds to the mean quantity produced, $\bar{Q}$. Notice that if the demand curve is not linear, a symmetric price trigger band determines a nonsymmetric quantity trigger band (and vice versa). In Figure 4–1 the quantity produced is Q, and without any intervention the price would fall to P, which is below the predetermined lower limit P_2. If sufficient storage space is available then the quantity $(Q - Q_2)$ is put into storage and the price rises to P_2. In that case consumers lose the amount designated by the shaded area $(A + B)$. Producers, however, gain the amount designated by the areas $(A + B + C)$. Government expenses on purchasing the grain equal the amount designated by the areas $(C + D)$. (These expenses do not include transportation or handling costs.) Hence the net economic loss is the amount designated by the areas $(B + D)$.

In Figure 4-2 the quantity produced is Q, and without any intervention the price would fall to P, which is above the upper limit P_1. If there is sufficient grain in storage then the quantity $(Q_1 - Q)$ is released from storage and the price falls to P_1. In that case consumers gain the amount designated by the shaded areas $(F + G)$, while producers lose the amount designated by the area F. Government revenues from the sales of grain in storage are designated by the area H. The net economic gain is therefore the amount designated by the areas $(G + H)$.

DATA AND PARAMETERS

The simulation model was designed to represent a typical developing country, not any specific country. However, most of the parameters of the model were deliberately selected to approximate the structural parameters of a South Asian country such as India. Furthermore, the analysis is not confined to any specific type of foodgrain. For this reason production levels and prices are specified in terms of index numbers instead of actual levels. Thus, both the mean production and the mean price were normalized at 100 at the initial period.

In the simulation experiments themselves, a time horizon of thirty years was assumed. This was found to be long enough in the sense that succeeding events had only negligible effects on the outcome.[5] Every simulation experiment involved 300 iterations of a thirty-year sequence of random production events. The total sample therefore consists of 9,000 observations drawn at random from a specified probability distribution.[6] The specific parameters of the model are production, consumption, and storage operation.

Production. The country is assumed to produce an average of 100 million metric tons (MMT) annually. The coefficient of variation in the country is 7 percent of the mean, and the random disturbances in production are assumed to be normally distributed. At the mean level of production the price is also set to be 100. At this mean level the price elasticity of supply is assumed to be 0.25 and the risk response coefficient, or the elasticity of supply with respect to a change in the standard deviation, is assumed to be 0.5.

Consumption. Consumers in the country are grouped into three categories: low-income urban consumers, middle- to high-income urban consumers, and rural consumers. Table 4–1 lists the specific demand parameters assumed in the simulation experiments.

Storage Operation. The decision variables that determine the storage operation are the storage capacity and the two trigger prices. For the storage capacity we consider a number of levels ranging from 3 up to 15 percent of mean annual production. For the price band we consider each of the three possible storage rules shown in Table 4–2.

The first two rules specify a symmetric band centered on the mean price, the only difference between them being in the width of the band. The third, the insurance-oriented storage rule, specifies a nonsymmetric band. It necessitates storing as much grain as possible so as to offset the most severe shortages.

For the storage operation we assume a handling charge of $5 per ton when the grain is loaded into storage. No allowance is generally made in the tables for capital costs. A separate table is presented, however, that lists the main financial indicators of the storage operation and includes the capital costs. For the calculation of capital costs we have considered several types of storage facilities. Table 4B–1 in Appendix 4B provides two illustrative examples. They show that in a silo where highly mechanized techniques are used capital costs can be as high as $215 per ton capacity (1978 prices), whereas in a warehouse where grain is stored in bags the capital costs can be as low as $40 per ton capacity. The calculations in this chapter assume the latter, simpler facility considered in Appendix 4B, which is used widely in developing countries.

The rate of interest in all financial accounts as well as in the calculation of the present value of the welfare gains is assumed to be 8 percent. The sensitivity of the results to other rates is considered as well, however.

Table 4-1. Country Demand Parameters.

	Low-Income Urban Consumers	Middle-to High-Income Urban Consumers	Rural Consumers	Total Population
Mean quantity consumed as percentage of total consumption	30	40	30	100
Price elasticity of demand at the mean				
$P > 100$	0.55	0.3	0.25	0.36
$P < 100$	0.55	0.4	0.35	0.43

Table 4-2. Storage Rules.

Storage Policy	Percentage Deviation from the Mean	
	Upper Limit	Lower Limit
Storage rule B (10,10)	+ 10	− 10
Storage rule B (5,5)	+ 5	− 5
Storage rule B (10,0)	+ 10	0

No grain is assumed to be in storage during the first year of operation of the facility in most cases. For the first few years the storage authority will thus have to purchase grain in the market before it can sell grain in years of shortage and thus work to lower the price. During these early years the storage authority can therefore only contribute to raising the price. Because of the discounting factor, these initial effects may outweigh the latter effects of the storage operation. To examine the influence of the discounting factor, an analysis of the buffer stocks operation assuming different initial amounts of foodgrain in storage is presented. Finally, the following specific performance measure for evaluating the gains from storage is defined: *Food insecurity (10 percent)* is the probability that the quantity consumed by the urban poor falls by more than 10 percent below their normal consumption, defined as consumption in a stable year.

STOCKS OPERATION
WITH ALTERNATIVE STORAGE RULES

Figure 4–3 parts a–g illustrate the stabilizing effects of buffer stocks under the three sets of storage rules. A number of general observations stand out. First, increasing storage capacity contributes to an increase in both stability and food security. However, successive increases of the storage capacity have diminishing effects on these goals. Thus, for instance, under storage rule B(5,5) a storage facility of 3 MMT (or 3 percent of the average annual production) lowers the variability of the price from a coefficient of variation of 17.6 percent to 15.3 percent, a reduction of some 15 percent. It lowers the level of food insecurity from 16.9 percent to 13.6 percent, a reduction of some 20 percent. An increase of the storage capacity by 3 MMT from 12 to 15 MMT would lower the variability of the price by only 4 per-

Figure 4-3.   Policy Analysis: Alternative Storage Rules.

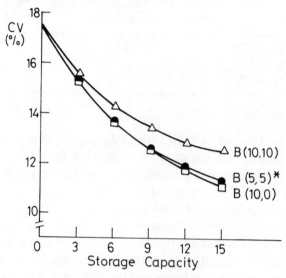

(a) Variability of Price (Coefficient of Variation).

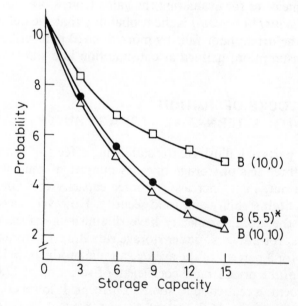

(b) Probability that Price Falls by More than 20 Percent below Normal Price.

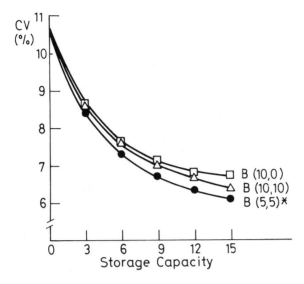

(c) Variability of Farmers' Income (Coefficient of Variation).

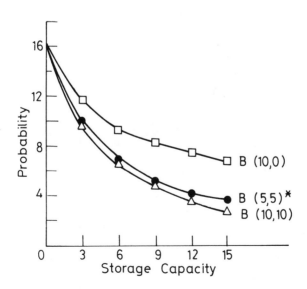

(d) Probability that Farmers' Income Falls by More than 10 Percent below Their Normal Income.

Figure 4-3. *(continued)*

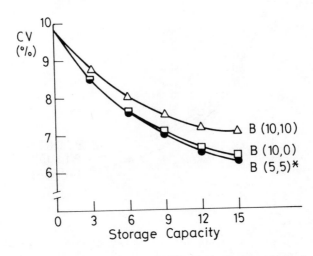

(e) Variability of Supply to the Poor (Coefficient of Variation).

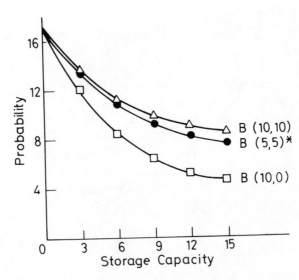

(f) Probability that Supply to the Poor Falls by More than 10 Percent below Their Normal Consumption.

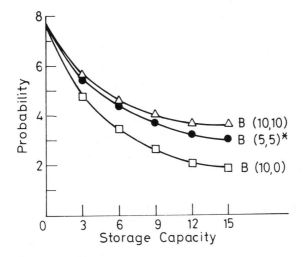

(g) Probability that Total Supply Falls by More than 10 Percent below Normal Supply.

---

cent and the level of food insecurity by 5 percent. This diminishing productivity of buffer stocks is manifested by the concavity of the curves describing the effects of increasing levels of stocks on the various performance measures. The slope of these curves describes the marginal effect of an additional unit of storage on the given performance measure, or its marginal productivity. The monotonic and at times sharp decrease in the slope thus manifests the decrease in the marginal productivity of buffer stocks.

Second, as the price band becomes narrower the rate of utilization of the storage facility increases and buffer stocks thus become more effective in increasing stability and food security. These effects resulting from the width of the price band become more pronounced at higher levels of storage capacity, since at low levels the capacity of the storage facility is usually the binding constraint on the level of storage activities. However, by comparing storage rule B(10,10), which defines a price band of 20 percent, with storage rule B(5,5), the base case, which defines a price band of 10 percent, we can see that some performance measures are considerably more sensitive than others. Thus, for instance, the variability of farmers' income is relatively little affected by the width of the price band and even at a level of 15 MMT (15 percent of average annual production) the coefficient of variation of farmers' income decreases from 6.4 percent under rule B(10,10) to 6.1 percent under rule B(5,5), a decrease of 5 percent. At that level of storage, the price variability decreases by 10 percent and the variability of supply to the poor decreases by 13 percent as the price band is reduced from 20 to 10 percent.

Third, the nonsymmetric insurance-oriented storage rule B(10,0) is more effective for some purposes but less effective for others. Relatively little difference exists in the coefficient of variation of price, supply, or farmers' income between rule B(10,0) and the symmetric rule B(5,5), both having the same width. Significant differences do exist, however, in the probabilities at the tails. The probability that the total supply and even more so that the supply to the poor would fall below the critical level of 90 percent of the average is markedly reduced by changing the storage rules from B(5,5) to B(10,0).

At the same time, however, the insurance-oriented rule has very little stabilizing effect on the market price and on farmers' income. The probability that the price falls below 20 percent of the normal (stable) price with a 15 MMT storage capacity is only 2.7 percent under storage rule B(5,5) but more than 5 percent under storage rule B(10,0). Similarly, the probability that farmers' income falls below 10 percent of the normal (stable) income is only 3.8 percent under storage rule B(5,5) and slightly less than 7 percent under storage rule B(10,0).

The stabilizing effects of buffer stocks are most vividly demonstrated in the histogram showing the price without storage and with a storage capacity of 15 MMT, in Figure 4-4, illustrating the results for storage rule B(5,5). The frequency distribution of the price becomes considerably more condensed as an effect of the storage operation. Without storage the probability that the price falls within the range of 20 percent around the stable level is 42.8 percent. With a storage capacity of 6 MMT this probability rises to 64.6 percent, and with a storage capacity of 15 MMT it rises to 78.1 percent.

The economic gains and losses of the various groups as a result of the storage operation are expressed as a percentage of the annual expenditures by consumers on that commodity (and thus also of the annual income of farmers from that commodity) in a normal (stable) year. Table 4-3 summarizes the expected annual gains from

Figure 4-4. Probability Distribution of the Price.

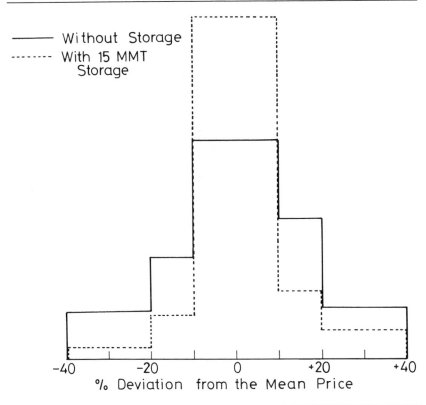

— Without Storage
------- With 15 MMT
       Storage

-40   -20   0   +20   +40
    % Deviation from the Mean Price

operating a storage facility of 6 MMT (6 percent of production in a normal year), under the three sets of storage rules. In all cases consumers lose on average from the storage operation while producers gain. The magnitude of the gains and losses, however, depend on the price elasticities of demand, as will be seen later on. The magnitude of the gains also depends on the storage rule, as we see by comparing the results for storage rules B(10,10) and B(5,5) with those for storage rule B(10,0). The nonsymmetric (insurance-oriented) rule B(10,0) leads to nonsymmetric buying and selling operations. Since the probability that the price exceeds the upper trigger price is much smaller in this case than the probability that the price falls below the lower trigger price, the number of selling operations is much smaller than the number of buying operations. In addition, the number of

Table 4-3. Expected Annual Gains or Losses due to 6 MMT Buffer Stocks under Different Storage Rules (as Percentage of Annual Expenditures in a Normal Year).

Policy	Economic Gains			
	Consumers	Producers	Storage Operation[a]	Total Economy
Storage rule B (10,10)	−.49	+.53	−.17	−.11
Storage rule B (5,5)	−.44	+.54	−.19	−.09
Storage rule B (10,0)	−.65	+.74	−.22	−.13

[a]Including amortization costs.

times that the market price is reduced due to sales out of storage is much smaller than the number of times the price is raised due to purchases into storage. Hence consumers' losses and producers' gains are larger under the nonsymmetric storage rule.

Another noteworthy result in Table 4–3 is that the private sector (producers and consumers combined) is likely to experience net gains as a result of the storage operation. Moreover, even the storage authority is likely to have some operating gains, despite the fact that its expenses include handling charges. Only the inclusion of the amortization costs turns these operating gains into net losses large enough to outweigh the gains of the private sector. At the same time it should be remembered that the amortization costs assumed are those of a primitive warehouse whose capital costs per ton capacity are less than one-fifth of the capital costs in a modern silo. The foregoing results further emphasize the importance of taking the capital costs into account in calculating the desirability of price stabilization through storage.

Still, the net economic gains or losses should not by any means be the sole criterion for evaluating the desirability of price stabilization. Instead we regard these costs as an insurance premium that society pays in order to secure price stabilization and the availability of food. Figures 4–5 parts a and b illustrate the cost effectiveness of buffer stocks, costs that society must bear in order to increase price stabilization and food security through storage under the three storage rules. Thus, for instance, a reduction of 15 percent in the price variability would cost the economy an amount equal to 0.02 percent of the normal annual expenditures on that commodity under rule B(5,5), 0.06 percent under rule B(10,10), and 0.085 percent under rule B(10,0). A further reduction of 15 percent in the price variability would require an *added* cost of 0.12 percent under rule B(5,5), of 0.09 percent under rule B(10,0), and 0.18 percent under rule B(10,10). These results as well as the increasing slope of the trade-off curves vividly demonstrate the decreasing marginal productivity and hence the increasing marginal costs of storage.

An increase of 25 percent in food security (a reduction of 25 percent in the probability of a shortage in the supply to the urban poor in excess of 10 percent of their normal consumption) would cost the economy an amount equal to 0.025 percent of the normal annual expenditures on that commodity under storage rule B(5,5), 0.05 percent under rule B(10,10), and 0.075 percent under rule B(10,0). A further

Figure 4-5. Economic Costs of Stabilization under Different Storage Rules.

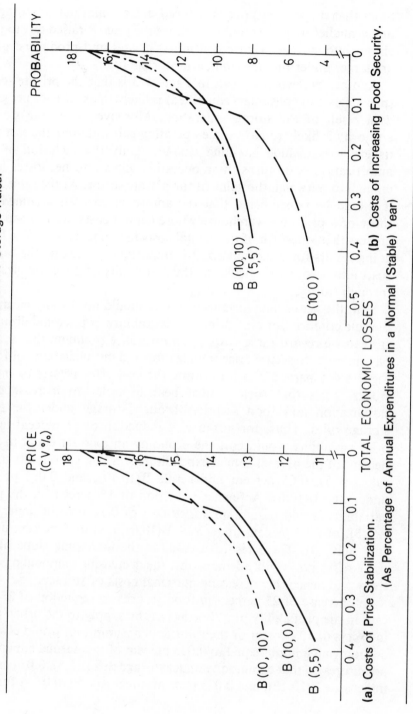

(a) Costs of Price Stabilization.   (b) Costs of Increasing Food Security.

(As Percentage of Annual Expenditures in a Normal (Stable) Year)

Figure 4-6.   Economic Gains and Losses of Stabilization.

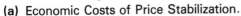

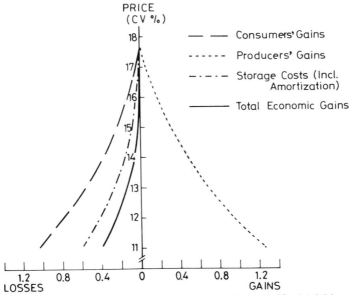

(As Percentage of Annual Expenditures in a Normal (Stable) Year)

(a) Economic Costs of Price Stabilization.

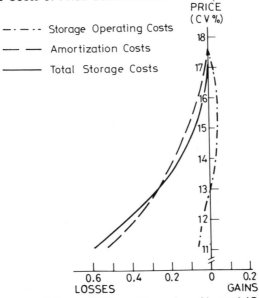

(As Percentage of Annual Expenditures in a Normal (Stable) Year)

(b) Storage Costs of Price Stabilization.

Figure 4-6. *(continued)*

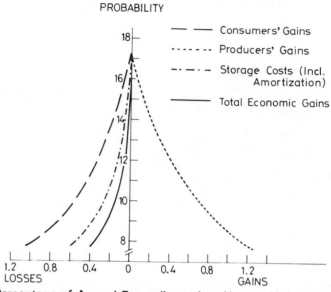

(As Percentage of Annual Expenditures in a Normal (Stable) Year)

(c) Economic Costs of Increasing Food Security.

increase of food security by 25 percent would cost the economy an *additional* amount equal to 0.125 percent under rules B(5,5) and B(10,10), but only 0.04 percent under rule B(10,0).

By comparing Figures 4–5a and 4–5b we can obtain a partial ordering of the three storage rules. Notice that in Figure 4–5a rule B(5,5) is uniformly superior to the other rules in that it provides the same level of price stabilization for the lowest costs. In Figure 4–5b this storage rule is superior only up to a certain level of food security; thereafter, rule B(10,0) becomes superior. Thus if we want to rank the storage rules according to the three criteria: economic costs, price stabilization, and food security, we can conclude that the two rules B(5,5) and B(10,0) are both efficient in the sense that neither is uniformly superior to the other. We can unequivocally conclude, however, that storage rule B(10,10) is uniformly *inferior*. Hence widening the price band makes the storage operation less cost effective. Moving the band in the direction of one of the tails makes the storage operation more cost effective in terms of the objective defined by events which occur at that tail.

Figures 4-6 parts a-c illustrate the cost effectiveness of buffer stocks under storage rule B(5,5) for each sector of the economy. They show that the net losses to the economy at large are due to the amortization costs of the storage facility. In Figure 4-6b we can see that up to a certain level the storage authority has operating gains, and only increasing the storage capacity (and thus also reducing the price variability) above that level may produce operating losses.

BUFFER STOCKS OPERATION UNDER DIFFERENT FORMS OF THE SUPPLY FUNCTION

As noted in Chapter 2, a number of propositions derived from the simple model put forward by Massell may not hold under different forms of the supply function. Thus, for instance, Turnovsky (1974), who examined the case of adaptive expectations, could only state that nothing conclusive can be inferred in regard to the distribution of the gains from stabilization until the various parameters of the model are specified.

In this section the stabilizing effects of buffer stocks under three different forms of the supply function are examined. As noted earlier, each form of the supply function represents a different expectational form about future prices. The three forms examined in this section are rational, adaptively rational, and adaptive expectations.

Figure 4-7 parts a-f illustrate the stabilizing effects of buffer stocks under these three forms of the supply function. A number of observations stand out. First, when there is no storage facility and the random disturbances are serially uncorrelated, the adaptive supply lead to far greater instability than do either of the two rational supply functions; the coefficient of variation of the price is 17.5 percent under rational supply and 22.5 percent under the adaptive supply (that is, some 30 percent higher). The level of food insecurity (the probability that supply to the poor falls below 10 percent of normal, or stable, supply) is almost 40 percent higher and the probability that farmers' income falls by more than 10 percent below their normal income is more than 40 percent higher under the adaptive supply than under the rational supply.

Because instability is greater under the adaptive supply, buffer stocks are much more effective in this case and contribute considerably more to stabilizing the economy than under the rational

Figure 4-7. Stabilization Effects of Storage under Different Forms of the Supply Function.

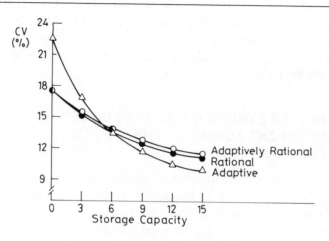

(a) Variability of Price (Coefficient of Variation).

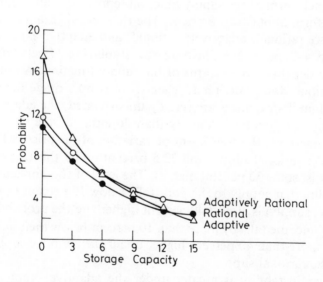

(b) Probability that Price Falls by More than 20 Percent below Normal Price.

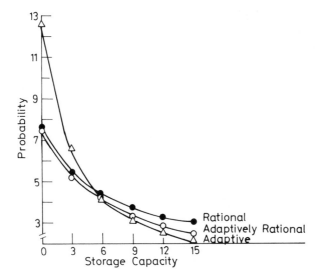

(c) Probability That Total Supply Falls by More than 10 Percent below Normal Supply.

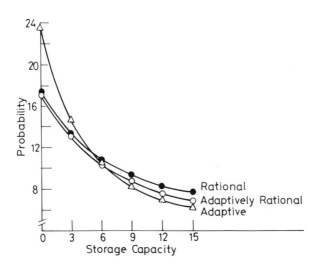

(d) Probability that Supply to Poor Falls by More than 10 Percent below their Normal Consumption.

Figure 4-7. *(continued)*

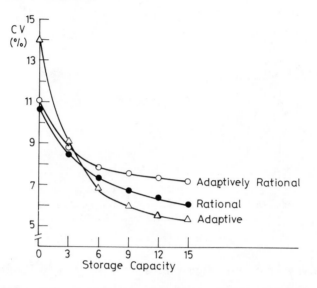

(e) Variability of Farmers' Income (Coefficient of Variation).

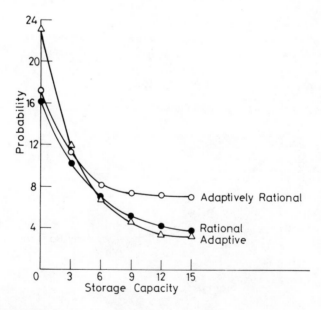

(f) Probability that Farmers' Income Falls by More than 10 Percent below their Normal Income.

supply. This is reflected by the slope of the corresponding curves in the figures, which is much steeper under the adaptive supply, indicating that the marginal productivity of storage, as defined earlier, is much larger in this case. Thus, for instance, a 6 MMT storage facility would reduce the coefficient of variation of the price by almost 40 percent (from 22.5 percent to less than 14 percent) under adaptive expectations and only by 22 percent (from 17.5 percent to 13.6 percent) under rational expectations. This storage facility would also reduce the level of food insecurity by 55 percent under adaptive expectations and only by 35 percent under rational expectations.

The adaptively rational supply function, which does not use the information about the probability distribution of the output and is influenced by random disturbances, nonetheless leads to only a slightly greater instability than does the rational supply. Thus, for instance, without stocks the variability of the price is 3 percent higher and the variability of supply is about 1 percent higher under adaptively rational supply than under rational supply.

The cost effectiveness of buffer stocks under the different forms of the supply function is illustrated in Table 4-4 and Figure 4-8. Table 4-4 summarizes the expected annual gains from operating a storage facility of 6 MMT. It shows that there are very small differences in the economic and financial consequences between the rational and the adaptively rational supply functions. There are however considerable differences between these results and those obtained with the adaptive supply. The greater volatility associated with the adaptive supply raises the stabilizing role of buffer stocks and increases its cost effectiveness. Thus, for instance, the operation of 6 MMT buffer stocks, which would cause net economic losses of 0.09 percent of normal expenditures under the rational supply, would bring net economic *gains* of 0.57 percent of normal expenditures with the adaptive supply. Figure 4-8 shows, however, that the rapidly rising marginal costs of storage under the adaptive supply would outweigh the net gains of the private sector at larger storage capacities.

Thus far we have assumed that the storage authority, having perfect knowledge about the probability distribution of output and all the demand characteristics, determines the trigger prices for the storage intervention on the basis of the true mean price. We now suppose, however, that this knowledge is not available, and the authorities must estimate the mean price. One likely estimate is a weighted average of past observations. In the latter case the storage interven-

Table 4-4. Expected Annual Gains or Losses due to 6 MMT Buffer Stocks under Different Forms of the Supply Function
(As Percentage of Annual Expenditures in a Normal Year).

| | Economic Gains | | | |
Policy	Consumers	Producers	Storage Operation[a]	Total Economy
Rational	– .44	+ .54	– .19	– .09
Adaptively rational	– .40	+ .53	– .21	– .08
Adaptive	– .54	+ 1.24	– .13	+ .57

[a]Including amortization costs.

Figure 4-8. Economic Gains and Losses of Price Stabilization
with Rational and Adaptive Expectations.

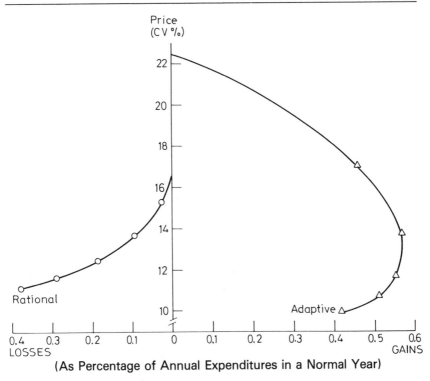

(As Percentage of Annual Expenditures in a Normal Year)

tion rule is termed an adaptive band rule and in the case where the
storage intervention rule is determined in reference to a fixed price it
is termed a fixed price rule.

In the experiments presented here, the mean price was estimated as
a simple average of the past five years' prices. Figure 4-9 parts a and
b illustrate some of the main results under this assumption. By comparing these figures with the ones previously presented we can make
the following observation: under the adaptive band rule the stabilizing effects of stocks would be only slightly weaker than those under
the fixed band. Thus with a 15 MMT storage facility, for instance,
the variability of the price would decline by 37 percent with the fixed
band and by 35 percent under the adaptive band; the probability that
the price falls by more than 20 percent below the normal price is

Figure 4-9.   Stabilizing Effects of Storage under Different Forms of Band Determinations.

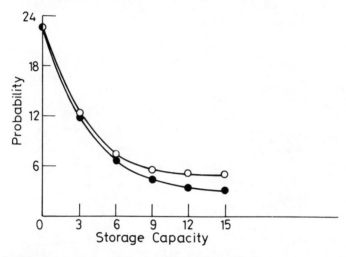

(a) Probability that Price Falls by More than 20 Percent below Normal Price.

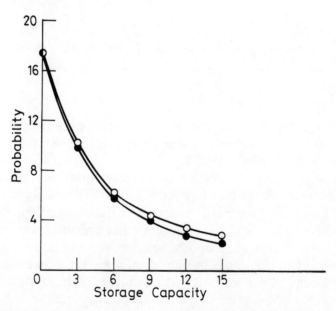

(b) Probability that Farmers' Income Falls by More than 10 Percent below their Normal Income.

reduced to 2 percent with the fixed band rule and to 3 percent with the adaptive band (note that there is almost no difference up to 9 MMT storage capacity). These differences can be regarded as the cost of information in terms of these two performance measures. When we return to these two storage rules subsequently it will be shown that in a different economic environment than the one assumed thus far there are more significant differences in the performance of the storage operation depending on the storage rule.

SUPPLY RESPONSE AND EFFICIENCY GAINS FROM STORAGE

When risk-averse producers respond to a reduction in the variability of the price by increasing their supply, the effects of the storage operation will be manifested not only by a general decrease in instability but also by an increase in supply and by the resulting decrease in price. The difficulty facing the storage authority in this case is how to determine the trigger prices. If prices are determined on the basis of the prices prevailing prior to the storage operation and without taking into account the supply response, then with the increase in supply the storage authority will be forced to purchase increasing quantities of grain unless the trigger prices are adjusted.

Let us again consider the two options of band determination: the fixed-band rule, which determines the trigger prices symmetrically around a fixed price, and the adaptive-band rule, which determines the trigger prices symmetrically around an *estimated* mean price, where this estimate is based on the past five observations.

Although the adaptive band does not explicitly take the supply response into account, it nevertheless automatically incorporates its effects. This is because the estimates of the mean price as moving averages of past observations must reflect the gradual decrease in price with the supply response, and as a result there will also be a gradual adjustment in the trigger prices. Hence, with supply response the adaptive band becomes more effective than the fixed band, since the latter involves a bias in the estimates. For this reason the fixed-band rule cannot in fact be regarded as rational in the sense of Muth (1961) even when the price is fixed at the true mean. This is so because the information set, on the basis of which the subjective estimates are made, does not contain knowledge of the correct structural equations of the model as required by the rationality assump-

Figure 4-10.   Efficiency Gains: Change in the Level of the Main Performance Indicators due to Storage.

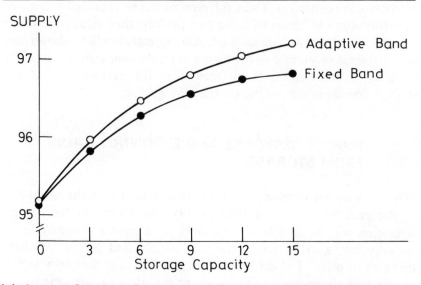

(a) Average Supply as Percentage of Supply in a Stable Market.

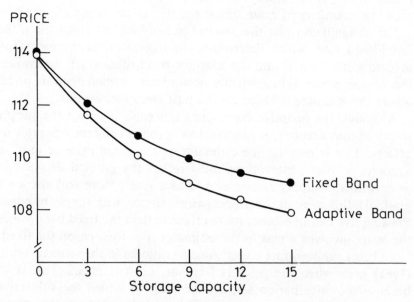

(b) Average Price as Percentage of the Price in a Stable Market.

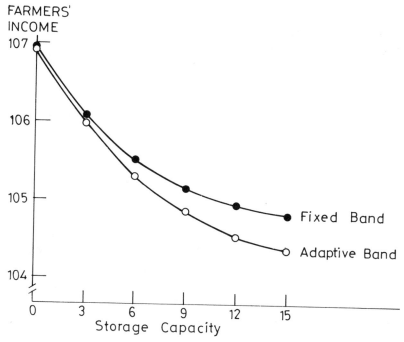

(c) Farmers' Average Income as Percentage of the Income in a Stable Market.

tion; specifically it disregards the behavioral response of producers to the reduction in risk. On the other hand it should be noted that prior to the implementation of any stabilization scheme, this supply response cannot be observed. A priori, therefore, there can be no way for the government or for private agents to learn about the magnitude of the supply response or even about its existence and incorporate this knowledge in their information set. By rigidly adhering to fixed trigger prices and by ignoring the accumulating evidence about changes in the mode of behavior of producers, the fixed-band rule may lead to persistent and consistent errors over time. This can be seen as a direct application of what has become known as the Lucas critique (1976), namely that reduced forms of economic models are not invariant to the policy regime being followed.[7]

The fixed-band rule is of interest because of experience with past stabilization schemes of primary products, in which the rules were usually determined prior to the actual implementation. Once these rules were agreed upon, they were extremely difficult to change. A number of international commodity agreements have run into considerable difficulties because of this type of rigidity, and their very existence has been jeopardized as a result of changes in the behavior of producers and consumers following the agreement.

Figure 4-10 parts a–c illustrate the effects of the storage operation on the levels of the quantities supplied and the resulting effects on the price level and on farmers' income. In the absence of any storage operation, the quantity produced will be 5 percent less than the quantity produced in a stabilized market, and the price will be 14 percent higher because the instability deters risk-averse producers from increasing the area committed to that crop. With the introduction of buffer stocks price instability will diminish, the quantity produced will increase, and the market price will gradually decline. A storage capacity of 15 MMT will induce a 5 percent decline in the average price.

Figure 4-11 parts a and b illustrate the stabilizing effects of buffer stocks. With a storage facility of 6 MMT the price variability declines by some 20 percent (depending on the storage rule). Producers respond by increasing their supply by 1 to 1.5 percent and the average price declines by about 3 percent. For the farmers this decline in price more than offsets the increase in output, and their average income thus declines by about 1.5 percent.

These results vividly demonstrate the higher efficiency of the adaptive-band rule. A storage facility of 15 MMT would reduce the variability of the price by less than 25 percent under the fixed-band rule but by more than 30 percent under the adaptive-band rule. As a consequence average supply would increase by about 1.4 percent under the former and by 2.2 percent under the latter. The average price would thus decline by 4.3 percent under the fixed-band rule and by 5.4 percent under the adaptive band. The stabilizing effects of buffer stocks under the adaptive band would contribute initially to a greater stability also of farmers' income, as can be seen in Figure 4-11b. Beyond a certain level, however, as the price becomes more stable for increasing storage capacities, farmers' income would be destabilized under the adaptive band as the fluctuations in production become the dominating factor.

The most important findings from the experiments with the risk-responsive supply function are the substantial magnitudes of the efficiency gains that are far more significant than the distribution gains.

Figure 4-11.   Efficiency Gains: Change in the Variability of the Main Performance Indicators due to Storage.

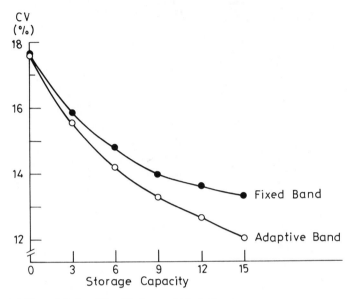

(a) Variability of Price (Coefficient of Variation).

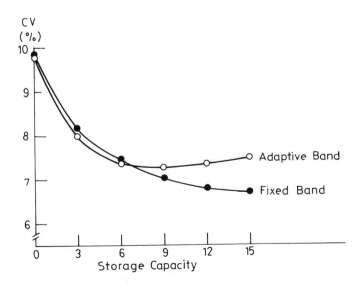

(b) Variability of Farmers' Income (Coefficient of Variation).

Table 4-5. Expected Annual Efficiency and Distribution Gains due to 6 MMT Buffer Stocks (as Percentage of Annual Expenditures in a Normal Year).

Storage Rule	Consumers	Producers	Storage Operation[a]	Total Economy
Fixed band rule				
Efficiency gains	+3.11	−1.13	+0.02	+2.00
Distribution gains	−0.44	+0.54	−0.19	−0.09
Total gains	+2.67	−0.59	−0.17	+1.91
Adaptive band rule				
Efficiency gains	+3.42	−1.14	+0.03	+2.31
Distribution gains	−0.40	+0.53	−0.21	−0.08
Total gains	+3.02	−0.61	−0.18	+2.23

[a]Including amortization costs.

Figure 4-12.   Economic Gains and Losses of Price Stabilization with Efficiency Gains.

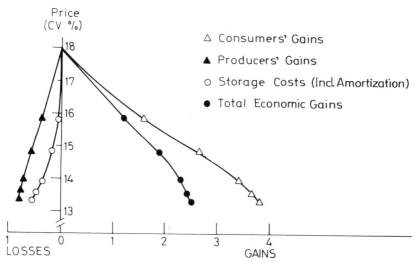

(As Percentage of Annual Expenditures in a Normal (Stable) Year)

These results confirm and strengthen the results presented in Chapter 2. Table 4-5 summarizes the economic and financial gains from a 6 MMT capacity storage operation. It distinguishes the efficiency gains, resulting from the reduction of risk, from the distribution gains, resulting from the transfer of purchasing power as an effect of stabilization. These calculations were made for the two storage rules.

The gains for the economy at large from a 6 MMT storage operation are 1.9 to 2.2 percent of the normal annual expenditures on the product, depending on the storage rule. The distribution effect of shifting purchasing power with stabilization is a miniscule loss of less than 0.1 percent of the normal annual expenditures. As expected, the economic gains under the fixed-band rule are smaller than under the adaptive-band rule.

Finally, Figure 4-12 illustrates the cost effectiveness of buffer stocks. It shows that with supply response the storage policy is beneficial both in reducing the variability of the price and in generating substantial economic gains. The losses of producers are far outweighed by the gains of consumers as a result of the increase in the quantity produced.

STOCKS OPERATION UNDER
SERIAL CORRELATION

The presence of serial correlation should reduce the effectiveness of buffer stocks. If, because of serial correlation, a bad year is more likely to be followed by another bad year, and a good year by another good year, then the probability is higher that the storage facility will remain either empty (in a series of bad years) or full (in a series of good years) and thus idle for longer periods of time. As a result of the serial correlation, therefore, storage activities will be fewer and their overall effect on the price will be smaller.

Figure 4-13 parts a-d illustrate the effects of different levels of buffer stocks on the main stability indicators with and without serial correlation (denoted in the figures by W/SERCOR and NO SER-COR) and under the assumptions of the rational expectations supply function. The figures clearly demonstrate that the presence of serial correlation (with a correlation coefficient of $R^2 = 0.3$) considerably reduces the stabilizing effects of buffer stocks. Thus, for instance, with a 6 MMT storage facility the probability of a shortfall in domestic supply in excess of 10 percent of the normal supply is reduced from 7.7 to 4.4 percent when there is no serial correlation, but from 7.8 to only 6.6 percent when there is serial correlation. With the same storage facility, the probability of a fall in price by more than 20 percent below the normal price is reduced by 50 percent when there is no serial correlation, and by only 25 percent when serial correlation exists.

Figure 4-14 parts a-d illustrate these effects of buffer stocks under the assumption of the adaptively rational expectations supply function. Again, the results show that the presence of serial correlation considerably reduces the stabilizing effects of buffer stocks. Similar results were obtained under the assumption of the adaptive expectations supply function, as illustrated in Figure 4-15 parts a-d.

Figure 4-16 parts a – d illustrate the stabilizing effects of storage in the presence of serial correlation under each of the three assumed forms of the supply function. The most interesting phenomenon is the larger variability existing with the rational supply function as compared with the other expectational form. These results are the opposite of those when there is no serial correlation (see Figure 4-7). As noted earlier, the rational supply function assumes the long-run price, the mean of the price distribution, to be the best predicter of the next period's price. If there is no serial correlation, this assump-

Figure 4-13.   Sensitivity Analysis: Rational Expectations with and Without Serial Correlation.

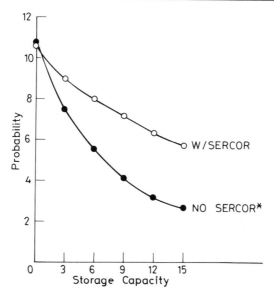

(a) Probability that Price Falls by More than 20 Percent below Normal Price.

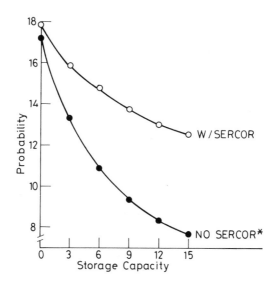

(b) Probability that Supply to the Poor Falls by More than 10 Percent below their Normal Consumption.

Figure 4-13. *(continued)*

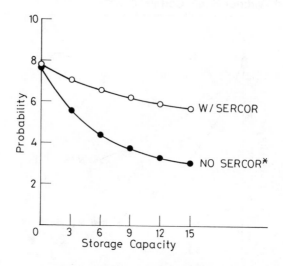

(c) Probability that Total Supply Falls by More than 10 Percent below Normal Supply.

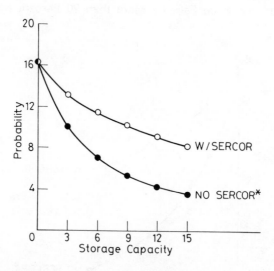

(d) Probability that Farmers' Income Falls by More than 10 Percent below their Normal Income.

Figure 4-14. Sensitivity Analysis: Adaptively Rational Expectations with and without Serial Correlation.

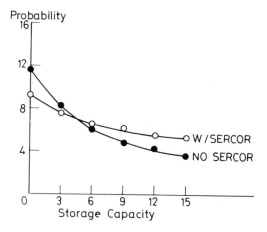

(a) Probability that Price Falls by More than 20 Percent below Normal Price.

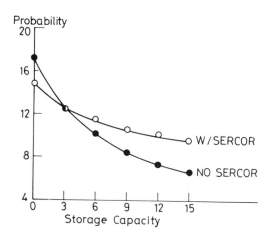

(b) Probability that Supply to the Poor Falls by More than 10 Percent below Their Normal Consumption.

Figure 4-14. *(continued)*

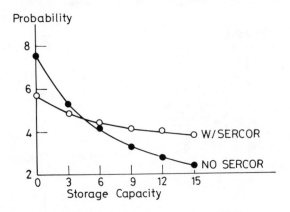

(c) Probability that Total Supply Falls by More than 10 Percent below Normal Supply.

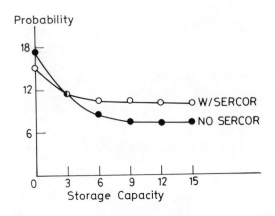

(d) Probability that Farmers' Income Falls by More than 10 Percent below Their Normal Income.

tion is correct and the expectations in that case are indeed rational in the sense of Muth.

If serial correlation exists, however, the long-run price will no longer be the best predicter of the next period's price once the current price is known. The reason is that the *conditional* probability of

Figure 4-15.   Sensitivity Analysis: Adaptive Expectations with and Without Serial Correlation.

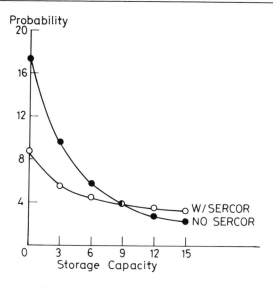

(a) Probability that Price Falls by More than 20 Percent below Normal Price.

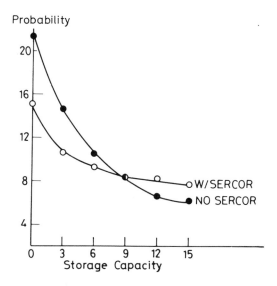

(b) Probability that Supply to the Poor Falls by More than 10 Percent below Their Normal Consumption.

Figure 4-15. *(continued)*

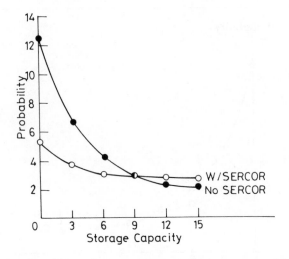

(c) Probability that Total Supply Falls by More than 10 Percent below Normal Supply.

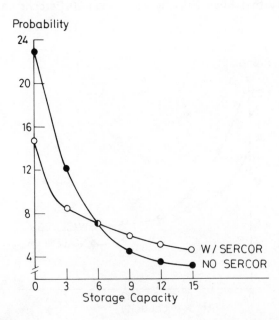

(d) Probability that Farmers' Income Falls by More than 10 Percent below Their Normal Income.

Figure 4-16. Stabilizing Effects of Storage under Different Forms of the Supply Function and With Serial Correlation.

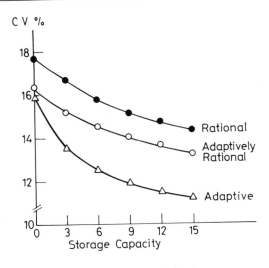

(a) Variability of Price (Coefficient of Variation).

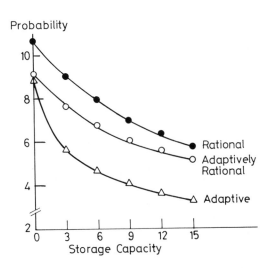

(b) Probability that Price Falls by More than 20 Percent below Normal Price.

Figure 4-16. *(continued)*

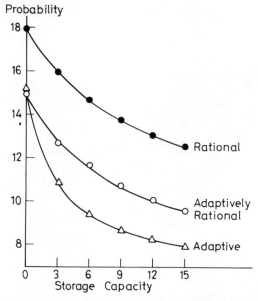

(c) Probability that Supply to the Poor Falls by More than 10 Percent below Their Normal Consumption.

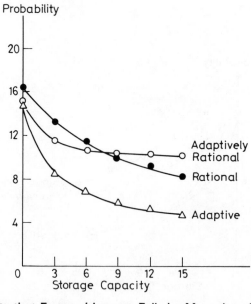

(d) Probability that Farmers' Income Falls by More than 10 Percent below Their Normal Income.

Table 4–6. Expected Annual Gains or Losses due to 6 MMT Buffer Stocks under Different Supply Specifications

(As Percentage of Annual Expenditures in a Normal Year).

	Consumers	Producers	Economic Gains		
			Storage Operating Costs	Storage Total Costs[a]	Total Economy
No Serial Correlation					
Rational	– .44	+ .54	+ .02	– .19	– .09
Adaptively rational	– .40	+ .53	.00	– .21	– .08
Adaptive	– .54	+1.24	+ .08	– .13	+ .57
With Serial Correlation ($R^2 = 0.3$)					
Rational	– .51	+ .54	– .04	– .25	– .22
Adaptively rational	– .34	+ .44	– .07	– .28	– .18
Adaptive	– .36	+ .57	– .03	– .24	– .03

[a] Including amortization costs.

Figure 4-17. Economic Losses due to Price Stabilization with Buffer Stocks when Expectations Are Adaptive with and without Serial Correlation.

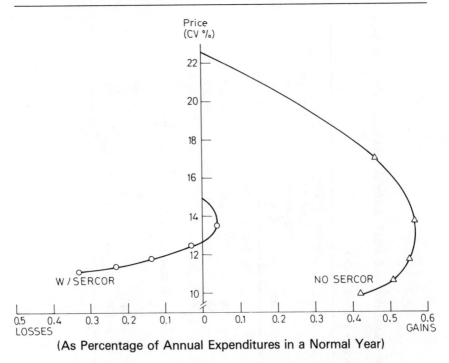

(As Percentage of Annual Expenditures in a Normal Year)

having a certain price in the next period, given the actual price in the current period, is different, in the presence of serial correlation, from the unconditional probability. (If there is no serial correlation the two probabilities are obviously equal.) The adaptively rational expectations and even more so the adaptive expectations automatically incorporate the serial correlation and can therefore predict more accurately the future's price, thus reducing this source of instability. For instance, without any storage the coefficient of variation of the market price will be 17.6 percent under rational supply function but only 16 percent under adaptive supply. Food insecurity will be 17.8 percent under rational supply function and 15.1 percent under both adaptive and adaptively rational supply.

Also noteworthy is the substantial difference in the stabilizing effects of storage between adaptive and adaptively rational supply. A storage capacity of 6 MMT will reduce the price variability by 22 percent under adaptive supply, but only by 11 percent under adaptively rational supply.

As the stabilizing effects of buffer stocks become smaller in the presence of serial correlation, the resulting economic and financial costs of the program increase. This is especially pronounced with the adaptive supply function, where a net gain to the economy resulting from 6 MMT buffer stocks in the absence of serial correlation turns into a net loss when serial correlation is present. These results are given in Table 4–6 for all forms of the supply function and in Figure 4–17 for the adaptive supply.

SOME SENSITIVITY ANALYSES

Having examined the sensitivity of the results to the assumed forms of the supply function and the presence of serial correlation, we now examine the sensitivity of the results to specific values of the parameters assumed in the simulation experiments. In particular let us examine their sensitivity to different levels of the demand elasticities, interest rates, and variability in production. Relaxing the assumption made in the base case whereby the process starts with no grain in storage, let us examine cases in which one-third and two-thirds of the storage capacity is full at the beginning of the process.

Sensitivity Analysis: Elasticities

The stabilizing effects of buffer stocks for different levels of price elasticity of demand are illustrated in Figure 4–18 parts a–e. The details of the three different sets of elasticities considered are summarized in Table 4–7.

The most noteworthy result is the potentially *destabilizing* effect of larger storage capacity on farmers' income at high levels of demand elasticities. In general, the higher the elasticities the more stable the price, and the more stable also farmers' income. As a result of the storage operation the price becomes even more stable (as seen in Figure

Figure 4-18.   Sensitivity Analysis: Different Levels of Elasticity.

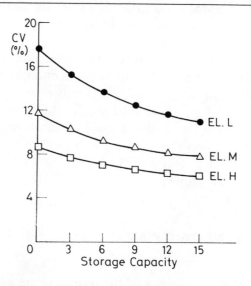

(a) Variability of Price (Coefficient of Variation).

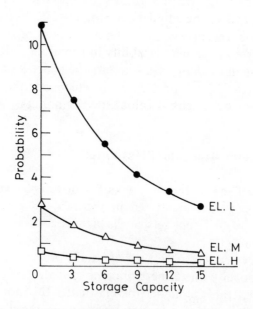

(b) Probability that Price Falls by More than 20 Percent below Normal Price.

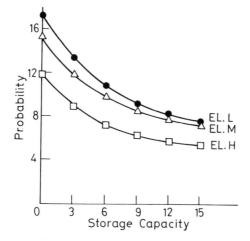

(c) Probability that Supply to the Poor Falls by More than 10 Percent below Their Normal Consumption.

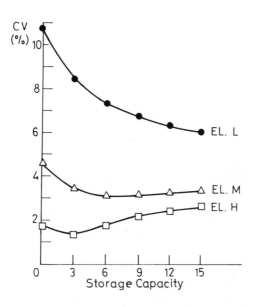

(d) Variability of Farmers' Income (Coefficient of Variation).

Figure 4-18. *(continued)*

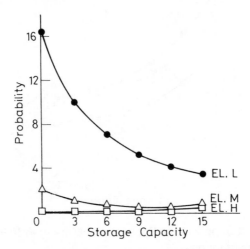

(e) Probability that Farmers' Income Falls by More than 10 Percent below Their Normal Consumption.

4-18a) but farmers' income may become *less* stable (as seen in Figure 4-18d).

In Chapter 2 we already noted that price stabilization need not lead to the stabilization of farmers' income and that the outcome depends on the relevant demand and supply elasticities. That conclusion was reached on the basis of a theoretical analysis that assumed linear supply and demand schedules and complete price stabilization. The results of the simulation experiments where nonlinear demand schedules and partial stabilization are considered suggest that within a certain range of elasticities further increase of the storage capacity beyond a certain level will still increase price stability but will only destabilize farmers' income. The reason is that as the price is further stabilized, the variations in income resulting from variations in output are no longer compensated for by corresponding price variations in the opposite direction.

Another noteworthy observation is the sensitivity of certain results to the specific demand parameters. As has already been noted, the higher the elasticities the more stable the price. As a result at higher elasticities the stabilizing effects of buffer stocks are likely to be smaller. In the low-elasticity case (EL.L), which is the base case, a

Table 4-7. Alternative Demand Parameters.

	Low-Income Urban Consumers	Middle- to High-Income Urban Consumers	Rural Consumers	Total Population
Mean quantity consumed as percentage of total consumption	30	40	30	100
Price elasticity of demand at the mean				
Low elasticity				
EL.L[a]				
P > 100	0.55	0.3	0.25	0.36
P < 100	0.55	0.4	0.35	0.43
Medium elasticity				
EL.M				
P > 100	0.75	0.50	0.35	0.53
P < 100	0.75	0.75	0.5	0.675
High elasticity				
EL.H				
P > 100	0.90	0.75	0.60	0.75
P < 100	0.90	0.90	0.75	0.855

[a]Base case.

Table 4-8. Expected Annual Gains or Losses Due to 6 MMT Buffer Stocks under Different Levels of Demand Elasticity
(as Percentage of Annual Expenditures in a Normal Year).

| | | | Economic Gains | | |
Elasticities	Consumers	Producers	Storage Operating Costs	Storage Total Costs[b]	Total Economy
EL.L[a]	−.44	+.54	+.02	−.19	−.09
EL.M	−.24	+.28	−.02	−.23	−.17
EL.H	−.26	+.30	−.03	−.24	−.20

[a]Base case.
[b]Including amortization costs.

storage facility of 15 MMT would reduce the coefficient of variation of the price by almost 40 percent. In the high-elasticity case (EL.H), this storage facility would reduce the coefficient of variation of the price by only 30 percent. With the same storage capacity the probability that the price will fall by more than 20 percent below the stable price is reduced from 10.9 percent to 2.7 percent in the low-elasticity case, whereas in the high-elasticity case this probability is only 0.6 percent even when there is no storage, and is reduced to 0.35 percent with a storage facility of 15 MMT.

Table 4-8 summarizes the main results with respect to the economic gains and losses due to a 6 MMT storage capacity (or 6 percent of annual average production). The gains or losses are expressed in the table as percentages of total annual expenditures on grain in a normal (stable) year. The results indicate an increase in the losses to the economy as a whole due to the storage operation as the demand elasticities increase. Both consumers and producers become less affected while the storage operating costs increase. The reason is that price variability at higher demand elasticities is considerably smaller, and thus the scope for storage operations is also smaller.

Sensitivity Analysis: Interest Rate

Differences in the rate of interest do not make any difference to the stabilizing effects of buffer stocks, of course. They do alter the discounted economic gains or losses due to buffer stocks, however, as illustrated in Table 4-9. For the private sector both the gains and the losses would be smaller the lower are the interest rates. An important reason for this is that the bias resulting from the fact that the process starts with no grain in storage and working against consumers and in favor of producers would be less pronounced at a lower interest rate. For the same reason the storage authority is likely to have much larger operating gains at lower interest rates. In addition there will be a decrease in the annual amortization costs from $3.5 per ton capacity with an interest rate of 8 percent to $2.6 with 5 percent. As a result both the storage authority and the economy at large are more likely to have gains at lower interest rates.

Sensitivity Analysis: Production Variability

Figures 4-19 a-d illustrate the main effects of increasing levels of storage capacity under different assumptions on the variability of

Table 4-9. Expected Annual Gains or Losses due to 6 MMT Buffer Stocks at Different Interest Rates (As Percentage of Annual Expenditures in a Normal Year).

	Economic Gains					
Interest Rate	Consumers	Producers	Storage Operating Costs	Storage Total Costs[b]	Total Economy	
5 percent	−.33	+.41	+.26	+.10	+.18	
8 percent[a]	−.44	+.54	+.02	−.19	−.09	

[a]Base case.
[b]Including amortization costs.

domestic production. Three levels of variability are considered: CV = 11 percent; CV = 7 percent (the base case); and CV = 3 percent.

The results indeed confirm both a priori expectations and common sense. As the variability of production increases the entire economy becomes less stable, as indicated by all the performance measures. A noteworthy observation is the change in the marginal productivity of buffer stocks, measured by the effect on the performance criteria of successive increases of the storage capacity. As noted earlier, there is a monotonous decrease in the marginal productivity, but the decrease is much steeper at smaller levels of production variability. This can be observed by the considerable differences in slope of the curves.

At higher levels of production variability the economic gains or losses due to buffer stocks will also be larger. Consumers' losses and producers' gains from the storage operations will increase. The storage authority is more likely to cover at least the operating costs as the level of production variability increases. (This is in part due to the nonlinearity of the demand curve, which leads to higher prices when grain is released from storage.) As a result the overall welfare losses to the economy are markedly smaller at higher levels of production variability, and there may even be small gains. These effects are summarized in Table 4–10.

Sensitivity Analysis: Initial Stocks

In the simulation experiments conducted so far we assumed that the process starts with no grain in storage. During the first few years of operation, the authorities must therefore build up stocks. During these years the storage intervention has to be one-sided, capable only of extracting excesses from the market and thus raising the price. Only later, when enough grain is accumulated in stocks, can the authorities intervene to lower the price by releasing grain to the market.

The following simulation experiments were designed to examine the sensitivity of the results to this assumption. Along with the base case assumption of no grain in storage at the beginning of the process (denoted by Init = 0), we considered a case in which one-third of the storage facility is full (denoted by Init = ⅓ · capac) and a case in which two-thirds of the storage facility is full (denoted by Init = ⅔ · capac).

Figure 4-19.   Sensitivity Analysis: Production Variability.

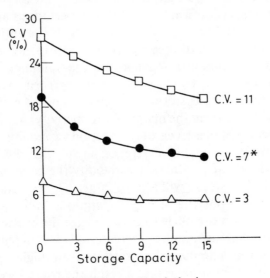

(a) Variability of Price (Coefficient of Variation).

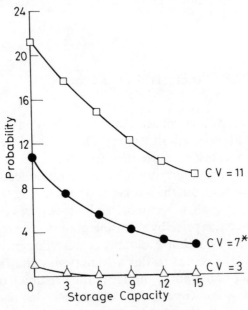

(b) Probability that Price Falls by More than 20 Percent below Normal Price.

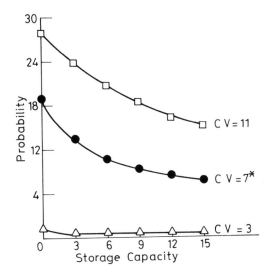

(c) Probability that Supply to the Poor Falls by More than 10 Percent below Their Normal Consumption.

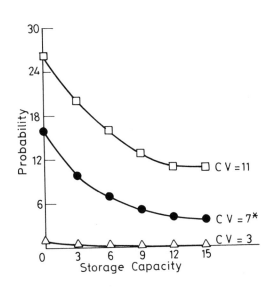

(d) Probability that Farmers' Income Falls by More than 10 Percent below Their Normal Income.

Table 4-10. Expected Annual Gains or Losses due to 6 MMT Buffer Stocks under Different Levels of Production Variability

(As Percentage of Annual Expenditures in a Normal Year).

| Production Variability[a] | Consumers | Producers | Economic Gains | | Storage Total Costs[b] | Total Economy |
			Storage Operating Costs			
CV = 3	−.30	+.32	−.01		−.22	−.20
CV = 7[c]	−.44	+.54	+.02		−.19	−.09
CV = 11	−.61	+.74	+.17		−.04	+.09

[a]Coefficient of variation.
[b]Including amortization costs.
[c]Base case.

Figure 4-20.   Sensitivity Analysis: Initial Stocks.

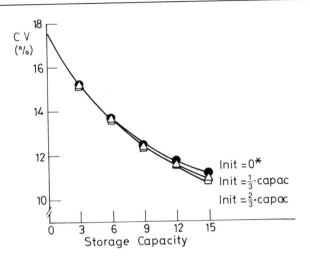

(a) Variability of Price (Coefficient of Variation).

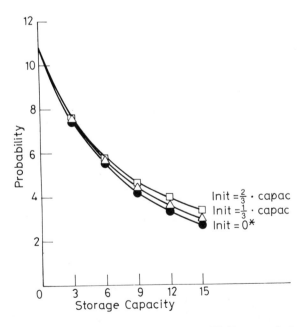

(b) Probability that Price Falls by More than 20 Percent below Normal Price.

Figure 4-20. *(continued)*

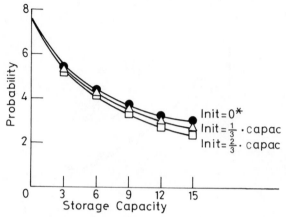

(c) Probability that Total Supply Falls by More than 10 Percent below Normal Supply.

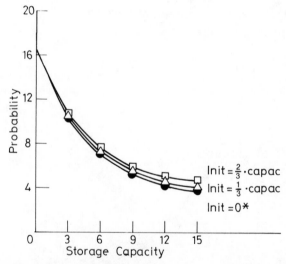

(d) Probability that Farmers' Income Falls by More than 10 Percent below Their Normal Income.

Figure 4-20 parts a–d illustrate the main stabilization effects of buffer stocks under these three assumptions. They show that altering the base case assumption of zero initial stocks does not change the stabilizing effects of buffer stocks in any significant way. Only at a relatively high level of storage will there be any noticeable difference.

Table 4-11. Expected Annual Gains or Losses due to 6 MMT Buffer Stocks at Different Levels of Initial Stocks

(As Percentage of Annual Expenditures in a Normal Year).

| | Economic Gains | | | | |
Initial Stocks	Consumers	Producers	Storage Operating Costs[a]	Storage Total Costs[b]	Total Economy
0[c]	−.44	+.54	+.02	−.19	−.09
2 MMT	−.06	+.15	+.18	−.05	+.04
4 MMT	+.34	−.24	+.33	+.08	+.17

[a]Not including purchase of initial stocks.

[b]Including purchases of the initial stocks and annual amortization.

[c]Base case.

Obviously, the larger the stocks at the beginning of the process, the larger would be the stabilizing effects on supply. Farmers' income may become less stable, however, when there is grain in storage at the beginning of the process, because during these first years the storage authorities are more likely to be active in lowering the price when shortages are revealed.

The volume of stocks at the beginning of the process will have, however, considerable impact on the distribution of the welfare gains from price stabilization. The results, summarized in Table 4–11 show that some of the effects are completely reversed when the process starts with two-thirds of the storage capacity full as compared with the base case starting with no grain in storage. The reason is clear: when there are no initial stocks, the first operations will be inventory accumulation which raises the price. Consumers will thus incur losses from storage during the first years, whereas producers will gain. When the storage facility is two-thirds full, the first storage operations will be inventory depletion, which lowers the price, thereby benefiting consumers at the expense of producers. In Table 4–11 we see that with no grain in storage at the beginning of the process consumers lose and producers gain from the storage operation, whereas with two-thirds of the capacity full at the initial stage consumers gain and producers are now losing. The table also indicates considerable differences in the storage operating profits. These differences are also due to the fact that with more grain in storage more of the grain will be sold early on in the process and the discounted value of the revenues will therefore increase.

CONCLUDING REMARKS

The main conclusion emerging from the simulation analysis is the strong dependence of the specific effects of buffer stocks on the economic environment within which they operate. The form of the supply function as determined by producing farmers' form of expectation, the degree of serial correlation in production, the values of the demand elasticities, and the degree of variability in production—all these have a strong impact on the extent to which buffer stocks will stabilize the price and secure a stable flow of supply, and on the economic gains or losses resulting from the storage operation. Thus, for instance, price stabilization through buffer stocks is likely to produce welfare losses when producers' expectations are rational but welfare gains when producers' expectations are adaptive. If there is serial correlation in production, however, the storage operation is likely to produce welfare losses even when expectations are adaptive.

Moreover, the initial conditions existing in the economy are strongly influenced by the endogenous parameters that define the economic system. Thus, for instance, the variability of the price is some 35 percent higher when expectations are adaptive than when they are rational. The stabilizing effects of buffer stocks are larger the greater the initial degree of instability. A 6 MMT storage facility reduces the price variability by some 45 percent when expectations are adaptive but only by 18 percent when expectations are rational.

In all cases, however, our results exhibit the diminishing marginal productivity and consequently the increasing marginal costs of buffer stocks. Successive increases of the storage capacity lead to higher stability but at a diminishing rate. Incremental increases in the degree of stability thus become increasingly costly. For example, a 6 MMT storage facility is likely to reduce the variability of the price by more than 20 percent when expectations are rational. Increasing this facility by an additional 6 MMT further reduces the variability of the price but this time by less than 12 percent.

The stabilizing effects of buffer stocks also depend very significantly on the form of the storage rules. The simulation experiments show a considerable difference in effects on storage activities between a symmetric price band and a nonsymmetric one. Under a symmetric band the storage operation performs better in reducing the coefficients of variation of price, supply, and farmers' income. Under a nonsymmetric band the storage operation performs better in reducing the probabilities of events that take place in one tail of the probability distribution. The notable example is the probability that total supply or, more specifically, the supply to the poor does not fall below a certain critical level. The latter criterion is intimately related to what many countries regard as the level of food security. The simulation results thus suggest that under a nonsymmetric band the storage operation is likely to render higher food security.

The second variation in the form of the storage rules that we have considered is the case when the mean price, in relation to which the price band is determined, is estimated adaptively on the basis of past observations. In contrast, most theoretical as well as empirical analyses of buffer stocks assume the mean price to be known. The simulation results indicate that there is a relatively small difference in performance of the buffer stocks when the assumption of a fixed band is replaced by the adaptive band. Moreover, in the presence of serial correlation the adaptive band performs better than the fixed band. The reason is that under the former rule the bands are adjusted continuously to any trend in the price series, thus automatically taking into account the effects of serial correlation ignored by the fixed band. The importance of this finding lies in the fact that most stock agreements determine a single reference price, which is normally assumed to be the mean of the price distribution. Changes in the reference price are sometimes extremely hard to make after the agreement is signed. The results suggest that a better procedure might be to agree on the principle according to which the reference price would be determined and to adjust this price continuously and automatically according to this principle. The latter procedure should ensure that any developments taking place after and sometimes as a result of the stock agreement will automatically be taken into account.

Finally, the analysis of the efficiency gains shows that if risk-averse producers respond to the reduction in the risk associated with unstable prices, then the *efficiency* gains resulting from the storage operation will be far more important than the gains usually attributed to this operation. The simulation experiments show that with the reduction in price variability due to a 6 MMT storage operation, average supply would increase by some 2.5 to 3 percent, even under rather conservative estimates of the degree of supply response, and average price would thus decline by some 7 to 8 percent (depending on the demand elasticities).

These consequences are far more important for enhancing food security and promoting farm production than all the other effects of buffer stocks. This will also be reflected by the welfare gains generated by the storage operation. In the absence of supply response, the operation of a 6 MMT storage facility is likely to produce net economic losses amounting to 0.05 percent of the average annual expenditures on the product. However, even with a moderate supply response the same storage facility is likely to produce net economic *gains* amounting to 3.82 percent of the average annual expenditures. An analysis of the degree to which producers are responding to the more stable environment by increasing their production is therefore a vital prerequisite for determining the desirability of buffer stocks.

APPENDIX 4A.
EVALUATING THE END PERIOD'S STOCKS

The simulation described is for a finite time horizon (assumed to be thirty years). Typically, at the end of the period there will still be some grain left in storage, the value of which must be taken into account when calculating the financial gains or losses from the storage operation.

The question is, at what price should the remaining stocks be evaluated? Obviously, even if we assume that beyond the time period considered in the simulation experiments the output remains stable at its mean, we still cannot take the corresponding stable price to be the price at which the remaining stocks should be evaluated. This is because as these stocks are released from storage the market price will fall below that level. Thus, the storage authority is unlikely to release the remaining stock at once and will instead seek an optimal strategy for selling the stock so as to maximize its (present discounted) value. To determine this strategy the following question is considered: Suppose that the storage authority is left with the quantity $\bar{S}$ of grains in storage. Suppose also that production is stable at its long-run mean. What would be the optimal policy for selling the quantity $\bar{S}$ if the storage authority is seeking to maximize the present value of its future receipts from these sales? This optimization problem can be written in a continuous time,

$$\text{Max} \int_0^T P_t \, S_t \cdot e^{-rt} \, dt$$

$$\text{Subject to (i) } P_t = a - b\,(\bar{Q} + S_t)$$

$$\text{(ii)} \int_0^T S_t = \bar{S}.$$

The first constraint determines the market price as a (linear) function of the quantity $\bar{Q}$ produced plus the quantity S_t released from storage. The second constraint shows that the sum of the quantity released from storage during the time $[0,T]$ must be equal to the initial amount $\bar{S}$ in storage. The length of the time period $[0, T]$ during which grain is to be released must itself be dertermined as part of the optimal strategy.

To solve this problem we can write the Hamiltonian

$$H = e^{-rt} [a - b (\overline{Q} + S_t)] S_t - \lambda S_t .$$ (4A-1)

The conditions for dynamic optimization are given by

(i) $\dfrac{\partial H}{\partial S_t} = \overline{P} - 2bS_t - \lambda_t = 0$,

where $\overline{P} = a - b\overline{Q};$

(ii) $\dfrac{\partial H}{\partial X_t} = \dot{\lambda} - r\lambda = 0$,

where a dot denotes the time differential, and $X_t = \overline{S} - \int_0^t S_t.$

(iii) $\dfrac{\partial H}{\partial \lambda} = \dot{\overline{S}} = S_T .$

The latter condition simply ascertains that the second constraint in the optimization problem is satisfied.

When T itself is to be determined in the optimal solution, a fourth condition must be added, which is given by

(iv) $H (t = T) = 0 .$

Hence

$$P_T S_T - \lambda_T S_T = 0 ,$$ (4A-2)

and therefore

$$P_T = \lambda_T .$$ (4A-3)

The condition (ii) implies

$$\lambda_t = \lambda_0 e^{rt} .$$ (4A-4)

From (4A-3) and the condition (i) we get

$$S_T = \frac{\overline{P} - \lambda T}{2b}.$$

But if the second constraint in the optimization problem is satisfied we must have $P_T = \overline{P}$ and therefore also $S_T = 0$. Hence, from (4A-4)

$$\lambda_T = \lambda_0 e^{rT} = \overline{P} ,$$

which implies that

$$\lambda_0 = \overline{P} \cdot e^{-rt} .$$

Hence, from the condition (i) and (4A-4) we get

$$S_t = \frac{\bar{P}}{2b} [1 - e^{-r(T-t)}] . \qquad (4A\text{-}5)$$

This is the optimal strategy for releasing the remaining stocks from storage. The corresponding price path is given by

$$P_t = \frac{\bar{P}}{2} [1 + e^{-r(T-t)}] . \qquad (4A\text{-}6)$$

Thus the prices rise monotonically over time from the level of $P_0 = \frac{1}{2}$ $\bar{P}(1 + e^{-rT})$ until they reach the level of $\bar{P}$ at time T, and they then remain at that level.

To calculate the optimal time interval $[0,T]$ during which grain is to be released from storage, we compute

$$
\begin{aligned}
\bar{S} = \int_0^T S_t &= \int_0^T \frac{\bar{P}}{2b} (1 - e^{-r(T-t)}) \, dt \\
&= \frac{\bar{P}}{2b} [t - \frac{1}{r} e^{-r(T-t)}] \Big|_0^T \\
&= \frac{\bar{P}}{2b} (\frac{1}{r} - e^{-rT}) + \frac{\bar{P}}{2b} T .
\end{aligned}
$$

Thus we can make the following approximation

$$T \approx \frac{2b}{P} \cdot \bar{S} . \qquad (4A\text{-}7)$$

We can now calculate the value of the objective function given the values of $\bar{P}$, b, and $\bar{S}$.

APPENDIX 4B.
CAPITAL COSTS OF STORAGE

The cost of storage structures varies widely, depending on scale, location, construction materials, and other factors. Units of 40-ton capacity constructed of a welded mesh with a butyl liner, placed on a concrete slab, have been erected at a cost of $25 to $30 per ton capacity (1978 U.S. dollars). Corrugated metal stores holding 80 to 400 tons cost from $45 to $90 per ton capacity. Monolithic concrete silos holding 10,000–15,000 tons cost from $85 to $125 per ton capacity. To these costs must be added the costs for machinery, which in the case of bulk handling may raise the capital costs of storage by as much as 50 percent.

As an illustration let us consider the total capital cost and its main components of two types of storage facilities. One is silo storage, typical in the developed countries; the other is warehouse storage in bags, typical in developing countries. The different types of storage facilities require different handling technologies and thus also considerable differences in costs of machinery. The data in Table 4B-1 are given only as examples and should not be taken to have any general validity. Annual capital costs include depreciation of the building (twenty years for the warehouse; thirty years for the silo); depreciation of the machinery (ten years for machinery in the warehouse; fifteen years for machinery in the silo); interest (8 percent per annum) and loan amortization (over ten years).

Table 4B-1. Capital Costs of Grain Storage Facility.

	Silo 30,000 MT capacity	Warehouse 5,000 MT capacity
	U.S. dollars	
Total capital costs		
Building and site	300,000	155,000
Machinery	210,000	20,000
Other[a]	135,000	30,000
Total capital costs	645,000	205,000
per ton capacity	215	41
Annual overhead costs		
Annual capital costs	55,000	40,000
per ton capacity[b]	18.35	8
Other overhead costs	16,000	6,500
per ton capacity[c]	5.35	1.3
Total annual overhead costs	71,000	46,500
per ton capacity	23.7	9.3

[a]Other capital costs include service, installation, planning, and design.

[b]Including depreciation of building and machinery, interest, and loan amortization.

[c]Including permanent staff maintenance, etc.

NOTES

1. Pharaoh had his compensation from this undertaking; the Biblical story tells us that the people hit by the drought came to Joseph and begged: "Give us bread; for why should we die in thy presence? for our money faileth! And Joseph said: Give your cattle, and I will give you bread for your cattle, if money fail. And they brought their cattle unto Joseph. And Joseph gave them bread in exchange for the horses, and for the flocks, and for the herds, and for the asses; and he fed them with bread in exchange for all their cattle for that year."

2. In the closed economy model it is assumed that the economy is at a steady state, so that both production and consumption are growing at the same rate and consumption per capita remains constant. For all practical purposes we can therefore examine in this case the simpler stationary state.

3. The case of a quantity trigger band was also considered.

4. The band need not be centered symmetrically on the long-run equilibrium price, however; nonsymmetric intervention rules were also considered.

5. Note, however, that all financial and welfare performance measures are given by their present discounted values.

6. The results presented here assume a normal distribution, but the model can accommodate other distributions as well.

7. The proposition states that models designed and estimated under one set of policies may lead to consistent errors if used for prediction under a different set of policies because of possible changes in the very structure and in the values of the parameters of the model.

5 INTERNAL STABILIZATION PROGRAMS: SUBSIDIES, SUPPORT PRICES, AND BUFFER STOCKS

The theoretical analysis of price stabilization emphasizes the net social gains due solely to changing the flow of supply over time. Because the policy instrument that ensures such pure price stabilization is buffer stocks, the economic literature on the subject has emphasized this instrument much to the neglect of any other. In practice, however, the main policy instruments of stabilization employed in both the developed and the developing countries are various price and distribution programs. Moreover, decisions whether to operate buffer stocks and at what level are strongly influenced by the existing policies with respect to production and prices and by the specific means chosen to implement them.

Buffer stock policy differs fundamentally from price and distribution policies in two ways. First, the former applies to the general population, whereas the latter usually deliberately aim at or effectively apply to specific target groups. Subsidy programs are often confined to certain consumer groups only: price support is given to the producers of agricultural products; a public distribution system of staple foods is directed at low-income consumers; and so on. Second, the stock policy works by shifting consumption from one time period to another. Price and distribution programs work by shifting consumption, either directly or through the transfer of money income, from one group or sector to another within the same period; such programs therefore require differential fiscal transfers and involve considerable changes in the income distribution.

The subsidy programs are generally designed to provide the microeconomic unit, be it a household or a firm, with financial incentives aimed at encouraging or discouraging, according to the particular case, the purchase and use of certain goods or services or certain factors of production. Examples include subsidies to lower the price and encourage the sales of certain agricultural commodities or subsidies to encourage the purchases of certain factors of production (including credit). The important feature to emphasize is that subsidies represent a form of intervention that works through and within the framework of the market system and does not attempt to replace it.

The economic justification for subsidies comes in two forms. One emphasizes externality or merit good considerations and the role of subsidies in increasing economic efficiency. The other emphasizes the role of subsidies as an instrument of income redistribution.

As for the actual implementation of the subsidy program, traditional welfare economics has always stressed the superiority of direct cash transfers over price subsidies as a means of improving income redistribution. The main reason is that the cash transfers do not restrict the commodity choice of the beneficiary consumer, thus enabling individual recipients to attain the highest possible level of satisfaction. However, arguments in favor of subsidy programs in fact regard the restrictions imposed by these programs on the commodity choice to be their main advantage. Thus, for instance, a subsidy program can be more cost effective than direct cash transfers in encouraging the consumption of certain food items over other food or nonfood items or in redistributing consumption between the members of the household through the choice of specific goods. The merit good argument, which is sometimes mentioned in this context, emphasizes the long-run effects of malnutrition, especially in early childhood, on the level of adult productivity.

In Chapter 3 some of the reasons that have motivated governments to select these policy instruments were examined, and the specific cases of several countries were reviewed. The most important reason for selecting group-specific policies appears to be that goals such as stabilization and adequate nutrition are often defined in terms of group-specific targets. Food security, for example, is usually defined in terms of the nutritional needs of low-income consumers only. A distribution system that ensures sufficient food for the low-income consumers therefore provides the simplest and most effective way of achieving this goal. The solvency of the farm sector is another important goal, and price support or income maintenance programs are the most direct and obvious instruments for achieving it.

This chapter examines the effects of several price policies as well as effects of buffer stocks when these policies are implemented. The focus is on two types of programs: a price support program that applies to farmers only and a price subsidy program that applies to low-income urban consumers only. The direct and indirect effects of each individual policy are examined as well as the combined effect of various combinations of policies and the *marginal* effect of a given policy when it is implemented in conjunction with other policies.

Of the various ways of implementing each policy and program, only those typical of many developing countries are considered here. The price support program, for instance, can be carried out as a form of deficiency payment, which makes up the difference between the market price and the secured floor price without extracting any quantities from the market. Alternatively, the program can be carried out by procuring the excess supply and extracting it from the market, thereby raising the market price to the secured floor price; later on, in years of shortage (when price support is no longer needed) the quantities procured and stored can be released to the market and thus work to lower the price. The subsidy program can apply to all consumer groups as it does in Egypt and Israel, for instance, or it can apply, through food stamps or other forms of rationing, to specific groups only.

Each of these policies may also exert a lasting effect on the level of production in subsequent years via effects on prices, and thus influence the long-run growth trends of production. Both the immediate and the long-run effects of each policy and program are analyzed here.

SOME ECONOMIC CONSIDERATIONS REGARDING FOOD SUBSIDIES

Food subsidies can be analyzed at three levels: the nationwide, or macroeconomic level; the specific market for food products; and the household, or the elementary microeconomic, level. In this book we are mainly concerned with the level of the food market and the level of the household unit. As a prelude to this partial equilibrium analysis several other economic considerations that may influence the design of the subsidy programs must be mentioned.

From a macroeconomic point of view subsidies may be extremely important, especially in developing countries, both because they make up a substantial share of the government budget and because the subsidized commodities often account for a large portion of domestic production or personal consumption. Another macroeconomic consideration regarding subsidies is their consequence in terms of the balance of payments. This is a result of the significant role of imports in supporting and supplementing a subsidy program. Governments that have attempted to lower prices to consumers via subsidies have often had to increase their reliance on imports; countries such as Egypt, India and Indonesia, which are committed to comprehensive subsidy programs, have their trade balance and government budget largely dominated by these programs, as shown in the following tables.

Table 5-1 provides an indication of the budgetary costs of food subsidies in some developing countries, calculated as a percentage of the total government expenditure. The data are for the years 1972 and 1974.

The sharp rise from 1972 to 1974 in the budgetary costs of food subsidies is largely due to the exceptional rise in world prices, which forced governments to increase both the quantities distributed under the subsidy programs and their payments for the quantities procured from domestic sources and abroad for this purpose.

Table 5-2 presents the implications for the balance of payments of these subsidies. From a microeconomic point of view a subsidy pro-

Table 5-1. Budgetary Costs of Food Subsidies
(As Percentage of Total Government Expenditure).

Country	1972	1974
Burma	—[a]	8
Egypt	4	22
Indonesia	—[a]	13
Korea	4	14
Pakistan	1	13

[a] Dashes indicate expenditures of less than 1 percent.
Source: Davis (1977).

Table 5-2. Food Imports and the Balance of Payments (As *Percentage of X = Value of Exports and of M = Value of Imports*).

| | 1972 | | 1974 | |
Country	X	M	X	M
Egypt (all food)	30	19	59	29
India (cereals)	8	7	19	15
Mali (all food)	50	29	59	57
Morocco (all food)	25	20	31	27
Sri Lanka (rice, flour, and sugar)	33	30	51	41
Tanzania (all food)	13	9	41	19

Source: Davis (1977).

gram works to increase consumption of the subsidized product (say, food) through the substitution effect—by making food cheaper relative to nonfood products—and through the income effect. Many programs aimed at increasing food consumption above previous levels operate mainly by means of income transfer. Consider, for instance, the food stamp program in the United States. In its initial phase, from 1964 to 1971, qualifying recipients were entitled to obtain only food commodities and were required upon redeeming their stamps to purchase a certain minimum quantity of food against the stamp. Such a program is successful only if the purchasing of additional food is induced by these requirements. A family whose customary level of food consumption is well above the minimum specified requirement will treat the food stamps only as a source of extra income, however. Moreover, if food demand is not highly responsive to income, as empirical studies suggest, an income transfer, even when disguised in the form of food stamps, will not necessarily lead its recipients to purchase much more food. Only for those households whose purchase requirements are large relative to their presubsidy level of food consumption will the program effectively increase food consumption.[1] The sale of staple foods through the public distribution system at prices lower than the market prices also amounts in most cases to an income transfer. This is because the quantities sold to each household in the ration shops (see Chapter 3) are usually much smaller than the total quantities bought by the household. Thus the cheaper prices pertaining to only a fraction of its food consumption will not alter the household consumption decision.

Empirical studies also point to considerable differences in response to income between the different income groups. Table 5-3 illustrates these differences for the case of India. Given the high income elasticities of the low-income consumers and the larger shares of their budget allocated to staple foods, it is clear that even when the subsidy program works as an income transfer it is still likely to have considerable impact on the food consumption of these groups.

Another consideration at the household level is the propensity of consumers to move to higher quality, more expensive food products as their income goes up. As a result, subsidy as well as other income transfer programs often induce consumers to shift from cheap to more expensive varieties of food without increasing their caloric intake. Thus, for the subsidy program to be successful it must be linked, as far as possible, to specific types of food. An example of such a link, which is practiced successfully in several developing countries, is the distribution via the national ration shops of specific food products that are important nutrients for the poor but considered inferior by the more affluent consumers.

Identifying the food products consumed mostly by the poor and targeting the subsidies to these products can also be an effective means of raising the nutrition level of this segment of the population. The efficiency of such a program depends on the price responsiveness of consumers in the target group and on the degree of their consump-

Table 5-3. Budget Shares and Income Elasticity of Staple Foods in India.

Income Level as Proportion of Mean	Budget Shares			Income Elasticity		
	Rice	Wheat	Other Cereals	Rice	Wheat	Other Cereals
0.40	0.150	0.052	0.165	1.76	3.42	0.59
0.53	0.145	0.067	0.143	1.47	2.20	0.52
0.81	0.135	0.075	0.092	0.91	1.14	0.44
1.13	0.115	0.069	0.062	0.67	0.57	0.35
1.42	0.115	0.071	0.054	0.21	0.05	0.26
1.92	0.070	0.066	0.041	−0.86	−0.74	0.19

Source: Swamy and Binswanger (1980).

tion of the subsidized food product as a proportion of their total food consumption. Another way of directing the benefits to the poor is by identifying the nutritionally deficient households. This is commonly done by defining a poverty line, a minimum income level below which a family is assumed to lack the means to sustain a decent standard of living. Families below the line are then eligible for official help.

If the official help is given by awarding subsidies on specific food products to eligible families only, its effect will be to redistribute the existing supply more favorably between the different income groups. Such a program can achieve its goal of increasing the supply to the target group even without relying on additional imports or on an increase in domestic supply.

To analyze the effects of this program, consider a simple closed economy consisting of two consumer groups. Only one of these, say the second group, is eligible for help. Thus, if the market price of the food product is P, the eligible group pays only $P \cdot (1 - \theta)$, where θ is the rate of subsidy. Market clearing conditions are given by

$$D_1(P) + D_2[(1 - \theta)P] = S(P), \tag{5-1}$$

where D_i is the demand of the ith group ($i = 1,2$) and S is total supply. From this equation can be derived the effect of a change in the subsidy rate on the market price, given by

$$\frac{\partial P}{\partial \theta} \cdot \frac{\theta}{P} = \frac{\theta \, \eta_2 \, w_2}{\eta_1 w_1 + (1 - \theta) \, \eta_2 w_2 + \epsilon} > 0 , \tag{5-2}$$

where η_i is the price elasticity of demand of the ith group and w_i is the share of the ith group in the total consumption of that product. From Eq. (5-2) we can therefore conclude that the higher the subsidy rate the higher will be the market price to be paid by group 1, the nonbeneficiary group. Depending on their price responsiveness consumers in group 1 will then lower their demand for the product, thus allowing the shift of existing supply to the eligible group and hence a more desirable distribution of consumption. The larger the price elasticity of demand of the eligible consumers (η_2) and the larger their share in the consumption of the product (w_2), the larger the rise in price will have to be.

The trade-off in food consumption between the two groups is given by the ratio $\partial D_1 / \partial D_2$. This ratio indicates the amount of food that the nonbeneficiary group must relinquish in order to allow the beneficiary group one more unit of subsidized food. From (5-1) and (5-2) we can calculate this ratio:

$$\frac{\partial D_1 / D_1}{\partial D_2 / D_2} = - \frac{\eta_1 w_2}{(\eta_1 w_1 + \epsilon)} < 0 \qquad (5\text{-}3)$$

Hence, the smaller the price elasticity of demand of the nonbeneficiary group and the smaller their share in total consumption, the larger will be the amount of food that they will have to relinquish.

The costs of the subsidy to the government are given by

$$C = \theta \cdot P \cdot D_2 . \qquad (5\text{-}4)$$

After some algebra we can calculate

$$\frac{\partial C / C}{\partial \theta / \theta} = \frac{(1 + \theta \eta_2)(\eta_1 w_1 + \epsilon) + \eta_2 w_2}{\eta_1 w_1 + (1 - \theta) \eta_2 w_2 + \epsilon} > 0 . \qquad (5\text{-}5)$$

We can now calculate the cost effectiveness of the program. This is given by the ratio $\partial C / \partial D_2$, which indicates the marginal costs of delivering a unit of subsidized food to the eligible group. This cost is given, in elasticity terms, by

$$\frac{\partial C / C}{\partial D_2 / D_2} = 1 + \frac{1}{\theta \eta_2} + \frac{w_2}{\theta(w_1 \eta_1 + \epsilon)} > 1 . \qquad (5\text{-}6)$$

The additional costs above unity measure the excess burden of the program. This burden exists when the program works by shifting consumption from the ineligible to the eligible group, whereas when the additional consumption of the eligible consumers is imported the cost effectiveness would be $(\partial C / C) / (\partial D_2 / D_2) = 1$.

Despite these limitations, food subsidies represent a major instrument in many developing countries for changing the income distribution and influencing specific target groups. As will be seen in the simulation analysis, they can be highly efficient instruments for achieving certain objectives, particularly those defined in terms of the target groups. At the same time, however, the analysis indicates that these programs may involve very high economic costs and specifically high fiscal costs.

THE STRUCTURE OF THE INTERNAL PRICE PROGRAMS

The simulation model applied for the analysis of internal price policies is essentially the same as that developed in the previous chapter for the analysis of buffer stock operations. It also considers a closed economy, but now in addition to buffer stocks two other types of policies are considered: producers' support programs and consumers' subsidy programs. The decision principles in each of these programs are as follows:

Subsidy Program

The subsidy program is directed toward low-income urban consumers *only* and allows them to buy foodgrains at a discount price lower than the market price. The actual implementation of the program requires some form of rationing, either through special ration shops that sell only to eligible consumers or through other arrangements such as the food stamp program, which allows eligible consumers to buy foodgrains at a discount price in the usual retail outlets. It is assumed that the program becomes effective only when the market price rises above its mean level; that is, the program works only at the upper segment of the price distribution. It is further assumed that the program does not fix the subsidized price rigidly but adjusts it according to the prevailing market price. This is done, first, to prevent too large a gap between the market price and the subsidized price, which might lead to widespread abuses of the system, and second to reduce the fiscal burden of the subsidy payments. In the model this adjustment is assumed to take the form of a linear rule given by

$$P^s = \begin{cases} P + \alpha(\overline{P} - P) & \text{if } P > \overline{P} \\ P & \text{if } P \leq \overline{P} \end{cases}$$

where P and $\bar{P}$ are the current and the median prices, respectively, P^S is the subsidized price to the urban poor and $0 \leqq \alpha \leqq 1$.

It is easy to see that with this adjustment rule the effective price elasticity of demand of the urban poor becomes $(1 - \alpha)\, \eta_p$, where η_p is the regular price elasticity of this group. Hence, the policy has the effect of modifying the demand curve of the urban poor, making it less elastic above the median price. As a result the entire market demand curve becomes less elastic above the mean price. The subsidy decision rules are illustrated in Figure 5-1, where D_B is the demand schedule of the beneficiary group and D_S is the subsidy schedule. Thus when the market price is P_1 the subsidized price will be P_1^s. D_s therefore becomes the effective demand curve for the group and the total demand schedule shifts to D'. Hence, as supply falls below its

Figure 5-1.   Subsidy Decision Rules.

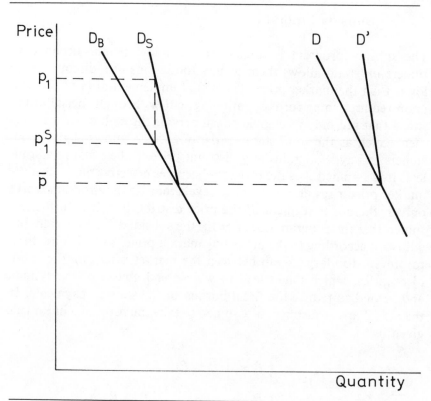

mean level, the price to nonbeneficiary consumers would be higher the less elastic the modified demand curve D'.

Price Support Program

The price support program is directed toward the farmers and takes the form of a deficiency payment; that is, the government makes up the difference between the market price and a prespecified floor price whenever the market price falls below that level. Consider two alternative decision rules for this program: one rule determines a fixed support price and does not allow the price to fall below that level; the other is a linear adjustment rule that allows the price paid to farmers to decline but at a lower rate than the decline in the market price. This rule is given by

$$P_{sup} \begin{cases} = P + \beta\,(\overline{P} - P) & \text{if } P < \overline{P} \\ = P & \text{if } P \geq \overline{P}\,, \end{cases}$$

where P_{sup} is the price support to farmers and $0 \leq \beta \leq 1$. This rule has the effect of modifying the *effective* demand curve the farmers face, making it more elastic at the lower segment of the price distribution. The price elasticity of demand that is effective for the farmers is then given by $\eta/(1 - \beta)$, where η is the regular price elasticity of the market demand.

As for the actual implementation of the program, we consider two versions: direct price support and government procurement. In direct price support the government supports the floor price without constraining production or removing any surplus from the market. In that case the program does not have any direct effect on the market price, hence has no effect on any of the other sectors and, specifically, no effect on consumers. It should be noted though that when production is affected by past prices, as in the case of adaptive expectations, this policy will have the long-run effect of inducing farmers to increase their production, to the benefit of all sectors in the economy.

Under government procurement, the government procures the excess supply and removes it from the market. The support price becomes the effective market price, and all sectors in the economy are thus directly affected. It is assumed that the government stores the surplus and releases it in later periods when the prices rise above their median level. In this version we thus analyze the stocks operating not as an independent policy instrument but as an *offshoot* or a *residual* of other price policies, specifically of the government procurement policy. It is also assumed that there is no capacity constraint on the amount extracted from the market and stored. Existing storage facilities will be filled first. Any remaining surplus is stored in temporary storage facilities or warehouses or even under cover in open areas. It is assumed, however, that the grain stored in temporary facilities or in the open is subject to greater losses, a considerable proportion of it being taken by rats and insects or spoiled in other ways. This is indeed the situation in many countries (both developing and developed) where the level of stocks is influenced by existing policies on production and prices and by the means chosen to implement them. An FAO expert committee estimated that storage losses for cereals were on average over 10 percent and in some cases as high as 25 percent.

Income Maintenance

An alternative to the price support program is the farmers' income maintenance program. Operated whenever farmers' income falls below a certain critical level due to a fall in either price or production, the program supplements their income up to the critical level. Farmers' income is then given by

$$
I_{\text{farmers}} = \begin{cases} P \cdot Q & \text{if:} P \cdot Q \geq I_{\text{critical}} \\ I_{\text{critical}} & \text{if:} P \cdot Q < I_{\text{critical}} \end{cases}
$$

MEASURING THE GAINS FROM POLICIES

When two or more policies are implemented by the government, two types of performance measures must be considered. The first is the total effect of a given combination of policies; the second is the *marginal* effect of a particular policy *given* that certain other policies have already been implemented. As will be seen, the marginal effect may be substantially different depending on what other policies are already in effect.

Consider first the welfare gains from the subsidy program, illustrated in Figure 5-2. When the subsidy program is in effect the demand curve of the beneficiary group, the low-income urban consumers, becomes D_S instead of their original curve D_B. This results also in a rightward shift of the aggregate demand curve from D to D'. In Figure 5-2a we can see that in the closed economy, when the quantity available for consumption is Q (which may include the quantity produced *and* the quantity released from storage) the market price for the nonbeneficiary group rises from P_0 to P_1, and when D_{NB} is their demand schedule they suffer welfare losses given by the shaded area A. Figure 5-2b describes the gains for the beneficiary group. Without the subsidy program they would have paid the market price P_0. With the program the market price rises to P_1, but they pay only P_S. Their welfare gains are therefore given by the shaded area D. As for the government expenditures on the subsidy payments, they are given by the shaded areas $(C + D + E)$. One more factor must be taken into account, namely, the effect of the program on farmers. Clearly, this program was not designed with the aim of aiding the farmers, and yet the rise in the market price from P_0 to P_1 increases their income and welfare. These welfare gains are given in Figure 5-2a by the shaded area $(A + B)$. At the same time it should be noted that the program is likely to increase the variability of prices, and this may have adverse effects on the farmers, which will partly offset their income gains.

As an illustration of the *marginal* gains from a policy consider Figure 5-3. In Figure 5-3a only a buffer stock policy is in effect. When production is Q and the quantity S is released from storage, the quantity $Q + S$ is then available for consumption. Let D and D_1 denote the total demand curve and the demand curve of the urban poor, respectively. With the release of grain from storage the price declines to P_m, and the urban poor gain the amount designated by the area A. If the subsidy program is already in effect, however, as illustrated in Figure 5-3b, the effective demand schedule of the urban poor becomes D_S. Without the storage operation the market price would have been P^s. When the quantity S is released from storage, however, the market price declines to P_m and the price to the urban poor declines further to P_m^s. The welfare gains of this group are des-

Figure 5-2. Gains and Losses from the Subsidy Program.

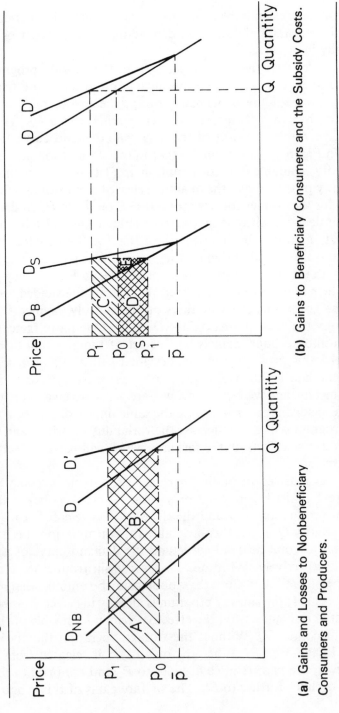

(a) Gains and Losses to Nonbeneficiary Consumers and Producers.

(b) Gains to Beneficiary Consumers and the Subsidy Costs.

Figure 5-3. Marginal Gains of "Poor" Consumers from Buffer Stocks.

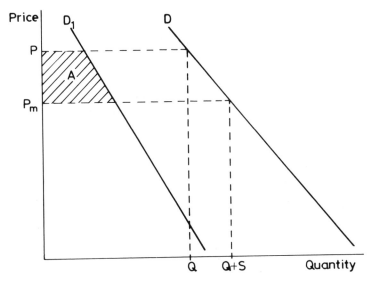

(a) Consumers' Gains when Stocks Only Are Operated.

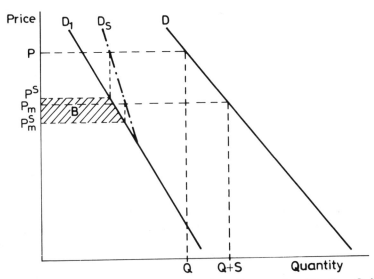

(b) Consumers' Gains when Stocks Are Operated with the Subsidy Program.

ignated by the shaded area *B* only. Clearly, these gains are significantly smaller than those obtained when the buffer stocks are operating alone.

DATA AND PARAMETERS

The structural parameters of the model are the same as those described in the previous chapter. Now, however, parameters specifying the decision rules relating to price support and the subsidy programs must be added.

Price Support

The following two alternative programs are considered:

Floor Price Program. The government maintains a constant floor price of 90; that is, the price is not allowed to fall by more than 10 percent below its normal level, where the normal level is its level in a stable year.

Partial Adjustment Program. The support price is determined each year according to the prevailing market price and the following adjustment rule:

$$P_{sup} = \begin{cases} P + 0.15\,(\bar{P} - P) & \text{if } P < 100. \\ P & \text{if } P > 100. \end{cases}$$

When the government procurement program is implemented and the excess supply of foodgrain is removed from the market and stored, the following assumptions are made: first, these stocks are released according to the existing storage rules; for example, when the price rises by more than 5 percent above the normal level. Second, when storage facilities exist, the excess removed from the market is stored first in these facilities up to their capacity. Any remaining surplus is stored in temporary facilities. This remaining surplus is assumed to decay at an annual rate of 10 percent. Third, loading costs in the temporary facilities are assumed to be $5 per ton, but there are no capital expenses on the facilities.

Income Maintenance

The government does not allow the income of farmers to fall by more than 10 percent below their normal income, that is, their income in a stable year.

Subsidy

The subsidy program is directed toward low-income urban consumers only. Their share in the total consumption of foodgrain is 30 percent, although their share in the population is much larger. This means that their per capita consumption of foodgrain is considerably smaller than that of the other consumer groups. The subsidy is awarded only when the price rises above its normal level (100). As explained earlier, the linear adjustment rule of the subsidy program has the effect of modifying the effective demand curve of the urban poor and thus also the aggregate demand curve at the upper segment of the price distribution, making them less elastic. Table 5-4 summarizes the price elasticities of the beneficiary group and of all consumers with and without the subsidy, under three different assumptions with regard to the level of intensity at which this program is implemented.

Performance Criteria

A smaller set of performance measures contains the following criteria: (1) *price instability,* measured by the coefficient of variation of

Table 5-4. Price Elasticities of Demand with the Subsidy Program
(Calculated at P = 100).

Subsidy Program	Beneficiary Group		All Consumers	
	Without Subsidy	With Subsidy	Without Subsidy	With Subsidy
Partial food security	0.55	0.25	0.36	0.27
Solid food security	0.55	0.10	0.36	0.225
Complete food security	0.55	0.00	0.36	0.195

the market price; (2) *food insecurity (5%)* measured by the probability that the quantity available for consumption by the urban poor falls by more than 5 percent below their normal consumption, that is, their consumption in a stable year; (3) *farmers' income insecurity,* measured by the probability that farmers' income falls by more than 5 percent below their normal income, that is, their income in a stable year.

PRODUCERS' SUPPORT PROGRAMS

The main objective of these programs is to stabilize farmers' income and prevent a sharp decline in their earnings to a level that may force some of them out of production. The programs will be evaluated by the degree to which they reduce the coefficient of variation of farmers' income and the insecurity of farmers' income as defined previously. Other benefits, if any, are only secondary to these main benefits. Table 5-5 summarizes the main stabilizing effects of the different support programs.

The results in Table 5-5 show that buffer stocks are capable of reducing both the variability of farmers' income and the variability of their price as much as or even more than the specific producers' support programs. Thus, with a storage facility of 6 MMT, the coefficient of variation of farmers' income is reduced from 10.7 percent to 5.4 percent. The floor price programs, through direct price support or government procurement, reduce this probability to 6.9 and 6.0 percent, respectively, and the income maintenance program reduces it to 8.7 percent. The latter programs are considerably more effective in reducing the insecurity of farmers' income, however.

With a 6 MMT storage facility there is still a probability of 7 percent that farmers' income will fall by more than 10 percent below their normal income, while with the producers' support program this probability is eliminated altogether. The difference lies in that buffer stocks work equally to reduce the probability of extreme events at both sides of the income probability distribution, whereas the price and income programs operate only at one side of this distribution and are therefore more effective in influencing events that occur at that side. The partial adjustment programs designed for these experiments are less effective in reducing the instability of farmers' income. Yet these programs are much less costly, as will be shown shortly.

Table 5-5. Main Stabilizing Effects of Producers' Support Programs.

	No Policy	Buffer Stocks 6 MMT	Direct Price Support		Government Procurement		Income Maintenance
			Floor Price	Partial Adjustment	Floor Price	Partial Adjustment	
Variability of farmers' income, CV (%)	10.7	5.4	6.9	9.2	6.0	8.7	8.7
Variability of farmers' price, CV (%)	17.6	13.6	13.8	16.3	12.2	15.7	17.6
Probability that farmers' income falls by more than							
5 percent of normal income	30.5	14.3	9.6	24.9	10.6	24.9	30.5
10 percent of normal income	16.2	7.0	0.0	10.6	0.0	10.6	0.0

In addition to their effect on the variabilities of the various distributions, the policies also affect their means. Thus, for instance, with the floor price program the average farmers' price is 2.5 percent higher than the average price with no policy, and their average income is 3 percent higher. With the government procurement program both farmers' price and income are only 1 percent higher than their price and income when there is no policy. The reason for this difference between the two programs is that with the government procurement program the excesses removed from the market in the good years are released from storage in the bad years, thereby causing the price, along with farmers' income, to decline.

Another difference between the programs is in their effect on the welfare of the various sectors in the economy. A direct price support program affects only the price to producers; an income maintenance program affects only their income without altering the market price. Consumers therefore will not be directly affected by these policies since they merely involve transfers from the government to producers. There are indirect effects, however. First, the money allocated for these programs could have been spent on other programs and thus represents a welfare loss to other groups or sectors. Second, the programs are likely to change producers' expectations about future prices and about the risk involved in production and hence change their production decisions. The procurement program will in addition have direct effects on consumers, because it works by changing the market price to producers and consumers alike. Table 5-6 summarizes the economic gains and losses to the different sectors arising out of the different support programs.

The results in Table 5-6 show that the direct price support and the income maintenance programs are by far the most costly for the government. The procurement and stocks programs are much less costly because of the revenues from sales of the procured grain during years of high prices (even after allowing for amortization cost and losses due to decay of the grain). The procurement and buffer stocks programs may involve considerable losses to consumers, however.

Comparison of the producers' direct support programs with the buffer stocks program shows that the latter is more cost effective in reducing the variability of farmers' income and the instability in their price. Even after allowing for amortization costs, buffer stocks of 6 MMT (or 6 percent of annual production) cost the government less than either one of the floor price programs or the income mainte-

Table 5-6. Expected Economic Gains and Losses due to Producers' Support Programs (As Percentage of Annual Expenditures in a Normal Year).

Economic Sector	Buffer Stocks 6 MMT	Direct Price Support		Government Procurement		Income Maintenance
		Floor Price	Partial Adjustment	Floor Price	Partial Adjustment	
Consumers	- .44	0	0	- 1.34	- 0.36	0
Producers	+ .54	+ 2.94	+ 1.15	+ 1.49	+ 0.38	+ 1.10
Government	- .19[a]	- 2.94	- 1.15	- 0.27	- 0.02	- 1.10
Total economy	- .09	0	0	- 0.12	0	0

[a]Including amortization costs.

nance program. Yet stocks are more effective in reducing the variabilities in income and price. Special producers' support programs may still be needed, however, because even with 6 MMT buffer stocks farmers suffer from a degree of income insecurity that may be deemed unacceptable by the government. The economic and financial costs involved in eliminating this insecurity by introducing a floor price program may thus be regarded as a form of insurance payment made to prevent these extreme events. The desirability of the programs should therefore be weighed against the repercussions of a critical fall in farmers' income.

To examine some of the long-run effects of the price policies resulting from their lasting effects on production consider the consequences of these policies when producers' expectations are affected by them. In the case of adaptive expectations in production a rise in producers' price with government support changes not only the current year's price but also the level of production and hence also the price in the following year, and consequently the whole production series varies. Tables 5-7 and 5-8 summarize the relevant stabilization and economic indicators when expectations are adaptive.

The long-run effects of the producers' support programs are demonstrated most vividly by the effects of the direct price support program on consumers' price, because the program is directed only to the producers. Table 5-7 shows that it has the effect of reducing the variability of the consumers' price by more than 10 percent through its long-term effects on production. Table 5-8 shows that consumers

Table 5-7. Stabilization Effects of Producers' Support Programs: Adaptive Expectations.

Stability Indicator, CV (%)	No Policy	Buffer Stocks 6 MMT	Floor Price	
			Direct Support	Government Procurement
Variability of farmers' income	14.0	6.8	7.0	5.5
Variability of producers' price	22.6	13.6	14.4	11.8
Variability of consumers' price	22.6	13.6	20.0	11.8

Table 5-8. Expected Economic Gains and Losses due to
Producers' Support Programs: Adaptive Expectations
(As Percentage of Annual Expenditures in a Normal Year).

| Economic Sector | Buffer Stocks 6 MMT | Floor Price | |
		Direct Support	Government Procurement
Consumers	− .54	+ 1.35	− 1.22
Producers	+ 1.25	+ 3.57	+ 2.07
Government	− 0.13	− 4.41	− 0.27
Total economy	+ 0.58	+ 0.51	+ 0.58

are likely to gain considerably from the lasting changes in production as an effect of the direct support program and that the economy as a whole is now likely to experience net gains.

Comparison of the stabilizing effects of buffer stocks with those of the procurement program shows that with adaptive expectations the latter, which unlike the storage operation has no capacity constraint, now becomes more effective in reducing the instability. The economic and financial data in Table 5-8 show, however, that the government procurement program involves more massive income transfers from consumers to producers than the storage operation and that the fiscal costs of the procurement program are double the costs of buffer stocks. Still, because the economy at large is likely to gain more from the procurement program, it is superior to buffer stocks in terms of both its stabilizing effects and its economic impact.

The direct price support program is the most beneficial of the three in terms of net gains to the economy at large. But it involves very large fiscal costs (more than sixteen times those of the procurement program), which are distributed directly to producers and spill over via the effect on production to consumers. The high fiscal costs may be a deterrent, which perhaps explains why many developing countries tend to prefer procurement programs.

A comparison of the results of Table 5-8 with those of Table 5-6 shows that the gains and losses from the various programs are extremely sensitive to the form of expectations in supply. Net economic losses with rational expectations have turned into net gains with adaptive expectations; government expenses on the direct price support program are 50 percent higher with adaptive than with rational expectations (although they are approximately equal in each of the other two programs); producers' gains are considerably larger in all three programs when expectations are adaptive.

The long-run effects of the producers' support programs are much larger and even more telling when risk-averse producers respond to the ensuing reduction in risk by increasing their production. Tables 5–9 and 5–10 summarize the relevant stabilization and economic indicators for the case with supply response. (See Chapter 4 for the supply function [Eq. (4–7)] and the parameters.)

The reduction in the variability of farmers' price with the direct price support program also leads to more stable conditions in the other segments of the economy, and the variability of the market price, though not directly affected by the program, is reduced by more than 15 percent as a result of the long-run effects on prices. The main gains from the programs are, however, the economic gains resulting from the increase in production. Table 5–10 shows that with supply response consumers have the main gain from the support programs, whereas without supply response it is the producers who gain since in the short run the programs mainly involve a transfer from the government to producers. These gains far outweigh both the losses to producers (resulting from the price decreases) and the fiscal costs, leaving the economy with substantial net gains.

Table 5-9. Stabilization Effects of Producers' Support Programs: Supply Response.

| Stability Indicator, CV (%) | No Policy | Buffer Stocks 6 MMT | Floor Price | |
			Direct Support	Government Procurement
Variability of farmers' income	10	7	8	8
Variability of producers' price	18	15	16	15
Variability of consumers' price	18	15	17	15

Table 5-10. Expected Economic Gains and Losses due to Producers' Support Programs: Supply Response (As Percentage of Annual Expenditures in a Normal Year).

Economic Sector	Buffer Stocks 6 MMT	Floor Price	
		Direct Support	Government Procurement
Consumers	+2.67	+2.05	+2.00
Producers	−0.59	+0.50	−0.30
Government	−0.17	−1.33	−0.06
Total economy	+1.91	+1.22	+1.64

Note again that the losses incurred by producers are essentially actuarial losses since they do not take into account the larger utility and the smaller insurance payments existing in a more stable environment. A comparison of the economic gains from the programs with and without supply response, in Tables 5-10 and 5-6, respectively, proves that the extent to which producers are affected by instability is a crucial factor influencing the effects and desirability of the programs.

PRODUCERS' SUPPORT PROGRAMS AND BUFFER STOCKS

When a producers' support program is implemented together with buffer stocks, the marginal effect of each individual program will be entirely different from its independent effect. Thus, for instance, when the procurement program is implemented, most of the storage operations are already carried out as part of this program.[2] Buffer stocks are then essentially a residue of the procurement program and, to a lesser degree, of the direct price support and income maintenance programs. The economic justification of the storage operation should thus be based on its *marginal* effects on the relevant economic variables over and above the effects of the existing programs. In this section the effects of combinations of producers' support and buffer stocks policies are analyzed.

Figure 5-4. Stabilization Effects of Producers' Support Programs and Buffer Stocks.

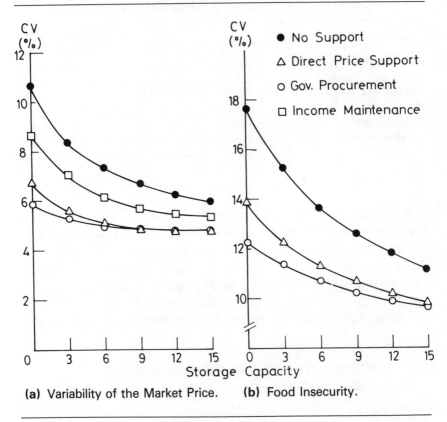

(a) Variability of the Market Price.   (b) Food Insecurity.

Figure 5-4 parts a and b demonstrate the stabilizing effects of different producers' support programs and buffer stocks policies on producers' income and price. The most noteworthy observation is that the larger the independent stabilizing effect of the support program the smaller will be the added stability achieved through buffer stocks and the more rapid will be the decline in the marginal productivity (expressed in terms of the stabilizing effects) of additional storage units. Thus, for instance, a storage facility of 6 MMT would reduce the variability of farmers' income by 31 percent when no support program is in effect, by 26 percent when a direct price support program is in effect, and by only 15 percent when a procurement program is in effect. Increasing this facility to 12 MMT would reduce the variability of farmers' income by 13 percent when no support price is in effect but only by 4 percent when a procurement program is in effect. Another noteworthy observation is that the diminishing marginal productivity of buffer stocks, that is, the decreasing stabilizing effects of additional units of storage, may still make a support program necessary because no reasonable amount of storage will be sufficient to secure the required level of stability. This is clearly demonstrated in Figure 5–5.

Figure 5-5. Stabilization Effects of Producers' Support Programs and Buffer Stocks: Farmers' Income Insecurity.

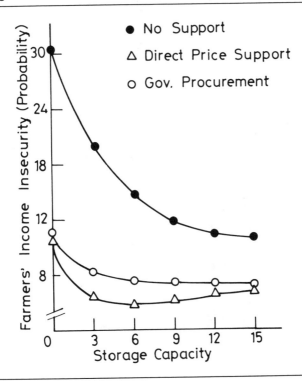

For the purpose of preventing a decline in farmers' income below a certain critical level, buffer stocks alone are of very limited value. Even a storage facility of 15 MMT (or 15 percent of annual production) can reduce farmers' income insecurity only to about 10 percent, a level that may still be considered unacceptable. A price support program and a storage facility of 6 MMT reduce this insecurity to less than 3 percent. (Note in Figure 5–5 that further increases in storage capacity only increase this probability as the yield instability outweighs the stabilizing effects of stocks on the price.)

Government procurement and buffer stocks policies have been analyzed thus far only with respect to their effect on producers. Their effects on the other sectors in the economy must be taken into account as well, even though these effects might be secondary in im-

Figure 5-6.   Secondary Stabilization Effects of Producers' Support Programs and Buffer Stocks.

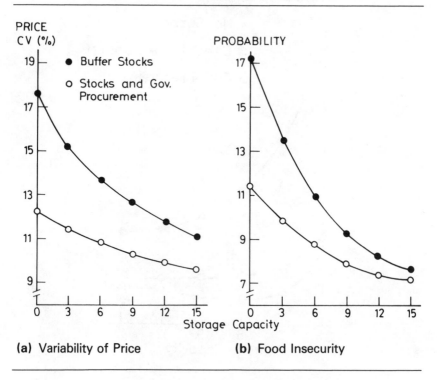

(a) Variability of Price   (b) Food Insecurity

portance. Of special interest are the stabilizing effects of these policies on prices and on the flow of supply, as presented in Figure 5-6.

The figure shows that the procurement program has considerable
stabilizing effects. As an outcome of this program the variability of
the price is reduced by 30 percent, a reduction that only a storage facility of 9 MMT is capable of securing; the probability of a shortage
in supply to the urban poor in excess of 10 percent below their normal
supply is reduced by 35 percent. The added stability due to buffer
stocks when the procurement program is in effect is much smaller
compared with the stability when buffer stocks only are operated,
however. This is reflected by the substantial difference in the slopes
of the corresponding curves in Figure 5-6.

The critical parameter for evaluating these two policy combinations
is their cost effectiveness. From the point of view of the food security
objective, for instance, cost effectiveness is measured by the total
economic costs of reducing the probability that supply to the poor
falls by more than 10 percent below their normal consumption. These
costs are presented in Figure 5-7, which shows that up to a certain
level of food security, buffer stocks alone are more cost effective
than the combination of buffer stocks and a procurement program,
whereas above that level the latter combination becomes more cost
effective.

Another important parameter concerns the *marginal* effectiveness
of a certain policy *given the other policies* already in effect. Figure
5-8 presents the marginal cost effectiveness of buffer stocks with and
without the procurement program. The results indicate that if a procurement program is already being implemented, buffer stocks become considerably less cost effective. Thus the cost of reducing food
insecurity by 1 percent by introducing buffer stocks is 35 to 50 percent higher when the procurement program is already in effect.

Price stabilization and food security are only secondary considerations in evaluating the procurement program. The main consideration is the cost effectiveness of this and the other support programs in
stabilizing farmers' income. Figure 5-9 demonstrates the cost effectiveness of buffer stocks in combination with the different support
programs. Obviously, buffer stocks alone is the least cost-effective
policy compared with the other combinations. This is because these
combinations are directed toward the target group—farmers—in

Figure 5-7.   Economic Costs of Raising Food Security with Buffer Stocks and the Government Procurement Program.

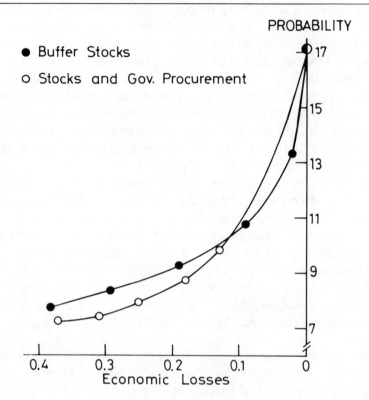

(As Percentage of Annual Expenditures in a Normal (Stable) Year)

terms of which the cost effectiveness is measured. Among these combinations, the one that includes price support appears to be the most cost effective, probably because it involves less government purchasing and no losses due to the decay of the procured grain. However, the marginal productivity of buffer stocks when a price support program is in effect declines more rapidly than when a procurement program is in effect, since with the latter program the storage operation saves on costly government purchases and prevents losses due to the decay of grain that would have occurred if no suitable storage facility had existed.

Figure 5-8.   Marginal Economic Costs of Raising Food Security via Buffer Stocks, with and without the Government Procurement Program.

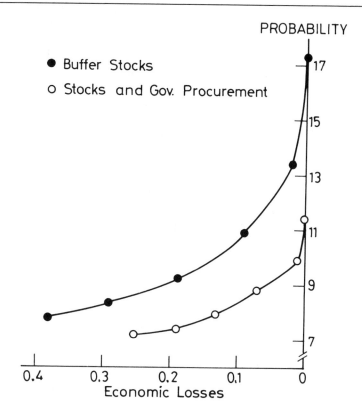

● Buffer Stocks

○ Stocks and Gov. Procurement

(As Percentage of Annual Expenditures in a Normal (Stable) Year)

Figure 5-10 illustrates the marginal cost effectiveness of buffer stocks when different producers' support programs are in operation. In general, the larger the reduction of instability as an effect of the support programs the smaller will be the stabilizing effects of buffer stocks and the smaller their cost effectiveness.

Finally, Figures 5-11 and 5-12 show the gains and losses to the different sectors in the economy due to the existence of a storage operation when the two main support programs are in effect. In Figure

Figure 5-9. Economic Costs of Raising the Security of Farmers' Income with Buffer Stocks and a Producers' Support Program.

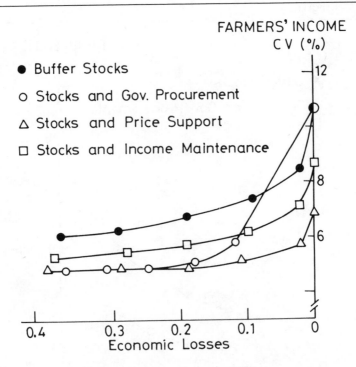

FARMERS' INCOME
C V (%)

● Buffer Stocks

o Stocks and Gov. Procurement

△ Stocks and Price Support

□ Stocks and Income Maintenance

Economic Losses

(As Percentage of Annual Expenditures in a Normal (Stable) Year)

5-11 a direct price support program is in effect. In this case the chief effect of buffer stocks would be to reduce the fiscal costs of the program. Without buffer stocks the price support program costs the government some 3 percent of total income from the crop in a normal year. With a storage facility of 6 MMT the fiscal costs are reduced to 1.4 percent even though they now include the storage costs (with amortization). The losses to producers from the storage operation are merely a reduction in their gains from the support program. With a storage facility of 6 MMT their combined gain from the two policies is still some 2 percent of their normal income (compared with a gain of 3 percent from the support program alone). Consumers are

Figure 5-10. Marginal Economic Costs of Raising the Security of Farmers' Income with Buffer Stocks when Different Support Programs Are in Effect.

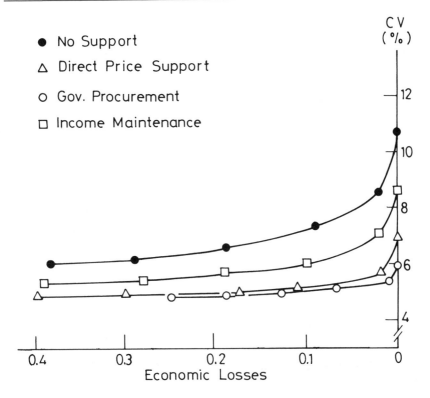

(As Percentage of Annual Expenditures in a Normal (Stable) Year)

not affected by the price support program, and their losses are due only to the storage operation.

In Figure 5-12 a government procurement program is in effect. In this case the storage operation does not bring any savings in the program's budget. This is because the purchases and sales of grain by the storage authority mostly replace purchases and sales that were previously carried out as part of the procurement program. The storage facility saves by preventing the decay of procured grain but adds

Figure 5-11. Marginal Economic Gains and Losses of Price Stabilization with Buffer Stocks when a Direct Price Support Program Is in Effect.

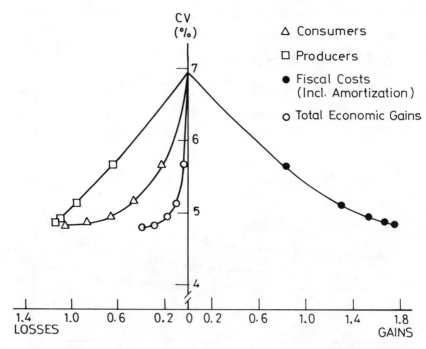

(As Percentage of Annual Expenditures in a Normal (Stable) Year)

amortization costs. Nevertheless the additional fiscal costs of operating the storage facility when the procurement program is in effect are less than 50 percent of the costs of operating a storage facility when there is no other program.

Producers initially lose and consumers gain from buffer stocks at low levels of storage capacity. At these levels the storage operation is largely dominated by the procurement program, and most if not all of the purchases of the storage authority are merely transfers of the grain procured under the support program. The storage operation itself therefore has very little effect on raising the price when grain is put into storage. It does, however, have a larger effect on lowering

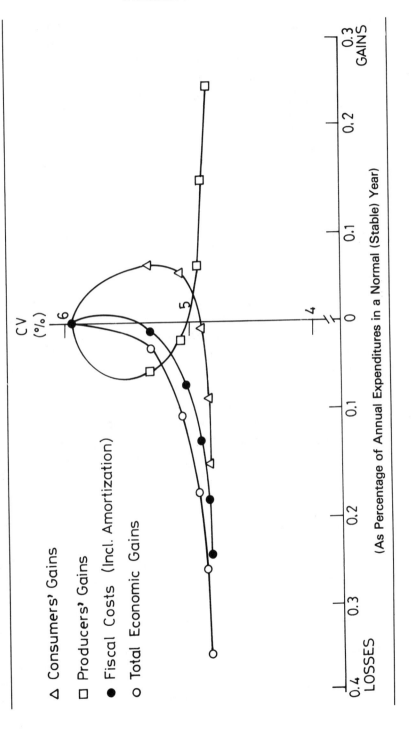

Figure 5-12. Marginal Economic Gains and Losses of Price Stabilization with Buffer Stocks when a a Government Procurement Program Is in Effect.

△ Consumers' Gains

□ Producers' Gains

● Fiscal Costs (Incl. Amortization)

○ Total Economic Gains

(As Percentage of Annual Expenditures in a Normal (Stable) Year)

the price when grain is released from storage by saving grain that would have been damaged in the absence of a suitable facility. The storage operation together with the procurement program thus results in net gains for consumers and net losses for producers. At larger capacities the storage operation becomes dominant, resulting in net losses for consumers and net gains for producers, as in the case in which buffer stocks alone are in operation.

SUBSIDY PROGRAMS

Earlier it was noted that the subsidy program raises the price to the nonbeneficiary consumers. Indeed, this is the very mechanism by which the program achieves the redistribution of consumption, since the rise in price forces the nonbeneficiary consumers to forego some of their consumption, thereby allowing the beneficiary consumers, who enjoy a subsidized price, to increase their consumption. This rise in price results in welfare losses to the nonbeneficiary consumers but brings gains not only to the beneficiary consumers but also to producers. Furthermore, in addition to the increase in the mean price due to the subsidy program, there is also an increase in its variability and an increase in the variability of farmers' income. These increases are obviously an undesirable outcome of the program.

In this section we consider three subsidy programs that are similar in their operating rules but different in level of intensity. The intensity of the programs is determined by the elasticity of the target demand curve set for the beneficiary group. The following expressions denote the different programs:

Type of subsidy program	Target elasticity
Partial food security	$EC(P) = 0.25$
Solid food security	$EC(P) = 0.10$
Complete food security	$EC(P) = 0.00$

where $EC(P)$ denotes the price elasticity of the target demand of the beneficiary consumers (the urban poor) calculated at the median price.

Table 5-11 summarizes the main effects of the subsidy programs. It demonstrates the inevitable trade-off between price stability and food security associated with the program. With the solid program

Table 5-11. Main Stability Effects of Subsidy Program.

| | Subsidy Program to Low-Income Consumers | | |
	No Subsidy	Partial EC(P) = 0.25	Solid EC(P) = 0.10[b]	Complete EC(P) = 0.00
Market price				
Mean	101.4	104.0	106.1	108.0
CV (%)	17.6%	20.4%	22.7%	24.7%
Farmers' income				
Mean[c]	100.0	102.5	104.4	106.1
CV (%)	10.7%	13.3%	15.3%	17.2%
Food insecurity[a]	32.6%	22.0%	5.4%	0.0%

[a]The probability that the quantity available to the urban poor falls by more than 5 percent below their normal consumption.
[b]The base case policy.
[c]Mean income as percentage of their normal income.

$[EC(P) = 0.10]$, for instance, the level of food insecurity is reduced from 32.6 percent to 5.4 percent. At the same time, however, the price variability rises by almost 30 percent, and the variability of farmers' income rises by close to 45 percent. The trade-off between food insecurity and price instability associated with the different subsidy programs is illustrated in Figure 5-13, which shows that eliminating food insecurity altogether (with the complete food security program) involves an increase of 40 percent in price variability (and an increase of more than 60 percent in the variability of farmers' income). In Table 5-11 we can see that the complete food security program involves, in addition, an increase of 6.5 percent in the mean price. Farmers would have substantial gains from this increase and their average income rises by more than 6 percent.

Table 5-12 summarizes the economic gains and losses due to the subsidy programs. It shows the income transfers implicit in the transfers of consumption from the nonbeneficiary to the beneficiary consumers. The welfare losses to the economy at large represent the excess burden of the program and highlight its inefficiencies compared with programs of direct income transfer.

The nonbeneficiary consumers (middle to high income) would shoulder most of the burden, for two reasons. First, they would suf-

Figure 5-13. Trade-off between Price Stability and Food Security due to the Subsidy Programs.

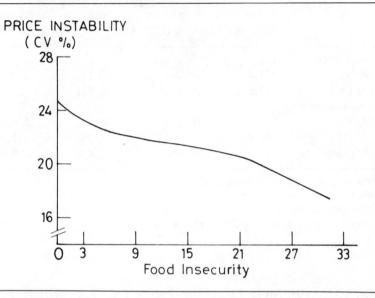

PRICE INSTABILITY
(CV %)

Food Insecurity

fer direct income losses as a result of the increase in the price that they pay for the products. Second, they would probably pay most if not all of the fiscal costs associated with the programs through their income taxes.

The total economic losses due to the subsidy programs cannot be taken as an indication of whether the programs are desirable or not,

Table 5-12. Expected Economic Gains and Losses due to the Subsidy Program
(As Percentage of Annual Expenditures in a Normal Year).

	Subsidy Program to Low-Income Consumers		
	Partial	*Solid*	*Complete*
Economic Sector	*EC(P) = 0.25*	*EC(P) = 0.10*	*EC(P) = 0.00*
Beneficiary consumers	+0.83	+1.53	+2.20
Nonbeneficiary consumers	−1.68	−3.00	−3.82
Producers	+2.39	+4.34	+6.06
Government	−1.57	−2.96	−4.35
Total economy	−0.83	−0.13	−0.29

however; they should rather be regarded as the costs involved in providing food security for the vulnerable sections of the population. Whether or not the program is desirable depends on the importance that society attaches to the provision of food security and the prevention of famine. Its desirability also depends on the ability of the government to implement other programs (such as direct income transfers) that can achieve the same goals, and on the cost effectiveness of these programs relative to that of the subsidy program.

Figure 5-14 describes the increase in costs involved in increasing the level of food security. The net losses to the economy at large are rather small, and the main effects are on the income distribution, described in Figure 5-15. For instance, increasing the level of food security from 80 percent to 95 percent would "cost" the economy only 0.1 percent of the total annual expenditures on the products. However, it would cost the nonbeneficiary consumers 1.32 percent of total expenditures (2.00 percent of *their own* expenditures), and it would cost the government an extra 1.39 percent.

Figure 5-14.   Economic Costs of Raising Food Security with the Subsidy Programs.

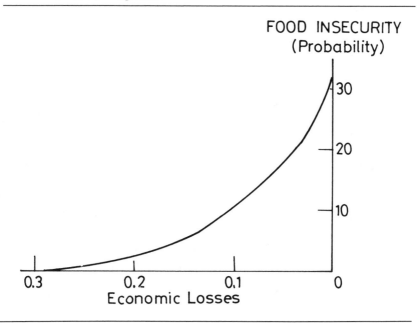

Figure 5-15. Costs and Benefits by Economic Sector of Raising Food Security with the Subsidy Program.

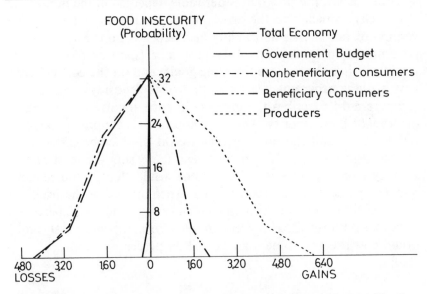

FOOD INSECURITY
(Probability)

——————— Total Economy
— — — Government Budget
—·— —·— Nonbeneficiary Consumers
—— ··· —— Beneficiary Consumers
········· Producers

.32

24

16

8

| 480 320 160 | 0 | 160 320 480 640 |
LOSSES   GAINS

(As Percentage of Annual Expenditures in a Normal (Stable) Year)

SUBSIDIES AND BUFFER STOCKS

A subsidy program is only one way of achieving food security in a country, and its cost effectiveness should be measured against the costs of attaining the same level of food security by other means. Another way of ensuring a stable flow of supply is by utilizing buffer stocks. As noted earlier, the stocks policy applies to the entire population and works to stabilize the total flow of supply, whereas the sub sidy programs (in the form considered here) apply only to a specific target group: low-income urban consumers. The subsidy program thus discriminates between these consumers and the rest of the population. This apparent deficiency in the program is also its strength when goals such as food security are specified in terms of group-specific objectives, as will be shown. Figure 5–16 describes the level

Figure 5-16. Stabilization Effects of Buffer Stocks with and without the Subsidy Program: Food Security.

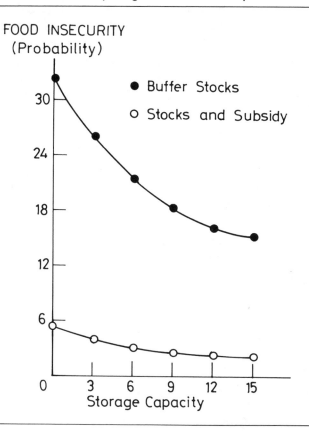

of food security attained with buffer stocks alone and with buffer stocks together with the solid subsidy program [$EC(P)$ = 0.10]. It shows that no reasonable amount of stocks can provide the same level of food security as can the subsidy program. Thus, for instance, with a storage capacity of 15 MMT the level of food security would rise from 67 percent to 85 percent. Increasing the storage capacity above that level would contribute only a marginal addition to food security. The solid subsidy program alone, on the other hand, can provide food security of 95 percent.

Figure 5-17 shows the cost effectiveness of buffer stocks, alone and in conjunction with subsidy programs, in reducing food insecurity. It shows clearly that the group-specific subsidy policy is far more cost effective when the objective is specified in terms of that specific target group. Thus, for example, a reduction in the level of food insecurity from 33 percent to 15 percent by means of buffer stocks would cost the economy 0.4 percent of its annual expenditures on the products. The same reduction by means of a subsidy program would cost the economy only 0.07 percent.

Both Figure 5-16 and Figure 5-17 show that when a subsidy program is implemented, the addition of buffer stocks would be extremely cost ineffective and would contribute only marginally to the level of food security already attained by the subsidy program. For instance, a storage facility of 6 MMT would reduce the level of food insecurity by 11.2 percent in the absence of any other program but

Figure 5-17. Economic Costs of Raising Food Security with Different Subsidy Programs and Buffer Stocks.

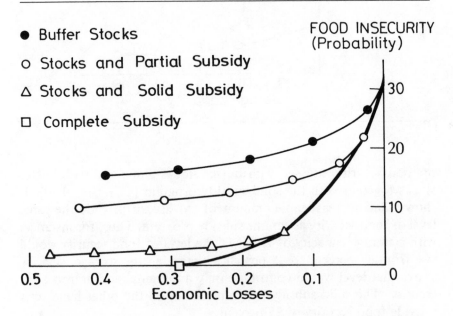

(As Percentage of Annual Expenditures in a Normal (Stable) Year)

only by 2.4 percent when the solid subsidy program is in effect. Nevertheless, buffer stocks play an important role as part of the overall government policy. Previously it was noted that a subsidy program would raise the variability of the market price. Buffer stocks can then be highly effective in reducing this variability and can thus moderate the undesirable consequences of the subsidy program. Figure 5-18 demonstrates these effects of buffer stocks when the solid subsidy program [$EC(P)$ = 0.10] is in effect. Two storage rules

Figure 5-18.   Stabilization Effects of Buffer Stocks with Different Storage Rules and a Subsidy Program: Variability of the Market Price.

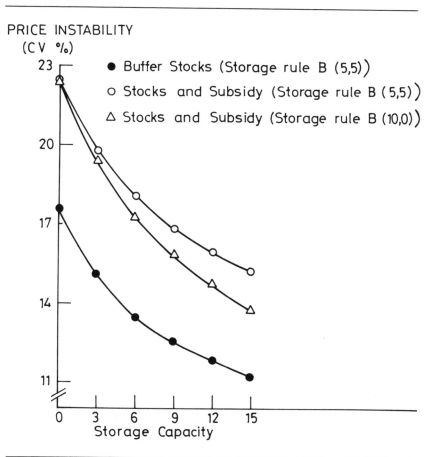

PRICE INSTABILITY
(C V °/o)

• Buffer Stocks (Storage rule B (5,5))

○ Stocks and Subsidy (Storage rule B (5,5))

△ Stocks and Subsidy (Storage rule B (10,0))

Storage Capacity

have been examined: one the symmetric rule B(5,5); the other the nonsymmetric rule B(10,0), which concentrates on the upper tail of the price distribution. Because the subsidy is given only when the price rises above the median (which is also the normal or stable price) the nonsymmetric rule is more effective in reducing the variability of the price. This is demonstrated even more clearly in Figure 5-19, which shows the probability of a price rise by more than 20 percent above its normal level under the stocks and subsidy policies. Thus, for instance, with the solid subsidy program and a 6 MMT storage facility, storage rule B(10,0) would reduce this probability by 15 percent *more* than rule B(5,5). The economic and financial gains or

Figure 5-19. Stabilization Effects of Buffer Stocks with Different Storage Rules and Subsidy Programs: The Probability that the Price Would Rise by More Than 20 Percent above the Normal Price.

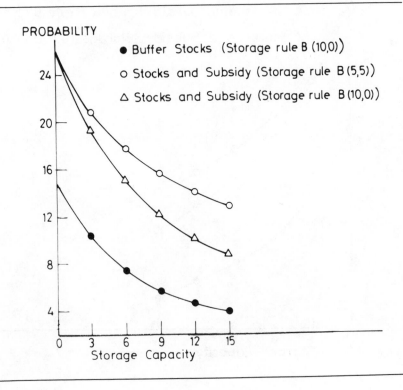

losses due to the storage operation are also quite different depending upon whether or not a subsidy program is implemented.

Table 5-13 summarizes the marginal gains and losses due to the storage operation. We can see that the net losses of the nonbeneficiary consumers when buffer stocks are operated alone turn into net gains when buffer stocks are operated in conjunction with a subsidy program. These gains actually represent a reduction in the losses sustained by the consumers under the subsidy program. Similarly, the losses of the beneficiary consumers and the producers are in effect a reduction in their gains from the program. These gains and losses are the result of storage operations that, by intervening to lower the market price whenever it rises above a certain critical level, reduce the subsidy payments and lower the extent to which the subsidy program affects the market price. This is also the reason for the substantial gains of the government, which reflect its savings on the subsidy payments. Hence, when a subsidy program is in effect, the government may have a strong interest in buffer stocks not only because of their stabilizing effect on the market price but also because of the savings they allow in the subsidy payments. Figure 5-20 demonstrates the gains and losses to the various sectors due to the reduction in the variability of the price by means of buffer stocks.

Since the subsidy program implies trading price stabilization for food security, the storage operation in conjunction with the subsidy

Table 5-13. Expected Economic Gains and Losses due to 6 MMT Buffer Stocks

(As Percentage of Annual Expenditures in a Normal Year).

| | | Type of Subsidy Program in Effect | |
Economic Sector	No Subsidy	Solid Food Security $EC(P) = 0.10$	Complete Food Security $EC(P) = 0.00$
Beneficiary consumers	− 0.16	− 0.31	− 0.69
Nonbeneficiary consumers	− 0.28	+ 0.32	+ 0.68
Producers	+ 0.54	− 0.45	− 1.05
Government[a]	− 0.19	+ 0.43	+ 0.96
Total economy	− 0.09	− 0.01	− 0.10

[a]Including amortization costs.

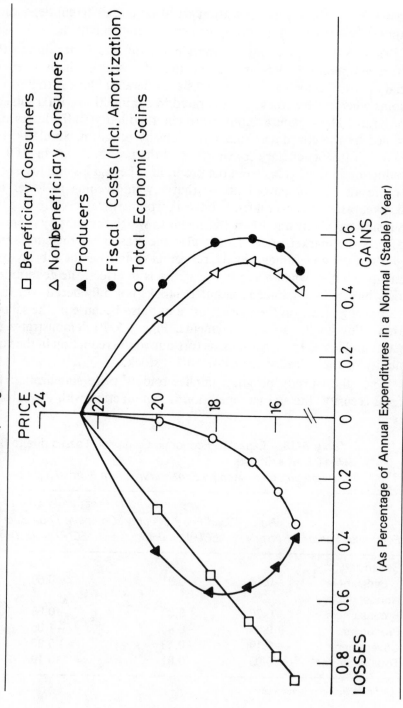

Figure 5-20. Economic Costs and Benefits by Economic Sector of Raising Price Stability with Buffer Stocks when a Solid Subsidy Program Is in Effect.

□ Beneficiary Consumers
△ Nonbeneficiary Consumers
▲ Producers
● Fiscal Costs (Incl. Amortization)
○ Total Economic Gains

PRICE

GAINS

LOSSES

(As Percentage of Annual Expenditures in a Normal (Stable) Year)

program contributes to reduce the instability effects of the program. Figure 5-21 demonstrates this trade-off between food security and price stabilization. The heavy line connects the points corresponding to subsidy programs without storage. The thinner lines originating from the heavy line denote the effects of increasing levels of stocks together with one of the subsidy programs. The figure shows that even with the program of complete food security, buffer stocks may still have an important role in correcting the instability effects of the program. Finally, Figure 5-22 demonstrates the trade-off between food security and price stability associated with the subsidy programs at three levels of storage capacity. The trade-off curves cannot cross each other, and their slopes indicate the marginal rate of transformation between these two objectives at different levels of storage capacity.

Figure 5-21. Trade-off between Price Stability and Food Security due to the Subsidy Programs and Buffer Stocks.

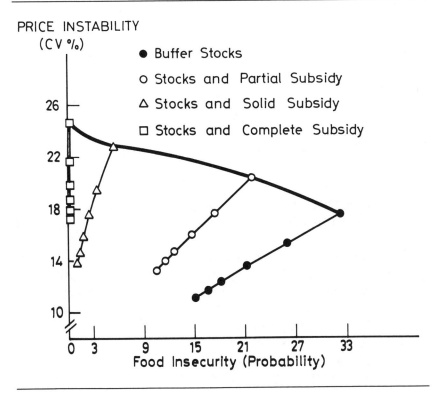

Figure 5-22. Trade-off between Price Stability and Food Security due to the Subsidy Programs at Different Levels of Storage Capacity.

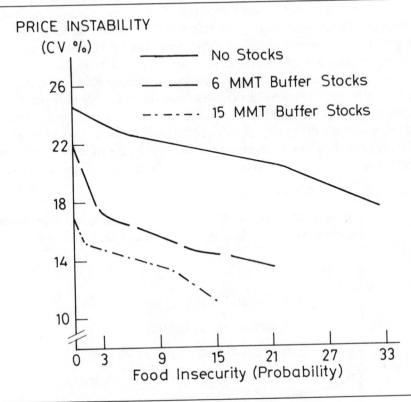

MULTIPLE POLICY COMBINATIONS AND SENSITIVITY ANALYSIS

Table 5-14 summarizes the main stability effects of different combinations of the three groups of policies analyzed thus far: producers' support programs, consumers' subsidy programs, and buffer stocks. The results show that the combination of subsidy and either one of the producers' support programs is highly effective in reducing both food insecurity and farmers' income insecurity.

Combining a subsidy program and a price support program raises the price variability by almost 30 percent. Adding buffer stocks to

Table 5-14. Stability Effects of Different Policy Combinations.

	No Policy	Subsidy and Price Support[a]	Subsidy, Price Support and 6 MMT Stocks[a]	Subsidy and Gov. Procurement	Subsidy, Gov. Procurement, and 6 MMT Stocks[a]
Market price, CV (%)	17.6	22.7	18.1	17.3	15.5
Farmers' income, CV (%)	10.7	12.1	9.6	10.6	9.3
Farmers' price, CV (%)	17.6	19.2	18.3	17.3	15.5
Food insecurity (5%)[b]	32.3	5.4	3.8	3.5	2.9
Farmers' income insecurity[c]	30.5	9.6	3.4	10.4	5.7

[a]The solid subsidy program with $EC(P) = 0.10$.

[b]Probability that supply to the urban poor falls by more than 5 percent below their normal consumption.

[c]Probability that farmers' income falls by more than 5 percent below their normal income.

this combination helps not only to reduce food insecurity (by 30 percent) and farmers' income insecurity (by 65 percent) but also to lower the price variability (by 20 percent) and the variability of farmers' income (by 20 percent).

The government procurement program together with a subsidy program is another efficient policy combination. Here the sales during years of poor harvest of stocks previously procured by the government help to lower the price and thus reduce the subsidy payments. With this policy combination the variability of the market price is slightly lowered instead of being raised as with the combination of subsidy and price support programs. The addition of 6 MMT buffer stocks further reduces the instability in the market price as well as food insecurity and farmers' income insecurity.

This last combination—subsidy, government procurement, and buffer stocks—is revealed to be the most powerful in stabilizing the domestic market. To examine the cost effectiveness of this and the other policy combinations see Table 5-15, which presents the expected economic gains due to the various policies. The results show that while the economy at large loses from all policy combinations, these losses are rather small. Far more substantial are the implied effects on the income distribution among the various groups and sectors in the economy.

Of special interest from the decisionmaker's point of view are the fiscal costs of the program. Here again the combination of subsidy, government procurement and buffer stocks is revealed to be superior to all the other combinations in that it provides the highest level of stability at the lowest costs.[3]

Finally, simulation experiments were conducted to examine the sensitivity of the results to the assumed parameters of the model. The results of some of these experiments are presented in Table 5-16, which summarizes the stability effects, and in Table 5-17, which shows the economic gains and losses due to the policy combination considered.

In Table 5-16 we can see that if expectations are adaptive, the variability of the market price would be more than 20 percent larger than with rational expectations (the base case assumption). The other stability indicators show only small differences. There would be, however, very substantial differences in regard to the distribution of the welfare gains from the policy, as can be observed in Table 5-17. With adaptive expectations the gains of the beneficiary consumers would

Table 5-15. Expected Economic Gains or Losses due to Different Policy Combinations (As Percentage of Annual Expenditures in a Normal Year).

Economic Sector	Subsidy and Price Support	Subsidy, Price Support, and 6 MMT Buffer Stocks	Subsidy and Gov. Procurement	Subsidy, Gov. Procurement and 6 MMT Buffer Stocks
Beneficiary consumers	+1.53	+1.01	+0.80	+0.67
Nonbeneficiary consumers	-3.00	-2.53	-3.21	-2.81
Producers	+7.24	+5.11	+4.75	+4.28
Government	-5.91	-3.79	-2.55	-2.35
Total economy	-0.14	-0.20	-0.21	-0.25

Table 5-16. Sensitivity Analysis: Main Stability Indicators.

| | | Policy: Consumers' Subsidy and Producers' Price Support | | |
	Base Case	Adaptive Expectations	Larger Production Variability[a]	Higher Demand Elasticity[b]
Market price, CV (%)	22.7	27.6	34.5	10.8
Farmers' income, CV (%)	12.1	12.1	15.1	3.3
Farmers' price, CV (%)	19.3	20.0	27.3	10.1
Food insecurity	5.4	5.6	15.0	0.0
Farmers' income insecurity	9.6	7.9	6.0	0.0

[a]Coefficient of variation of 11 percent compared with 7 percent in the base case.
[b]See Table 4–11 for values of the demand elasticities. On average the elasticities of the various groups in this case are 25 to 40 percent higher than in the base case.

Table 5-17. Sensitivity Analysis: Economic Gains and Losses due to Policy Combinations
(As Percentage of Annual Expenditures in a Normal (Stable) Year).

Economic Sector	Base Case	Policy: Consumers' Subsidy and Producers' Price Support		
		Adaptive Expectations	Larger Production Variability[a]	Higher Demand Elasticity[a]
Beneficiary consumers	+ 1.53	+ 2.59	+ 2.42	+ 1.00
Nonbeneficiary consumers	− 3.00	− 0.30	− 4.52	− 0.64
Producers	+ 7.24	+ 6.73	+ 12.21	+ 1.86
Government	− 5.91	− 9.21	− 11.41	− 1.95
Total economy	− 0.14	− 0.19	− 1.30	+ 0.27

[a]See footnotes in Table 5-16.

be larger, the losses of the nonbeneficiary consumers smaller, and the gains of producers only slightly smaller than with rational expectations. The net gains of the private sector (all consumers and producers) would therefore be 55 percent higher with adaptive expectations than with rational expectations. At the same time, however, government expenditures on the two programs would be 55 percent higher with adaptive expectations.

In Table 5-16 we can also see the effects of a larger variability of production on the major stability indicators. With larger production variability (the coefficient of variation in production being more than 50 percent larger than in the base case), the instability of the market price would be 25 percent higher and the level of food insecurity almost three times higher than in the base case. However, the insecurity of farmers' income is actually reduced. Table 5-17 shows that the net losses to the economy at large as a result of the subsidy and support programs would be much larger in this case. Even more significant would be the effects of the income transfers associated with these programs when the variability of production is higher. Producers' expected gains would be almost 70 percent larger and the gains of the beneficiary consumers would be almost 60 percent larger. At the same time, the expected losses of the nonbeneficiary consumers would be 50 percent larger and government expenditures would almost double.

Finally, we can see in the tables the effects of higher demand elasticity. As noted in the previous chapter, other things being equal, with higher demand elasticities the economy should be more stable. As a result, the stabilizing effects of the policies would be much smaller, and the ensuing gains or losses therefore considerably reduced.

In conclusion it should be noted that with different values of the parameters and hence under different structures of the economy, the stability and economic effects of the policies might be quite different from those in the base case. In most cases, however, these differences would only be in the values of the various indicators and not the direction in which the policies affect them.

SUMMARY AND CONCLUSIONS

The objectives of price policies in primary food products are often diverse and incompatible. To varying degrees governments are concerned with securing a stable flow of supply to the population, an adequate level of nutrition for consumers at the poverty level, stable prices, and an adequate income level to farmers. To cope with the problems of food insecurity and price instability, governments can implement several policies that fall into two main categories, namely those that apply to the general population, and those that apply to specific groups or sectors. The former are exemplified by buffer stocks and trade policies, and the latter by various support programs to producers and subsidy programs to specific consumer groups.

The analysis of the several group-specific price policies examined in this chapter, operated alone or in conjunction with other price policies and buffer stocks, points to one general conclusion: when the objectives of the policy are defined in terms of group-specific variables, the most powerful and cost-effective policies are group-specific programs targeted on those variables. When the objective of the policy is, for instance, to stabilize the price to the farmers or prevent a sharp fall in their income, the most efficient programs are those that directly support either the price to producers or their income. When the objective of the policy is to ensure that consumption by the poor does not fall below a certain minimum subsistence level, a subsidy program targeted on these consumers is more effective than any of the programs that apply to the general population.

In analyzing producers' support programs, three different types of policies were considered. One involves direct price support, with the government making up any difference that might exist between the market price and a prespecified floor price. The second is a government procurement program in which the government procures the excess supply and removes it from the market, thereby raising the market price to the floor price. The third is an income maintenance program, in which the government makes up the difference between farmers' actual income and a prespecified minimum income. Our simulation analysis indicates that all of these programs are extremely efficient in stabilizing farmers' income and in reducing or even totally eliminating the probability that their income falls below a certain critical level. In contrast, no reasonable amount of storage can provide the farmers with a comparable degree of security. The three support programs are also highly cost effective in that they can provide the farmers with the required level of security at far lower cost than any of the general programs.

A significant difference exists between the procurement program and the two other support programs in that the latter merely involve income transfer from the government to producers, leaving the market price and thus also consumption unchanged (at least in the short run). The procurement program, on the other hand, affects the market price and thus also consumption. As a consequence, the producers' gains from the procurement policy are mostly a result of income transfers from consumers to producers associated with the price changes, and the fiscal costs of the program are relatively small. In contrast, with the other two support programs producers' gains are direct transfers from the government, and their fiscal costs can be very substantial; government expenses are four times higher with the income maintenance program than with the procurement program and eleven times higher with the price support program. This may explain why governments in many developing countries favor the procurement program.

The analysis of the subsidy program demonstrates very clearly the trade-off between food security and price stabilization. In essence the subsidy program works via the price system to redistribute a given quantity of food more favorably between consumers. By allowing low-income consumers to buy food at a lower price, the program forces the other consumers to pay higher prices for their food supply and thus also to forego some of their consumption (depending, of course, on their income elasticity of demand). Thus, under the program there would be a rise not only in the mean level of the market price but also in its variability. With the subsidy programs, the level of food insecurity would be reduced by 85 percent. At the same time, however, the mean market price would rise by 6.5 percent and its variability would rise by 30 percent. Farmers would have substantial gains from the rise in the market price, and their average income would rise by more than 6 percent, but the variability of their income would rise by 45 percent. The subsidy program would thus cause massive changes in income distribution from the nonbeneficiary consumers and the government to the beneficiary consumers and, even more, to the producers.

The presence of internal price policies dramatically changes the role and effects of buffer stocks. When, for instance, a procurement program is in operation, most of the storage activities are automatically carried out through it. A storage facility is then only an instrument of the procurement policy, and the stocks policy is meaningful only to the extent that it changes rules of intervention defined by the price band.

When any of the other producers' programs is in operation it is already working to stabilize farmers' income, and the addition of buffer stocks contributes very little to stabilizing it further. In that case, however, buffer stocks would play another role in addition to that of stabilizing the market price and temporizing the flow of consumption. As a result of the storage operation the need for further assistance to producers is markedly reduced, and the fiscal burden thus decreases. For example, the fiscal costs of the support price program would be cut in half for a storage facility of 6 MMT, even after allowing for the operating and amortization costs of the facility.

When a subsidy program that applies only to part of the consumers is in operation, it raises the market price to the other consumers and increases its variability. Buffer stocks can then be very effective in stabilizing the price, even though in so doing they assist the nonbeneficiary (mostly the affluent) consumers. Even more important is the effect of the storage operation on the fiscal costs of the combined policies. Thus, for instance, with a 6 MMT storage facility the fiscal costs of the subsidy program plus buffer stocks would be 15 to 22 percent *lower* than the costs of the subsidy program alone (depending on the type of the subsidy program). Thus, government savings on subsidy payments resulting from the storage operation far outweigh the operating and amortization costs of the storage facility.

Finally, an analysis of different policy combinations brings us to the well-known conclusion usually discussed in a macroeconomic context, namely, that when a government sets itself more than one objective it requires more than a single policy instrument to achieve them. For the purpose of stabilizing farmers' income and securing an adequate food supply for the poor, the combination of buffer stocks, subsidy, and government procurement was found to be superior to any individual policy or other policy combinations. A subsidy program alone only increases the instability of the market price and of farmers' income while enhancing food insecurity. The various producers' support programs have only limited or no effect on the market price and on food security. Buffer stocks favorably affect all three objectives, but are very costly and the levels of food security and stability of farmers' income achieved by any reasonable amount of stocks may still be considered inadequate in many countries. A policy combination consisting of group-specific policies would thus be most effective in securing the diverse objectives of a government's overall food policy.

NOTES

1. It should be noted, however, that by dropping the purchase restriction and allowing free substitution between food and nonfood products, the program is likely to increase the satisfactions of these households. In this case the subsidy will amount to an ordinary cash transfer.

2. The only differences between the two are: (1) the price band within which the procurement program is operated can be different from the band for the storage operation; (2) the procurement program is not constrained by the storage capacity; and (3) when a suitable storage facility exists, the decay of the grain in storage will occur to a much smaller extent. At the same time the amortization costs of the storage facility will have to be added to the costs of the combined program.

3. Except for the criterion of farmers' income insecurity, where the probability would be slightly lower under a combination of subsidy, price support, and stocks.

6 STABILIZATION AND INTERNATIONAL TRADE

In the writings on international trade, both classical and modern economists have strongly endorsed policies of free trade. They have emphasized that the efficient allocation of resources across (and within) countries and specialization based on the principles of comparative advantage resulting from free trade will allow countries to achieve the highest possible level of welfare. Barring special cases such as countries large enough to influence their terms of trade and exploit their international monopoly power by increasing the relative price of their exports through tariffs,[1] all forms of intervention must involve some welfare losses, reflecting the excess burden of tariffs and other trade restrictions.

Given the strong theoretical justification for free trade it is both surprising and disquieting to find that high tariffs and other restrictive trade policies have always been, and still are, predominant in both developed and underdeveloped countries. In their review of historical movements in trade policy Cuddington and McKinnon conclude that "Free trade has been the exception rather than the rule in international commercial relations. While there have been ebbs and flows since the early 1800s, average tariff levels have generally been high. In practice, the policy recommendation of free trade has often been disregarded" (1979:7).

Recent writings in trade theory emphasize the role of ncneconomic arguments in explaining the level of protection, such as national defense, income distribution, and political powers. Tariffs are often a second-best policy in the sense that they are the best *viable* policy given the existing political or other constraints that prevent the authorities from choosing the optimal policy—free trade.

The theoretical evaluation of alternative trade systems is generally carried out in a deterministic world. It emphasizes the pattern of factor endowment in the trading countries and the different factor intensities in the commodities traded as the major factors explaining the commodity composition of trade. Even the recent writings on trade under uncertainty focus on these factors to explain the patterns of trade and production.

An important factor is still left unexplained and unaccounted for in these writings: the effect of *instability* on the patterns of trade and on the formation of trade policies. Since the early 1970s it has become increasingly evident that the trend toward more regulated international trade and the resurgence of protectionism is largely due to policies aimed at achieving internal stability through the control of imports and exports. In the European Community, for instance, the development of the Common Agricultural Policy (CAP) has emphasized the goals of supply and internal price stability, and has extensively employed various forms of trade interference as the main instruments of achieving these objectives. Shei and Thompson (1977) have demonstrated that world price changes have become larger and more volatile as more countries prevent world price signals from being reflected in domestic price changes.

In the developing countries free trade in agricultural food products is highly unpopular, and considerable efforts are made by the governments in these countries to *isolate* their economies from the world market and achieve self-sufficiency. Free trade is often accused of depressing agricultural production in importing countries, thus increasing their dependence on the exporting countries and exposing the importers to a higher risk of shortages in supply. Free trade is also accused of bringing in the instability in the world market because of the growing dependence on surpluses that may be temporary and thus augment the domestic instability. In many developed countries, most notably the European Economic Community (EEC), the tendency has been to *insulate* their economies from external instability through the use of variable levies and quota restrictions.

In the balance of this book the effects of international trade on domestic price stability and on food security are examined and the design of internal and trade policies aimed at securing domestic stability in an open economy analyzed. First let us review some theoretical aspects of the subject, the main interest being in the trade mechanism and its consequences in terms of welfare and balance of payments in an unstable world when supplies and demands in the trading countries may deviate temporarily from their long-run trends.

INSTABILITY AND THE GAINS FROM TRADE

The economic literature has long emphasized that nations can gain from international trade. Differences in relative endowment of factor inputs, differences in technology, and differences in tastes may produce variations in the relative prices of tradeable goods between countries. Such variations in turn trigger trading activities and make it beneficial for countries to specialize in the production of those commodities in which they have a comparative advantage.

A textbook exposition of the gains from trade that was employed extensively in the classical and early neoclassical writings is illustrated in Figure 6-1 (see Chambers, Letiche, and Schmitz 1979 for a review of this subject). Let S and D represent the supply and demand situation in the exporting country and S^* and D^* represent the supply and demand situation in the importing country. Without trade, price is P^* in the importing country and P in the exporting country. With trade and in the absence of transportation costs and other impediments, the world price is P^T. Heuristically, the movement to free trade results in net welfare gains equal to the two shaded areas. In the exporting country, the introduction of trade results in a loss of consumer surplus of BP^TPC, while producer surplus is increased by the area of AP^TPC. (The limitations of the economic surplus concept are well known and are discussed at some length in Chapter 2. Viner 1937:589–93 and Letiche 1959:71–73 note possible errors in using such Marshallian domestic-trade demand and supply curves for measuring the gains from trade. See also Chambers, Letiche, and Schmitz 1979.)

Recent studies on international trade under uncertainty have concluded that the standard theorems of international trade remain valid also under uncertainty. Mayer (1976) has proved the general validity

Figure 6-1.   Gains from Trade.

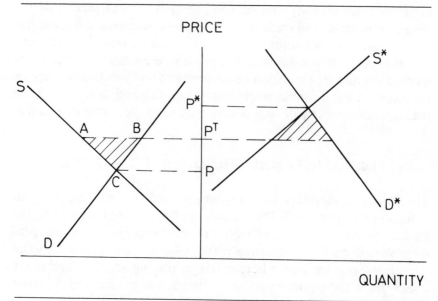

of the Rybczynski and the Stopler-Samuelson theorems. He has also shown that the conclusions of Batra whereby risk aversion invalidates these theorems apply to the intermediate run only, whereas in the long-run the theorems are still valid. Helpman and Razin (1978) and Baron and Forsythe (1979) have demonstrated that the existence of an international securities market is sufficient to yield all the standard theorems.

An important factor is still left unexplained by the usual relative cost advantage approach and is thus unaccounted for by the standard trade theory. This is the creation of trade flows between countries by the very existence of fluctuations in demand and supply, even when in the long run these flows are not justified on the basis of comparative advantage. Apart from their contribution to the risk involved in trade activities, these random fluctuations may create temporary gaps between the domestic price and the world price to an extent that can induce trade that would not normally occur. A shortfall in domestic production below the average level may raise the domestic price and thus induce imports, while a temporary glut in domestic production may lower the domestic price and thus induce exports.

Fluctuations in domestic demand or supply are not the only factors that can create these trade flows. Temporary aberrations in demand or supply in other countries can also produce price gaps between the domestic and the foreign markets that induce trade. Ample evidence suggests that a considerable portion of the trade in agricultural products is generated by temporary aberrations and that countries that in normal years are able to supply their own consumption of these products are forced at times to turn to the international market to eliminate or at least moderate domestic shortages or excesses. It is thus possible for a country that is self-sufficient in certain agricultural products and possibly even has a relative advantage in their production to become a net importer of these products in one year and a net exporter in another year.

To examine the effects of temporary aberrations in supply at home or abroad on a country's level of trade, balance of payments, and general welfare let us turn to a partial equilibrium model of the sector under consideration. (Fleming 1951 and Meade 1955 have made extensive use of this model especially in the context of optimal tariffs.) The basic model consists of linear demand and supply equations of the following form[2]:

$$S(P_t) = a + b\overline{P} + u_t \tag{6-1}$$

$$D(P_t) = c - dP_t \tag{6-2}$$

for the "home" country, and

$$S^*(P_t^*) = a^* + b^* \overline{P}^* + u_t^* \tag{6-3}$$

$$D^*(P_t^*) = c^* - d^*P_t^* \tag{6-4}$$

for the "foreign" country or "the rest of the world." In the absence of trade, the market clearing price in the home country is given by

$$P_t = \overline{P} - \frac{u_t}{d}. \tag{6-5}$$

Assume now that the country is opened to trade. Assume also that in a normal year, a year without random disturbances in either of the countries involved, there is no price differential between the two markets and thus no incentive for trade. Hence assuming away for the time being transportation costs, $\bar{P} = \bar{P}*$ and the world market clearing price is given by

$$P_t^T = \bar{P} - \frac{u_t + u_t^*}{d + d^*} .$$

(6-6)

As a result of trade, the degree of price variability declines in the trading countries and *both* can enjoy a greater stability. To see this we calculate the variance of the price in the closed economy, given by

$$\text{Var } (P) = \frac{\sigma^2}{d^2}$$

(6-7)

and the variance of the world price with trade, given by

$$\text{Var } (P^T) = \frac{\sigma^2 + \sigma^{*2}}{(d + d^*)^2} ,$$

(6-8)

where

$$\sigma^2 = E(u^2); \ \sigma^{*2} = E(u^{*2}); \ E(u,u^*) = 0; \ E(u) = 0; \ E(u^*) = 0.$$

It is easy to verify that when there are n trading countries the variance of the world price is given by

$$\text{Var } (P^T) = \sum_{i=1}^{n} \sigma_i^2 \bigg/ \left(\sum_{i=1}^{n} d_i \right)^2 ,$$

and we can write this as

$$\text{Var } (P^T) = \sum_{i=1}^{n} d_i^2 \cdot \text{Var } (P_i) \bigg/ \left(\sum_{i=1}^{n} d_i \right)^2 .$$

Hence the variance of the world price is a weighted sum of the variances of the closed country, which adds up to *less* than the weighted average of these variances. It is in that sense that we can regard international trade as a risk pooling arrangement that works to stabilize prices and potentially benefit all the trading countries. It is still possible, however, for certain countries to have their price destabilized as an effect of free trade. In Eq. (6-8) we can see that whether the country enjoys greater or less price stability under free trade depends on the degree of supply variability and the price elasticity of demand in each of the trading countries.

The random fluctuations in supply generate trade flows as commodities gravitate to that market where the price is higher, thus tending to equalize the world price. The balance of trade of the home country is given by

$$B^T = P^T [D(P^T) - S(P^T)] , \qquad (6\text{-}9)$$

and therefore, on average,

$$E(B^T) = \frac{d^* \sigma^2 - d\sigma^{*\,2}}{(d + d^*)^2}$$

$$= d \left[\text{Var}(P^T) - \frac{d}{(d + d^*)} \text{Var}(P) \right]$$

$$= \frac{dd^*}{(d + d^*)^2} [d \, \text{Var}(P) - d^* \, \text{Var}(P^*)]. \qquad (6\text{-}10)$$

Hence, whether the country is a net exporter or a net importer of the commodity depends on the degree of supply variability and the price elasticity of demand in each of the trading countries, as well as the share of each country in the total world consumption. Specifically,

$$E(B^T) > 0 < = = > \frac{\theta^* \cdot \eta^*}{\theta \cdot \eta} > \frac{\sigma^{*\,2}}{\sigma^2} ,$$

where η and η^* denote the income elasticity of demand at the mean price and θ and θ^* denote the share of the country's demand in total world demand at the mean price in the home and in the foreign country, respectively.

When there are n trading countries the balance of trade of the jth country is given by

$$E(B_j^T) = \frac{\displaystyle\sum_{i=1}^{n} (\sigma_i^2 d_i - \sigma_i^2 d_j)}{\left(\displaystyle\sum_{i=1}^{n} d_i\right)^2} \quad ; j = 1, \ldots, n$$

$$= \sum_{i=1}^{n} \frac{d_i\, d_j}{\left(\sum_{i=1}^{n} d_i\right)^2} [d_j\, \text{Var}\,(P_j) - d_i\, \text{Var}\,(P_i)]$$

and

$$E(B_j^T) > 0 <==> \sum_{i=1}^{n} \frac{\theta_i\, \eta_i}{\theta_j\, \eta_j} > \sum_{i=1}^{n} \frac{\sigma_i^2}{\sigma_j^2};\ j = 1, \ldots, n.$$

Finally, we calculate the gains from trade. Producers' gains are simply the change in their income. This is so because the supply functions assume producers to plan their production rationally on the basis of the expected price, being unable to adjust their production instantaneously to any change in the actual price.[3] Hence,

$$G_P^T = S(P^T) \cdot P^T - S(P) \cdot P\ ,$$

where G_P^T denotes the gains to producers from trade. We can now calculate

$$E(G_P^T) = \frac{d^*}{d\,(d + d^*)}\sigma^2$$

$$= \frac{d \cdot d^*}{(d + d^*)} \cdot \text{Var}\,(P) > 0\ . \tag{6-11}$$

Hence producers always gain from free trade if the motivation for trade is random fluctuations in supply. Notice, however, that producers' gains depend only on the level of their own supply instability and *not* on that in the foreign country and that their gains are *larger* the larger is *their own* supply instability.

Consumers' gains from trade, denoted by G_c^T, are given by

$$G_c^T = -\frac{1}{2}[D(P^T) + D(P)]\,(P^T - P)\ .$$

Hence

$$E(G_c^T) = \frac{d}{2}\left[\frac{\sigma^2 + \sigma^{*\,2}}{(d + d^*)^2} - \frac{\sigma^2}{d^2}\right]$$

$$= \frac{d}{2}\,[\text{Var}\,(P^T) - \text{Var}\,(P)]\ . \tag{6-12}$$

Hence, by combining Eqs. (6-7), (6-8), and (6-12), we get

$$E(G_c^T) > 0 < = = > \text{Var} (P^T) > \text{Var} (P) .$$

Thus, consumers gain from trade only if trade brings a *greater instability* in price.

Total welfare gains from trade for the economy at large are the combined gains for consumers and producers and are given, via (6-11) and (6-12), by

$$E(G_E^T) = \frac{d^2\sigma^{*2} + d^{*2}\sigma^2}{2d(d + d^*)^2}$$

$$= \frac{d}{2} [\text{Var} (P^T) + \frac{(d^* - d)}{(d^* + d)} \cdot \text{Var} (P)]$$

$$= \frac{dd^{*2}}{2(d + d^*)^2} [\text{Var} (P^*) + \text{Var} (P)] > 0 . \tag{6-13}$$

Hence the economy always gains from trade, and its gains are larger the larger the price instability in the two trading countries prior to free trade. These gains are illustrated in Figure 6-2. In the figure it is assumed that only supply in the home country is subject to random disturbances, where $\bar{S}$ is the average level of supply and S_1 and S_2 are its two equally probable random levels. When home supply falls to S_1 the price in the closed economy is P_1. If trade is permitted the country can bridge part of the gap by importing from the foreign country, and the international price becomes P_1^T. Producers' losses due to trade are given by the shaded area A. Consumers' gains are given by the shaded areas $(A + B)$. Net welfare gains from trade for the home country are therefore given by the shaded area B. Net welfare gains for the foreign country are given by the area E. Similarly, when home supply rises to S_2 the two closed markets are cleared at the prices P_2 in the home country and $\bar{P}$ in the foreign country, whereas with free trade the international market clearing price becomes P_2^T. Net welfare gains in the home country are given by the shaded area D and reflect the gains incurred by the producers, given by the area $(C + D)$, and the losses suffered by consumers, given by the area C. Net welfare gains in the foreign country are given by the shaded area F. In this particular example it is easy to see that over the long-run consumers

Figure 6-2.   Gains from Trade under Unstable Supply.

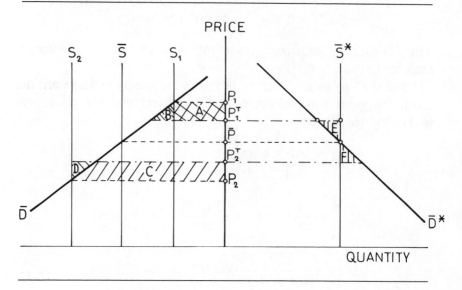

in the home country are expected to suffer losses [since the area C is larger than the area $(A + B)$], whereas producers are expected to gain. In the foreign country, however, it is expected that producers will lose and consumers will gain.

The welfare gains for the world as a whole are given by

$$E(G_W^T) = E(G_E^T) + E(G_{E^*}^T)$$

$$= \frac{d \cdot d^*}{2 (d + d^*)} \cdot [\text{Var } (P^*) + \text{Var } (P)] > 0 .$$

(6-14)

Although it is obvious that the model is highly stylized and that a general equilibrium framework is necessary in order to explore the overall effects of temporary aberrations in supply or demand on international trade and welfare,[4] two important observations emerging from our analysis appear to have a general validity. First, in a world that is dominated by wide fluctuations in demand and supply across all commodities, a significant part of international trade should be attributed to these factors rather than to factors that might account for the permanent cost advantage of a country. Secondly, the degree of instability in a country and, equally important, the degree to which this is correlated with the instability in its trading partners must be included among the factors that determine a country's comparative advantage, in the sense that they can help explain the flow of trade into and out of the country. Thus, for instance, the larger the positive correlation between fluctuations at home and abroad the smaller will be the trade flows created by these fluctuations and, correspondingly, the smaller the comparative advantage (or disadvantage, depending on the values of the other relevant parameters) of the home country. This point's quantitative significance will be demonstrated in the next chapter.

GAINS FROM STABILIZATION IN AN OPEN ECONOMY

In the previous section we saw that international trade may in itself have a strong stabilizing effect. As prices become less volatile when the country is opened to trade, gains from policies such as buffer stocks, which aim to further stabilize the prices, are likely to change considerably.

Hueth and Schmitz (1972) were the first to extend the analysis of the gains from price stabilization presented by Waugh, Oi, and Massell to international trade. They considered a two-country, one-commodity model and assumed that stabilization is achieved by means of international buffer stocks, which must therefore be sufficiently large (theoretically infinite) in order to be able to stabilize completely the world price of the traded commodity. Under this assumption we can employ the analytical model of the previous section to calculate the gains or losses from stabilization to each sector in a country and to the country and to the world at large.

Consider first Figure 6-3. Only supply is assumed to be unstable, with Q_1 and Q_2 being equally likely. The country faces an unstable world price and the two possible world prices, P_1 and P_2, are equally probable. The gains and losses from complete price stabilization for each of the possible random events are summarized in Table 6-1 in terms of the designated areas in the figure. In the figure it is assumed that the world prices determine the prices in the domestic market; that is, the country is small in relation to the world. It is also assumed that world prices and the country's production are both symmetrically distributed. In this case it is easy to see that producers have zero gains

Figure 6-3. Gains from Price Stabilization in an Open Economy.

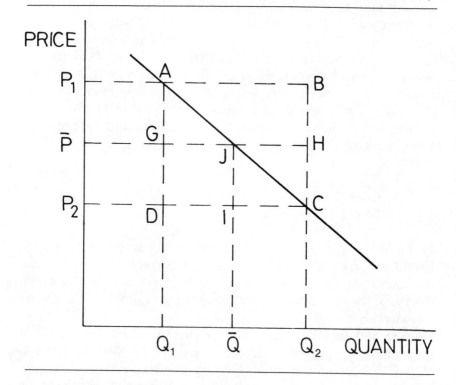

from price stabilization and consumers have net losses. In the more general case where the free trade price is determined as a clearing price of the two markets, the effects of price stabilization depend also on the demand parameters that define the structures of the two markets.

Producers' gains from price stabilization in an open economy are therefore simply equal to the resulting change in their income, given in the general case by

$$G^{ST}_P = S(\overline{P^T}) \cdot (\overline{P^T} - P^T),\tag{6-15}$$

where the superscript ST denotes a policy of perfect stabilization in an open economy. Their expected gains are thus given by

$$E(G^{ST}_P) = \frac{\sigma^2}{(d + d^*)} \cdot \tag{6-16}$$

Table 6-1.   Gains from Price Stabilization in an Open
Economy by Reference to Areas Shown in Figure 6-3.

Random Event		Welfare Gains		
World Price	Production	Producers	Consumers	Economy
P_1	Q_1	$- \bar{P}G\,A\,P_1$	$+ \bar{P}\,JA\,P_1$	$+ AG\,J$
P_2	Q_1	$+ \bar{P}\,GD\,P_2$	$- \bar{P}\,JC\,P_2$	$- G\,JCD$
P_1	Q_2	$- \bar{P}\,HB\,P_1$	$+ \bar{P}\,JA\,P_1$	$- J\,HBA$
P_2	Q_2	$+ \bar{P}\,HC\,P_2$	$- \bar{P}\,JC\,P_2$	$+ J\,HC$
Weighted Average		0	$- \frac{1}{2}\,GJID$	$- \frac{1}{2}\,GJID$

Notice that when supply in both countries is assumed to be determined rationally according to the expected long-run price, supply variability in one country does not affect the gains to producers in the other.

Consumers' gains from price stabilization in an open economy are given by

$$G_c^{ST} = \frac{1}{2}[D(P^T) + D(\bar{P}^T)]\,(P^T - \bar{P}^T) \,. \tag{6-17}$$

Their expected gains are thus given by

$$E(G_c^{ST}) = -\frac{1}{2}\,\frac{d}{(d + d^*)^2}\,(\sigma^2 + \sigma^{*\,2}). \tag{6-18}$$

Notice that from Eq. (6-8) we can write these gains as

$$E(G_c^{ST}) = -\frac{1}{2}\,d\,\mathrm{Var}\,(P^T) \,,$$

whereas in the closed economy, consumers' gains were given by

$$E(G_c^{S}) = -\frac{1}{2}\,d\,\mathrm{Var}\,(P) \,.$$

Hence, when demands are stable, consumers' gains depend only on the variability of the price and not on the source of the fluctuations in supply. Combining the producers' and consumers' expected gains we obtain the net expected gains for the economy, given by

$$E(G_E^{ST}) = \frac{(d + 2d^*)\sigma^2 - d\,\sigma^{*2}}{2(d + d^*)^2} \, . \tag{6-19}$$

Hence, a country engaged in trade *can lose from price stabilization.* This is the most noteworthy difference in results between the two-country free trade model and a closed economy. By combining (6-19) with (6-7) and (6-8) we can see that whether a country gains or loses from price stabilization depends on the variability of the price with and without trade and on the price elasticities of demand. Specifically,

$$E(G_E^{ST}) \lesseqgtr 0 \quad <==> \quad \frac{d^*}{d} \gtreqless \frac{\sigma^{*2} - \sigma^2}{2\sigma^2} \, .$$

From (6-10) we can also verify that if the country is on average a net importer of the product when it begins trading then it will always gain from price stabilization. Finally, from (6-17) we can calculate the total welfare gains for the two countries combined, given by[5]

$$E(G_w^{ST}) = \frac{1}{2} \frac{\sigma^2 + \sigma^{*2}}{d + d^*}$$

$$= \frac{1}{2}(d + d^*) \cdot \text{Var}\,(P^T) > 0 \, . \tag{6-20}$$

Hence the world at large always gains from price stabilization, and from a global point of view stabilization is indeed desirable. Table 6-2 summarizes the main results for the closed economy and for the open economy. One conclusion that emerges from this comparison is that those who gain from price stabilization gain less in the open economy, and those who lose, lose less in the open economy. This result is due to the stabilizing effect of free trade itself, which reduces the influence of further stabilization. Moreover, for the country as a whole we can easily verify the following proposition:

Total welfare gains from price stabilization are always *smaller in an open economy than in a closed economy, independent of whether trade stabilizes or destabilizes the domestic price.*[6]

Table 6-2.   Expected Welfare Gains from Price Stabilization.

Sector	Closed Economy	Free Trade
Consumers	$-\dfrac{1}{2}\dfrac{\sigma^2}{d}$	$-\dfrac{1}{2}\dfrac{d}{(d + d^*)^2}(\sigma^2 + \sigma^{*2})$
Producers	$\dfrac{1}{2}\dfrac{\sigma^2}{d}$	$\dfrac{\sigma^2}{(d + d^*)}$
Economy	$\dfrac{1}{2}\dfrac{\sigma^2}{d}$	$\dfrac{(d + 2d^*)\sigma^2 - d\sigma^{*2}}{2(d + d^*)^2}$
World	. . .	$\dfrac{1}{2}\dfrac{\sigma^2 + \sigma^{*2}}{(d + d^*)}$

GAINS FROM UNILATERAL STABILIZATION IN AN OPEN ECONOMY

The stabilization scheme considered in the previous section is one of complete price stabilization that should be achieved, according to Hueth and Schmitz, by international buffer stocks. The experience since the early 1970s casts serious doubt on the operational feasibility of such an undertaking. As a result there is an increasing tendency for countries to embark on a policy of unilateral price stabilization through national buffer stocks, an appropriate trade policy, or a combination of the two.

In this section the effects of unilateral price stabilization by a country engaged in trade with the rest of the world are analyzed. The country can achieve complete stabilization of the domestic price in one of two ways: it can design an appropriate tariff-cum-subsidy policy that will make foreign trade the instrument of stabilization, or it can operate its own buffer stocks.

The basic principles of the trade policy are as follows: if the world price rises above the stable price, the country subsidizes its imports (or taxes its exports) down to the level of the stable price. If the world price falls below the stable price, the country taxes its imports (or subsidizes its exports) up to the level of the stable price. The national buffer stock scheme requires certain restrictions on trade in order to be feasible. Thus, for instance, export should not be permitted when grain is released from storage. Similarly, imports should not be permitted when grain is put into storage. If these restrictions are not imposed then the national buffer stocks will in effect operate as an international stock. Table 6-3 gives the specific rules of the two stabilization schemes with reference to the random events illustrated in Figure 6-3.

To analyze the welfare and trade effects of unilateral price stabilization let us consider the scheme of stabilization through trade. If, say, country 2 (the foreign country) stabilizes its price at the mean, the market clearing equation becomes

$$D(P) - S(P) = S(\bar{P}^*) - D(\bar{P}^*) .$$

For the model described by Eqs. (6-1) to (6-4) we can solve the market clearing price,

$$P^U = \bar{P} - \frac{u + u^*}{d} , \qquad (6\text{-}21)$$

where the superscript U indicates the policy of unilateral stabilization. The variance of the price is given by

$$\text{Var} (P^U) = \frac{\sigma^2 + \sigma^{*2}}{d^2} \qquad (6\text{-}22)$$

and this variance is larger than both the variance of the free trade price [Eq. (6-8)] and that of the closed economy price [Eq. (6-7)]. Hence, the country that stabilizes its price unilaterally is in effect "exporting" its own instability to its trading partners. This policy can thus be termed "Destabilize Thy Neighbor". The trade flows generated under this trade policy are given by

$$B^U = [D(P^U) - S(P^U)] \, P^U$$

$$= [c - d \left(\bar{P} - \frac{u + u^*}{d} \right) - (a + b \bar{P} + u)] \left(P - \frac{u + u^*}{d} \right). \qquad (6\text{-}23)$$

Table 6-3. Policy Rules of National Stabilization Schemes with Trade by Reference to Events Shown in Figure 6-3.

Random Event		Policy Rules	
Country's Production	World Price	Scheme 1: Stabilization through Trade	Scheme 2: Stabilization through National Buffer Stocks and Trade Restrictions
Q_1	P_1	Subsidy of $(P_1 - \bar{P})$ to imports	The quantity $(\bar{Q} - Q_1)$ is released from storage. Export is prohibited.
Q_1	P_2	Tax of $(\bar{P} - P_2)$ on imports	Trade is permitted. Tax of $(\bar{P} - P_2)$ on imports.
Q_2	P_1	Tax of $(P_1 - \bar{P})$ on exports	Trade is permitted. Tax of $(\bar{P} - P_2)$ on exports.
Q_2	P_2	Subsidy of $(\bar{P} - P_2)$ to exports	The quantity $(Q_2 - \bar{Q})$ is put into storage. Import is prohibited.

Hence, on average,

$$E(B^U) = -\frac{\sigma^{*2}}{d} + [\bar{D}(\bar{P}) - \bar{S}(\bar{P})]\,\bar{P} \ , \tag{6-24}$$

where $\bar{D}$ and $\bar{S}$ indicate the normal (stable) levels of demand and supply, respectively.

Thus, if the country is on average self-sufficient so that $\bar{D}(\bar{P}) = \bar{S}(\bar{P})$, then the result of a unilateral stabilizing policy is on average a net export from the home country to the foreign country. Obviously the feasibility of the policy depends on the ability of the foreign country to finance this trade deficit. Notice that the extent of the surplus does not depend on the variability of supply in the home country but only on that in the foreign country. The reason is that a random increase in supply in the home country leads to a parallel decline in price, thus leaving the balance of trade unchanged. By comparing (6-24) with (6-10) we can see that this policy may actually increase the trade flows between the two countries. If the home country is a net importer under free trade, then this policy in the foreign country will actually increase its imports. If the country is a net exporter under free trade, then the policy will reduce its exports.

The gains from trade and from the trade policy under unilateral stabilization must be calculated separately for the two countries. For the foreign country that completely stabilizes its price, the gains from the policy are simply the gains from price stabilization in an open economy, calculated in the previous section. To these gains, however, we must add the net tax revenue of the government. These revenues, denoted by TX, are given by

$$TX^* = (P^U - \bar{P})\,[S^*(\bar{P}) - D^*(\bar{P})] \ . \tag{6-25}$$

Hence,

$$E(TX^*) = -\frac{\sigma^{*2}}{d} \ . \tag{6-26}$$

The government must therefore make, on average, net subsidy payments equal to its trade deficit. Taking these net payments into account the foreign country's total net gains from the stabilization policy are obtained by combining (6-19) and (6-26), yielding

$$E(G_{E^\cdot}^U) = \frac{d^2(\sigma^2 - \sigma^{*2}) + 2dd^*\sigma^2 - 2(d + d^*)\sigma^{*2}}{2d(d + d^*)^2} \cdot$$

(6-27)

Hence, whether or not this tax-cum-subsidy policy does indeed impose a burden on the foreign country in the sense of reducing its welfare depends on the demand parameters and the degree of supply instability in the two countries.

It can immediately be verified that the net welfare gains for the foreign country are larger the larger the degree of instability of the home production and the smaller the degree of instability of the foreign production. Although it is tempting to assume that governments would implement this type of unilateral stabilization only to the extent that they gain, it is important to emphasize that this need not be the case. Other considerations, some of them reviewed in Chapters 2 and 3, may cause governments to implement such a policy even when they involve welfare losses.

For the home country we calculate first the *marginal* welfare effects of the unilateral stabilization policy implemented in the foreign country. This is done by comparing the latter situation of restricted trade with that of free trade. Producers' gains in the home country are then given by

$$G_P^U = S(\bar{P})[P^U - P^T]$$
$$= (a + b\bar{P} + u)\left(-\frac{u + u^*}{d} + \frac{u + u^*}{d + d^*}\right)$$

(6-28)

Hence,

$$E(G_P^U) = \frac{-d^*}{d(d + d^*)} \cdot \sigma^2 < 0 \ .$$

(6-29)

Thus, when demand is stable, producers in the home country suffer losses as a result of the trade restrictions in the foreign country. (This result cannot be extended to the more general case in which both demand and supply are subject to random disturbances.) Consumers' gains are given by

$$G_c^U = -\frac{1}{2}[D(P^U) + D(P^T)](P^U - P^T) \ .$$

(6-30)

Hence

$$E(G_c^U) = +\frac{1}{2}\,\frac{2dd^* + d^{*2}}{d(d + d^*)^2}\,(\sigma^2 + \sigma^{*2}) > 0 \ .$$

(6-31)

Thus, consumers in the home country actually gain from the unilateral stabilization policy implemented in the foreign country. The home country's total expected welfare losses amount to

$$E(G_E^U) = \frac{d^*\,[(2d + d^*)\,\sigma^{*2} - d^*\sigma^2]}{2d\,(d + d^*)^2} \ .$$

(6-32)

Thus, the home country can either lose or actually gain from the unilateral stabilization in the foreign country, depending on the value of the relevant parameters, where

$$E(G_E^U) > 0 <==> \frac{2d + d^*}{d^*} > \frac{\sigma^2}{\sigma^{*2}}$$

$$<==> \frac{d}{d^*} > \frac{1}{2}\,\frac{\sigma^2 - \sigma^{*2}}{\sigma^{*2}} \ .$$

By combining (6-27) and (6-32) we get

$$E(G_W^U) = E(G_{E^*}^U) + E(G_E^U)$$

$$= \frac{(d^2 + 2dd^* - d^{*2})\,\sigma^2 + [d^{*2} + 2dd^* - d^2 - 2(d + d^*)]\,\sigma^{*2}}{2d\,(d + d^*)^2}$$

(6-33)

Hence, it is possible that the two countries combined will incur welfare losses as a result of this policy. In that case it will not be possible for the gaining country to compensate the one losing in order to encourage it to trade under the restrictions imposed by the policy.

The foregoing analysis considered the following question: what are the welfare effects on each of the two trading countries engaged in free trade if one of them decides to restrict the trade in a way that stabilizes its own domestic price? For many countries, however, this question is fairly irrelevant. Instead, the relevant question is whether it will be beneficial for them to engage in trade with a country that restricts its trade. To examine this question we compare the situation of restricted trade with that of no trade at all. Producers' gains in the home country are then given by

$$G^{UT}_P = S(\bar{P})\,(P^U - P)$$

$$= (a + b\bar{P} + u)\left(-\frac{u^*}{d}\right), \qquad (6\text{-}34)$$

where the superscript UT signifies that the comparison is with the case of no trade and P^U is the price defined in Eq. (6-21). Hence,

$$E(G^{UT}_P) = 0 \ . \qquad (6\text{-}35)$$

Thus, if there is no correlation between the levels of production in the two countries and the demands are stable then producers in the home country neither lose nor gain from this trade. Consumers' gains are given by

$$G^{UT}_c = -\frac{1}{2}\,[D(P^U) + d(P)]\,(P^U - P)$$

$$= -\frac{1}{2}\left[c - d\left(\bar{P} - \frac{u + u^*}{d}\right) + c - d\left(\bar{P} - \frac{u}{d}\right)\right]\left(-\frac{u^*}{d}\right) \ . \qquad (6\text{-}36)$$

Hence

$$E(G^{UT}_c) = \frac{1}{2}\,\frac{\sigma^{*2}}{d + d^*} > 0 \ . \qquad (6\text{-}37)$$

Hence, consumers in the home country will, on average, gain from trade with a country that unilaterally stabilizes its domestic price. These welfare gains to consumers will also be the welfare gains to the economy at large. We can therefore conclude that if one of the countries restricts its trade in order to stabilize its price, the other country will still be better off with trade than with no trade.

CONCLUDING REMARKS

In the 1970s international prices of most agricultural products displayed a volatility that has not been seen since the years of the

Great Depression. Worldwide inflation and repeated sharp increases in oil prices and other raw materials are likely to perpetuate these wide price gyrations in the foreseeable future. During these years an increasing portion of world trade has become dominated by random and temporary aberrations in supply and demand, and the sharp rise in the protectionist tendencies that we are now witnessing is largely due to efforts made by countries to protect themselves against the external instability.

In this chapter some of the theoretical issues in the process of international trade that is carried out in an unstable environment were analyzed. Specifically analyzed were the balance of payments and welfare implications of a trade process, triggered and enhanced by the fluctuations of supply and demand. The main conclusions can be summarized as follows:

1. International trade works in general to stabilize the national economies and serves as a type of risk pooling mechanism. It is possible, however, for one of the countries to suffer greater instability with trade than without trade.

2. International trade is still better for a country than no trade in that it allows the country to achieve a higher level of welfare even when the country becomes less stable as a result of free trade.

3. International price stabilization schemes will always be beneficial to the world as a whole. Some of the countries may, however, suffer welfare losses as a result of such schemes.

4. Total welfare gains from price stabilization are *always* smaller in an open economy than in a closed economy (provided that the costs of stabilization are the same) independent of whether trade stabilizes or destabilizes the domestic price.

5. Unilateral price stabilization by a single country through regulated foreign trade need not be beneficial to the country from the welfare point of view. (It is possible and indeed most likely that this policy is motivated by other factors. In that case the welfare losses to consumers and producers must be traded off against the other objectives.)

6. Unilateral stabilization by one country need not be detrimental to its trading partners from the welfare point of view although the internal instability in their markets is bound to increase considerably.

The main issue concerning the unilateral stabilization policy that amounts to "Destabilize Thy Neighbor" is whether the other countries will be willing and able to retaliate. If retaliation is possible and indeed probable, then the end result of this type of trade war may very well be less trade, larger instability and a lower level of welfare in all the trading countries.

APPENDIX 6A.
INSTABILITY AND THE GAINS FROM
TRADE: THE GENERAL MODEL

This section extends the analysis of the first section to allow also for random fluctuations on demand. In the home country the market model then consists of the following demand and supply equations:

$$S(\bar{P}) = a + b\bar{P} + u \qquad (6A\text{--}1)$$

$$D(P) = c - dP + v . \qquad (6A\text{--}2)$$

The market clearing price in the closed economy is given by

$$P = \bar{P} + \frac{v - u}{d} . \qquad (6A\text{--}3)$$

Suppose now that the country is engaged in free trade with a foreign country, having linear supply and demand equations of the form

$$S^*(\bar{P}^*) = a^* + b^* \bar{P}^* + u^* \qquad (6A\text{--}4)$$

$$D^*(P^*) = c^* - d^*P^* + v . \qquad (6A\text{--}5)$$

Assume that if there are no random disturbances the market clearing prices in the two (closed) economies and hence also the world market clearing price will be equal; that is, $\bar{P} = \bar{P}^* = \bar{P}^T$. Thus, in a normal year both countries are self-sufficient and no trade takes place. By combining the two markets we can derive the world market clearing price, given by

$$P^T = \bar{P} + \frac{V - U}{D},$$

(6A–6)

where $D = d + d^*$, $V = v + v^*$ and $U = u + u^*$.

In the absence of trade, price variability in the home country is given by

$$\text{Var}(P) = \frac{\sigma_V + \sigma_u}{d^2}.$$

(6A–7)

With free trade, the variability of the world market price is given by

$$\text{Var}(P^T) = \frac{\sigma_v^2 + \sigma_u^2 + \sigma_v^{*2} + \sigma_u^{*2}}{D^2}$$

$$= \frac{d^2}{D^2} \text{Var}(P) + \frac{d^{*2}}{D^2} \text{Var}(P^*).$$

(6A–8)

Hence, the variability of the free trade price is a weighted *sum* of the variabilities of the closed economy prices, with the weights adding up to *less* than unity.

The trade flows generated by the random disturbances are given, from the point of view of the home country, by

$$B^T = P^T[D(P^T) - S(P^T)].$$

(6A–9)

Hence, since the country is normally self-sufficient so that $\bar{D}(\bar{P}) = \bar{S}(\bar{P})$, then

$$E(B^T) = \frac{d^*}{(d + d^*)^2} (\sigma_v^2 + \sigma_u^2) - \frac{d}{(d + d^*)^2} (\sigma_v^{*2} + \sigma_u^{*2})$$

$$= d \left[\frac{d}{(d + d^*)} \text{Var}(P) - \text{Var}(P^T) \right]$$

$$= \frac{dd^*}{D^2} [d \, \text{Var}(P) - d^* \text{Var}(P^*)].$$

(6A–10)

The welfare gains to producers in the home country are now given by

$$G_P^T = S(P^T) \cdot [P^T - P]$$

$$= (a + b\bar{P} + u) \left[\bar{P} + \frac{V - U}{D} - \bar{P} - \frac{v - u}{d} \right] .$$ (6A-11)

Hence

$$E(G_P^T) = - \frac{\sigma_u^2}{D} + \frac{\sigma_u^2}{d} = \frac{d^*}{dD} \cdot \sigma_u^2 > 0.$$ (6A-12)

Consumers' gains from trade are given by

$$G_c^T = - \frac{1}{2} [D(P^T) + D(P)] (P^T - P) .$$ (6A-13)

Hence

$$E(G_c^T) = \frac{1}{2} \left[\frac{d}{(d + d^*)^2} (\sigma_v^{*2} + \sigma_u^{*2}) - \frac{d^{*2} + 2dd^*}{d(d + d^*)^2} (\sigma_u^2 + \sigma_v^2) \right]$$

$$+ \frac{d^*}{d(d + d^*)} \sigma_v^2$$

$$= + \frac{d}{2} [\text{Var}(P^T) - \text{Var}(P)] + \frac{d^*}{dP} \sigma_v^2 .$$ (6A-14)

Thus, total welfare gains from trade are given by

$$E(G_E^T) = E(G_c^T) + E(G_P^T)$$

$$= \frac{d^{*2}}{2d(d + d^*)} (\sigma_v^2 + \sigma_u^2) + \frac{d}{2(d + d^*)^2} (\sigma_v^{*2} + \sigma_u^{*2})$$

$$= \frac{d}{2} [\text{Var}(P^T) + \frac{(d^* - d)}{D} \text{Var}(P)]$$

$$= \frac{dd^{*2}}{2D^2} [\text{Var}(P^*) + \text{Var}(P)] > 0 .$$ (6A-15)

If we extend the model further and consider the case in which supply is a function of the actual market price, the supply functions in the home and the foreign countries will have the form

$$S(P) = a + bP + u$$ (6A-16)

$$S^*(P^*) = a^* + b^*P^* + u^* . \tag{6A-17}$$

The market clearing price in the closed economy will then be given by

$$P = \bar{P} + \frac{v - u}{e} , \tag{6A-18}$$

where $e = b + d$. The world market clearing price is given by

$$P^T = \bar{P} + \frac{V - U}{E} , \tag{6A-19}$$

where $E = e + e^*$.

The results with respect to price variability and the balance of payments are essentially similar to those obtained in (6A-8) and (6A-10) with e, e^*, and E replacing d, d^*, and D respectively, thus allowing for the effects of the supply elasticities. Producers' gains are now given by

$$G_P^T = \frac{1}{2}[S(P^T) + S(P)] (P^T - P) . \tag{6A-20}$$

Hence

$$\begin{aligned}
E(G_P^T) &= \frac{1}{2} \left[\frac{b}{E^2} (\sigma_v^2 + \sigma_u^2 + \sigma_v^{*2} + \sigma_u^{*2}) - \frac{b}{e^2} (\sigma_v^2 + \sigma_u^2) \right] + \frac{e^*}{eE} \sigma_u^2 \\
&= \frac{b}{2} [\mathrm{Var}(P^T) - \mathrm{Var}(P)] + \frac{e^*}{e \cdot E} \sigma_u^2 .
\end{aligned} \tag{6A-21}$$

Consumers' expected gains from trade are given by

$$\begin{aligned}
E(G_c^T) &= \frac{1}{2} \left[\frac{d}{E^2} (\sigma_v^2 + \sigma_u^2 + \sigma_v^{*2} + \sigma_u^{*2}) - \frac{d}{e^2} (\sigma_v^2 + \sigma_u^2) \right] + \frac{e^*}{e \cdot E} \sigma_v^2 \\
&= \frac{d}{2} [\mathrm{Var}(P^T) - \mathrm{Var}(P)] + \frac{e^*}{eE} \cdot \sigma_v^2 .
\end{aligned} \tag{6A-22}$$

Total welfare gains from trade are therefore given in this model by

$$E(G_E^T) = \frac{e^{*2}}{2eE^2} (\sigma_v^2 + \sigma_u^2) + \frac{e}{2E^2} (\sigma_v^{*2} + \sigma_u^{*2})$$

$$= \frac{e}{2} [\mathrm{Var}(P^T) + \frac{(e^* - e)}{E} \mathrm{Var}(P)]$$

$$= \frac{e \cdot e^{*2}}{2E^2} [\mathrm{Var}(P^*) + \mathrm{Var}(P)] > 0 \; . \tag{6A-23}$$

NOTES

1. This result is valid from a single country's point of view, whereas for the world as a whole this "optimum" tariff necessarily involves welfare losses resulting from the misallocation of resources.
2. Although the basic model developed in Chapter 2 is still employed here, note that in Appendix 6A we prove that, unless noted otherwise, all the conclusions mentioned in this chapter are valid also for the more general model and for the case in which demand too is unstable.
3. In Appendix 6A this specific assumption is relaxed and other forms of the supply function are considered.
4. Thus, for instance, only in a general equilibrium framework can we evaluate the resulting changes in relative prices and hence their effects on the balance of payments.
5. This result is very similar to the one obtained in Chapter 2 for the closed economy, for which total expected welfare gains from stabilization are given by $\frac{1}{2} d \, \mathrm{Var}(P)$.
6. From Eqs. (2–10) and (6–19) we can see that $E(G_E^S) > E(G_E^{ST})$ if and only if $(d + d^*)^2 \, \sigma^2 > d^2 (\sigma^2 - \sigma^{*2}) + 2dd^* \sigma^2$,
   and it is easy to see that the latter relation always holds.

7 DOMESTIC AGRICULTURAL POLICIES AND INTERNATIONAL TRADE

In the previous chapter we examined the stabilizing effects of free trade and showed how it functions as a risk pooling arrangement. Our analysis led us to conclude that all trading countries would gain from free trade, including those that would suffer from greater instability under free trade than under no trade. Trade would help the country to solve its adjustment problems arising from temporary aberrations in domestic supply or demand. Harvest failures, for instance, can be offset by imports, thus avoiding supply problems. In so doing the country in effect shifts the adjustment to its trading partners, who may then face temporary shortages. One notable example in the recent past was the huge purchases of wheat by Russia in 1972-73, which led to a large price increase for local consumers in the United States.

The mounting protectionist sentiments especially since the early 1970s could be attributed, at least in part, to measures taken in many countries to stabilize their own economies, which have caused larger instability in their trading partners. When world prices for grain rose sharply in 1972-73, the major trading countries pursued trade policies designed to insulate their economies from the effects of this foreign instability (see Grenns, Johnson, and Thursby 1978 for details). The EEC levy automatically fell to zero, export subsidies were eliminated, and exports to certain countries were restricted. The Japan Food

Agency abandoned its traditional tariff policy and sold grain purchased in the world markets to domestic millers below the world price. Argentina imposed a grain embargo, while Canada and Australia taxed their grain exports.

The analysis of free trade under conditions of instability in the previous chapter was carried out within the framework of a highly stylized model of the economy. The first objective of this chapter is to extend the analysis to a more generalized framework and examine the validity of the propositions in a more complex and thus more realistic economic environment. The second and more important objective is to examine the role and effects of domestic agricultural policies in an open economy and compare them with those in a closed economy. The domestic policies are those considered in Chapters 4 and 5, namely, buffer stocks, producers' support programs, and subsidy programs. The structure of the model, policy rules, and parameter values are generally those described in Chapters 4 and 5.

An open economy is exposed to a type of shortage that does not exist in a closed economy, namely, a shortage in foreign exchange. If the country does not have enough foreign exchange (or enough credit) to buy food in the world market, then it will not be able to supplement domestic supply in years of crop failure. Alternatively, if a country has to devote much of its foreign exchange to food purchases, it may have to forego some of its investment plans for which foreign exchange is required.

In short, in an open economy we give special attention to balance of payments considerations in each policy and program. In this chapter, no form of trade intervention is considered, however, and that discussion is postponed to the next chapter.

THE OPEN ECONOMY: MODEL AND PARAMETERS

The structure of the model in the open economy is similar to that described in Chapters 4 and 5 with the following modifications associated with foreign trade activities:

Trade between the country and the world is carried out in a free market subject to the restrictions of the government's trade policy. Thus, grain is imported when the domestic price exceeds the import price and exported when the export price exceeds the domestic price.

Import and export prices are determined by the world price and transportation costs (and tariffs, when applicable). World price is a random variable, determined from world production and world demand according to a simple model that transforms the frequency distribution of world production into a frequency distribution of the price. The model can accommodate year-to-year serial correlation as well as correlation between production in the country and in the world.

The only trade restriction considered in this chapter is one existing when buffer stocks are operated. We assume that in this case the government stipulates that in times of plentiful domestic harvest grain will be stored and only the excess beyond that may be exported; when domestic harvest is poor grain is imported as a first measure and only then will grain be released from storage. This constraint should afford extra security to the system. In addition, we assume that it will not be permitted for exports to lower supply below the level that triggers a release-from-storage operation or for imports to lower the price below the level that triggers an accumulation-into-storage operation. This rule is enforced by setting appropriate tariffs.

We consider three basic situations with regard to demand and supply conditions in the country:

1. The country is self-sufficient; that is, in a normal year, when domestic and world production are at their mean or stable levels, there is no price differential between the two and thus no incentive for trade.
2. The country is generally importing.
3. The country is generally exporting.

We also consider the following alternative assumptions with regard to the relationship between the country and the world:

1. The country is small, that is, its excess demand for imports or excess supply of exports have no effect on the world price.
2. The country is large and therefore affects the world price.

The specific parameters of the aforementioned features of the open economy model are as follows: world production is assumed to be normally distributed with a coefficient of variation of 5 percent. World demand of wheat is assumed to be kinked linear, thereby generating a skewed distribution of world prices. The elasticities,

Table 7-1.   A Country's Demand and Supply Characteristics.

Type of Country	Price[a]	Quantity Produced	Quantity Consumed
Self-sufficient	100	100	100
Generally importing	100	100	120
Generally exporting	100	100	80

[a]Transportation costs per unit of imports and exports are assumed to be 15 percent of the stable price.

calculated at the mean level of world production (for which the price is set to be 100 per unit) are

$$\eta_W = 0.6 \ \ \text{for } P \geqq 100$$

$$\eta_W = 0.75 \ \text{for } P \leqq 100 \ .$$

For the large country the world's mean production was assumed to be three times larger than the country's mean production. We also considered the case of a very large country (or a group of countries) whose mean production is equal to the world's mean production.

The country is self-sufficient when in a normal year there is no trade since the domestic stable market clearing price is then identical to the world's stable price. The country is generally importing when at the normal price it is on average only 80 percent self-sufficient, and generally exporting when at the normal price it is on average 120 percent self-sufficient. These characteristics are summarized in Table 7-1.[1]

TRADE CREATION AND THE GAINS
FROM TRADE

We begin the analysis with the self-sufficient country. By definition this country has neither advantage nor disadvantage in the production of foodgrains, and in a normal year there is no price differential between the country and the world and thus no incentive for trade. However, random fluctuations in production occurring in either the country or the world may create price gaps larger than the transportation costs and thus induce trade flows that can go in either direction, imports in some years and exports in others. The magnitudes of these flows depend on the market structure in the two trading countries, and especially on the size of the fluctuations, on the degree to which the fluctuations are correlated and on the level of the transportation costs (and tariffs, when applicable). Table 7–2 presents the main trade and balance of payments consequences of the trade relationships between the self-sufficient country and the rest of the world.

The most noteworthy observation is the considerable volume of trade generated by fluctuations in domestic production and in the world price. On average the quantities imported and exported account for slightly less than 1 percent of average annual production. For a country of the size of India, this means imports and exports of 2 to 2.5 million tons. However, the probabilities of having imports to and exports from the normally self-sufficient country are only 23 and 21 percent, respectively. This means that the average volume of imports for the period when goods are *actually imported* and the average volume of exports for the periods when goods are *actually exported* are approximately 4.3 percent of the annual production. The deficit in the balance of trade is on average 0.23 percent of the annual expenditures in a normal year, but there is a probability of 11 percent that the deficit exceeds 3 percent of normal expenditures. For a country the size of India and at the current world prices it means that once in ten years the deficit on food alone can exceed $1.25 billion. Similar effects on the trends of the trade flows would be revealed when there is a correlation in the sequence of good and bad years between the country and the world. Such a correlation can exist either when country and world production are both subject to similar weather conditions (as, for instance, is the case with most of the world trade in rice) or when the country is large enough to affect the world price (in which case the domestic prices would be correlated with the world prices even if there is no correlation in production). When a good year in the country coincides with a good year in the world and a bad year in the country coincides with a bad year in the world, the less the likelihood of trade activities. The volume of exports of a very large country, for instance, will be 40 percent smaller than that of a small country. The average volume of imports of a very large country will be 7 percent smaller (the difference in these effects on exports and imports is due to the price elasticities of demand in the country and the world and the consequent probability distributions of the prices), and the average trade deficit of a very large country is

Table 7-2. Trade Creation due to Supply Fluctuations in a Normally Self-sufficient Country.

	Volume of Trade[a]		Balance of Trade	
	Exports	Imports	Average Balance[b]	Probability that Deficit Exceeds 3% of Normal Expenditures
Free trade	0.94	0.98	−0.23	11%
Free trade with correlation[c]	0.44	0.55	−0.27	0
Large country	0.88	0.90	−0.22	10%
Very large country	0.58	0.91	−0.51	6%

[a]As a percentage of average annual production.
[b]As a percentage of annual expenditures in a normal year.
[c]A correlation coefficient (R^2) of 0.3 between the country's and the world's productions.

therefore 122 percent larger. However, the probability of having a large trade deficit, one in excess of 3 percent of normal expenditures, is only 6 percent in the very large country compared with 11 percent in the small country.

In an open economy, the possibility of supplementing domestic supply through imports in years of crop failure and eliminating surpluses through exports in years of plenty may contribute to a greater internal stability and a lower degree of food insecurity. Trade does not always stabilize the domestic market, however, and in some cases it can even *destabilize* it.[2] In the previous chapter it was shown that free trade results in a reduction in the global price instability by pooling the price fluctuations between the trading countries, even though in certain individual countries instability may actually increase. The final effect depends on the extent of the fluctuations in the country and in its trading partners and on their corresponding price elasticities of demand. Table 7–3 presents the stabilizing effect of free trade in the countries considered in the simulation analysis.

In all these countries the stabilizing effects of free trade are revealed to be very powerful. One effect is the reduction in price variability by 25 to 40 percent and in the variability of farmers' income by 35 to 55 percent. Even more important, the probability of extreme events is drastically reduced; the probability of food insecurity at the 10 percent level (the probability that supply to the poor falls by more than 10 percent below their normal supply) is reduced (in the base case) by more than 65 percent while the probability that the price falls by more than 20 percent below the normal price is reduced by 80 percent. These stabilizing effects of free trade are only slightly smaller in the other country cases presented in Table 7–3. In Table 7–4 the stabilizing effects of free trade are examined when the variability of production is greater in either the country or the world. Obviously, free trade contributes less to domestic stability when world production is more volatile. However, even when the world's production variability is doubled compared with the base case (and is then 40 percent higher than the country's production variability) the stabilizing effects of free trade are still very substantial. As production becomes less stable would more frequently price differentials between the country and the world be conducive to trade and the volume of exports and imports would thus expand. Table 7–5 shows that as production variability in the country increases by 55 percent the average volume of exports and imports rises by 125 percent and the

Table 7-3. Stabilizing Effects of Free Trade.

	No Trade	Free Trade	Free Trade with Correlation[a]	Large Country	Very Large Country
Price variability CV (%)	18	11	14	12	12
Probability that price falls by more than 20 percent below normal price	10.8	2.3	6.2	3.1	6.0
Food insecurity (10%)[b]	17.2	5.9	12.0	5.9	5.9
Variability of farmers' income, CV (%)	11	6	7	6	7

[a]With a correlation coefficient (R^2) of 0.3.
[b]Probability that supply to poor falls by more than 10 percent below 'normal' supply.

Table 7-4. Stabilizing Effects of Free Trade under Greater Production Instability.

	Price Variability, CV (%)	Probability That Price Falls by More than 20% below Normal Price	Food Insecurity (10%)	Variability of Farmers' Income, CV (%)
Base case[a]	11	2.3	5.9	6
Less stable world[b]	11	3.6	7.3	8
Less stable country[c]				
No trade	27	21.3	27.9	17
Free trade	13	4.7	9.7	7
Adaptive expectations				
No trade	23	17.5	24.0	14
Free trade	12	2.8	7.0	6

[a]The coefficient of variation in world's production is 5 percent.
[b]The coefficient of variation in world's production is 10 percent.
[c]The coefficient of variation in country's production is 11 percent compared with 7 percent in the base case.

Table 7-5. Trade Creation under Greater Instability.

| | Volume of Trade[a] | | Balance of Trade | |
	Exports	Imports	Average Balance[b]	Probability That the Deficit Exceeds 3% of Normal Expenditures, %
Base case	0.94	0.98	−0.23	11
Less stable world	1.28	1.25	+0.01	15
Less stable country	2.13	2.25	−0.63	20
Adaptive expectations	1.13	1.13	−0.23	13

[a]As percentage of average annual production.
[b]As percentage of annual expenditures in a normal year.

balance of trade is almost tripled. At the same time, the frequency of trade activities (imports or exports) rises from 43 percent to 60 percent (not shown in the table) and thus the average volume of either exports or imports *when these exist* is more than 7 percent of normal production.

The stabilizing effects of free trade are most vividly demonstrated in a histogram showing the probability distribution of the price in the closed and the open economies, given in Figure 7-1. The most drastic effect is on the probability of having extreme prices (relative to the normal price). Thus, for instance, the probability that the price deviates by more than 20 percent above or below the normal price is reduced by more than 75 percent as an effect of free trade.

Yet another aspect of free trade is its effect on national welfare and income distribution. In the previous chapter it was shown that each trading country gains from free trade, regardless of whether or not trade reduces instability in that country. We can now turn to the simulation analysis in order to examine these gains in a more general country model. Table 7-6 presents the gains from trade to the main sectors of the economy in several country cases. It shows that the economy always gains from free trade but that the distribution of the gains may differ substantially according to the specific conditions. In the small economy (the base case) producers gain from trade and the

Figure 7-1. Probability Distribution of the Price.

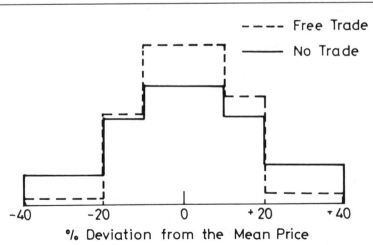

% Deviation from the Mean Price

larger the degree of instability the larger the gains. By contrast, in the very large country producers have, on average, substantial losses.

The main conclusion emerging from these data is that in an unstable economic environment a substantial volume of trade is generated quite apart from the traditional considerations of relative advantage. These flows of trade have a strong stabilizing effect on the domestic market, and they also affect the distribution of national income. The country at large always gains from trade, which not only stabilizes its markets but also raises its welfare. The costs to the country are manifested in the balance of payments; in order to allow free trade the country must relinquish some of its foreign exchange resources.

EXPORTING AND IMPORTING COUNTRIES

In a country that is generally an exporter there is usually a gap between the domestic market clearing price and the export price (calculated as the world price *minus* transportation costs). This price gap triggers outflow from the country, thus raising the domestic price to the level of the world price. If supply in that country is price responsive, then the rise in price will benefit the domestic producers and induce them to increase their output. Thus, for instance, in the exporting country considered in the simulation analysis—where the price elasticity of supply is assumed to be 0.25—the market clearing price in the closed economy is 66.3 and the quantity produced is 91.5. As the market is opened to trade, the price rises to 85 (the world price, 100, minus transportation costs, 15) and output rises to 96.25. At that price the quantity consumed is 85.2 and the quantity exported is 10.1. Table 7-7 presents the main effects of free trade when production is completely stable and when production in both the country and the world are randomly fluctuating. In the simulation analysis we have assumed that expectations are adaptively rational (see Chapter 4); that is, the supply gradually adjusts to price changes that last for several years and are thus considered by producers as permanent. A number of observations in Table 7-7 stand out. First, the exporting country enjoys far greater stability under free trade than with no trade, and the price variability under free trade is less than 30 percent of its variability under no trade. Second, when productions in the country and in the world are unstable, the volume of the trade flow and the value of the trade surplus are 20 percent larger than those in a

Table 7-6. Expected Economic Gains from Trade
(As Percentage of Annual Expenditures in a Normal Year).

	Free Trade (Base Case)	Free Trade with Correlation	Large Country	Very Large Country	Less Stable Country	Adaptive Expectations
Consumers	0.15	0.23	0.10	0.84	0.12	−0.20
Producers	0.03	−0.17	0.06	−0.72	0.56	1.12
Total economy	0.18	0.06	0.16	0.12	0.68	0.92

Table 7-7.   Effects of Free Trade in an Exporting Country.

	Stable Production		Stochastic Production	
	No Trade	Free Trade	No Trade	Free Trade
Country's price				
Mean	66.3	85.0	65.1	86.3
CV (%)	0	0	32.7	8.9
Quantity available for consumption				
Mean	91.5	85.2	92.0	84.7
CV (%)	0	0	7.8	3.1
Quantity exported[a]	. . .	10.1	. . .	12.1
Balance of trade[b]	. . .	+8.6	. . .	+10.6
Economic gains from trade[b]				
Consumers' gains	. . .	−16.5	. . .	−20.8
Producers' gains	. . .	+17.5	. . .	+23.4
Total economic gains	. . .	+1.0	. . .	+2.6

[a]As a percentage of annual production in a normal year.

[b]As a percentage of annual expenditures in a normal year.

stable situation. Put differently, only 80 percent of this country's trade should be attributed to its relative advantage in the production of foodgrains, and the rest should be attributed to stochastic factors. Third, in an unstable environment, producers' gains and consumers' losses from trade are 25 to 30 percent higher and the total economic gains from trade are 150 percent higher than in a stable environment. The usual measures of gains from trade, based as they are on a comparative static analysis, may therefore seriously understate the true value of these gains in a stochastic world.

In a country that is generally an importer, the import price is lower than the closed market clearing price and this price gap triggers trade inflow. As the market price is lowered to the import price (calculated as the world price *plus* transportation costs), the quantity consumed increases, but the quantity produced decreases. Table 7-8 summarizes the effects of free trade in an importing country for stable and for unstable production. The main conclusions noted for the exporting

Table 7-8. Effects of Free Trade in an Importing Country.

	Stable Production		Stochastic Production	
	No Trade	Free Trade	No Trade	Free Trade
Country's price				
Mean	129.3	115	130.5	114.8
CV (%)	0	0	12.6	6.5
Quantity available for consumption				
Mean	107.3	113.4	106.8	113.6
CV (%)	0	0	6.7	2.9
Quantity imported[a]	. . .	9.6	. . .	10.3
Balance of trade[b]	. . .	− 11.0	. . .	− 11.7
Economic gains from trade[b]				
Consumers' gains	. . .	+ 15.8	. . .	+ 18.2
Producers' gains	. . .	− 15.1	. . .	− 16.5
Total economic gains	. . .	+ 0.7	. . .	+ 1.8

[a]As a percentage of annual production in a normal year.
[b]As a percentage of annual expenditures in a normal year.

country are also valid for the importing one: first, free trade stabilizes the domestic market to a considerable extent, and second, an estimate of trade flows and gains from trade that is based on a comparative static analysis may lead to an underestimation of their true magnitude in an unstable environment.

Finally consider the case in which supply responds not only to the change in the level of the price but also in its variability. In that case, when the country is opened to trade there would be two conflicting effects on producers: the decrease in the mean price would depress supply while the increase in its stability would encourage it. With the parameters assumed in our supply function (a price elasticity of 0.25 and an elasticity with respect to the standard deviation of 0.5) the net effect would be a net increase in supply. Table 7–9 summarizes the effects of free trade in an importing country with supply response. The country under consideration is the one described in Chapter 4. It is a country that would have been self-sufficient in a stable situation, but

Table 7-9.   Effects of Free Trade with Supply Response.

	No Trade	Free Trade
Country's price		
Mean	114	105
CV (%)	18	11
Quantity available for consumption		
Mean	95	98
CV (%)	8	4
Quantity imported[a]	. . .	2.1
Balance of trade[b]	. . .	1.9
Economic gains from trade[b]		
Consumers' gains	. . .	7.4
Producers' gains	. . .	−3.6
Total economic gains	. . .	+3.8

[a]As a percentage of annual production in a normal year.
[b]As a percentage of annual expenditures in a normal year.

price instability due to fluctuations in production would cause supply to decline by an average of 5 percent and the price to rise by an average of 15 percent compared to their levels in a stable situation.

With free trade the average price in the country falls by 8 percent, but its standard deviation declines by 40 percent. As a result, supply rises by an average of more than 1.5 percent. As a result of this increase in domestic supply the level of imports and the trade deficit would be less than two-thirds of their level had producers not responded to the increase in price stability. The total economic gains from trade are much larger if supply response is exhibited, since consumers' gains far outweigh the (actuarial) losses registered by producers.

OPERATION OF BUFFER STOCKS IN AN OPEN ECONOMY

The stabilizing effects of buffer stocks in closed and in open economies should be analyzed against the background of a growing tendency in many nations to isolate their economies from the world market through prohibitive tariffs and to secure domestic stability by means of a comprehensive national stock policy. Measures to encourage domestic food production and self-sufficiency should, according to an often stated argument, reduce the country's dependence on unstable world markets and prevent the import of this instability through trade. The simulation analysis leads, however, to the opposite conclusion: in most cases the closed economy is bound to suffer far greater instability than the open economy, and no reasonable amount of stocks can achieve the same degree of stability as can free trade.

Figure 7–2 parts a and b illustrate the main stabilizing effects of buffer stocks in a closed and an open economy. In Figure 7–2b we can see that even a storage facility large enough to accommodate 15 percent of domestic production can reduce the level of food insecurity only to 7.7 percent. In an open economy the level of food insecurity is less than 6 percent even without any storage facility. Another noteworthy observation is the decrease in the marginal productivity of storage, expressed in terms of the added stability provided by an additional storage capacity and manifested in the figures by the slope of the curves. In an open economy, which is far more stable to begin with, the stabilizing effects of storage are much smaller and the decrease in its marginal productivity much more rapid. Thus, for instance, a storage facility of 6 MMT would reduce the level of price variability by 17 percent in the closed economy but only by 9 percent in the open economy.

Figure 7–3 illustrates the stabilizing effects of buffer stocks under different assumptions on the degree of production instability in the country and in the world. It shows that even when the variability of world production doubles, the degree of food insecurity in the country increases only marginally (from 5.9 percent to 7.3 percent) and there is no noticeable difference in the effect of buffer stocks. By contrast, as the variability of domestic production increases (by 55 percent) the degree of food insecurity more than doubles (to 13.1 percent compared with 5.9 percent in the base case). Still, this level of insecurity is less than half of its level in the closed (and less stable) economy. Interestingly, when domestic production is less stable in an open economy, buffer stocks are *less* effective in enhancing domestic stability in contrast to their effect in the closed economy. A storage facility of 6 MMT would reduce food insecurity by 45 percent in the base case but only by 13 percent with less stable production. This is because trade activities,

Figure 7-2.   Stabilization Effects of Buffer Stocks in a Closed and in an Open Economy.

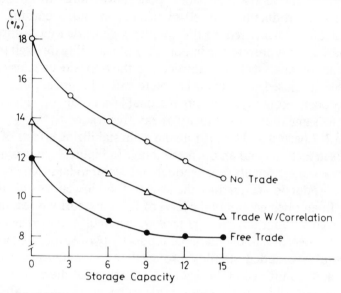

(a) Price Variability.

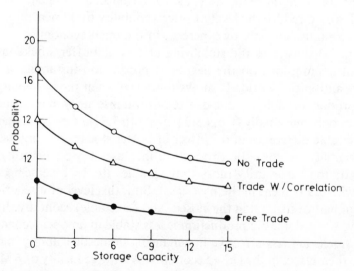

(b) Food Insecurity (10%)

Figure 7-3. Stabilization Effects of Buffer Stocks: Sensitivity Analysis of Production Variability.

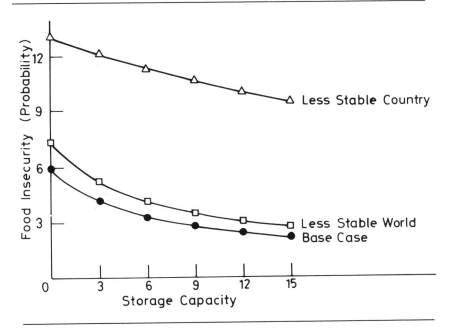

which become more extensive as the variability of domestic production increases, tend to replace the stocks activities.

Even though buffer stocks cannot secure the same level of stability as can free trade and although their stabilizing effect in an open economy is rather small, they can still play an important role in the economy even when free trade is permitted, the reason being their effect on the trade deficit; when domestic production declines, consumption and price can be stabilized either by an increase in imports or by inventory decumulation. Even when there is no restrictive trade policy, buffer stocks can reduce the country's dependence on imports in years of domestic harvest failure and high world prices. At such times, releasing grains from storage can provide the same stability less expensively and with substantial savings in foreign exchange.

Figure 7-4 illustrates the effects of operating buffer stocks of different capacities on the volume of trade. Thus, for instance, with a storage capacity of 15 MMT the average quantity imported is slightly

Figure 7-4. Volume of Trade at Different Levels of Storage Capacity.

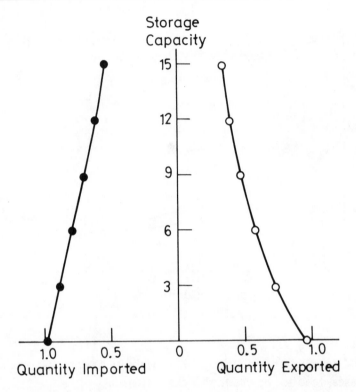

Storage
Capacity

15

12

9

6

3

1.0   0.5   0   0.5   1.0
Quantity Imported   Quantity Exported

(Expressed as a Percentage of Annual Product in a Normal Year)

more than one-half and the average quantity exported is one-third of the quantities traded when there is no storage facility. The large reduction in exports is mainly due to the restrictions imposed on trade when stocks are operated, even in the present context of an entirely open economy. According to these restrictions, described in the second section of this chapter, export is not permitted if at the same time grain is released from storage, since the acquisition of grain for storage must take precedence. Even more important is the contribution of buffer stocks to reduce a large trade deficit. Figure 7-5 illustrates the substantial reduction in the probability that a large trade deficit, in excess of 3 percent of the annual expenditures, will occur. In the base case such a deficit will occur once every ten years in the absence of stocks but only once every twenty years with 15 MMT stocks. If domestic production is less stable this frequency is reduced from once every five years in the absence of stocks to once every ten years with 15 MMT stocks.

Finally, we turn to examine the economic gains or losses from the storage operation and their distribution among consumers, producers, and the government. Table 7-10 presents the gains from a 6 MMT storage operation. In the base case the economic effects of buffer stocks on consumers and producers are very small because the storage operation will only rarely change the market price. In this case both consumers and producers will gain from the storage operations although the gains will now be markedly smaller. The total economic gains are dominated by the amortization costs of the storage facility. When price fluctuations in the domestic and the foreign markets are correlated, the stocks will more frequently be active; the economic gains will then increase and show greater resemblance to the results in the closed economy.

Table 7-11 presents the gains under different assumptions on the variability of production in the country and in the world. It shows that with larger instability in either the country or the world consumers gain from the storage operation while producers lose. By contrast, in the closed economy consumers lose and producers gain from storage, and these losses and gains increase as the variability increases.

Finally, Figure 7-6 shows that when supply responds to a reduction in price instability the stabilizing effects of buffer stocks would be much larger than with risk neutrality. As a result, domestic supply would increase and the country would become 99.1 percent self-sufficient with 15 MMT stocks instead of 98.4 percent self-sufficient in the absence of stocks. The economic gains from a 6 MMT storage operation with risk-averse producers are presented in Table 7-12. It shows that with supply response not only consumers gain from the storage operation but also producers. This is because the increase in output would outweigh the decrease in the average price and producers' earnings and thus also their net profits would rise.

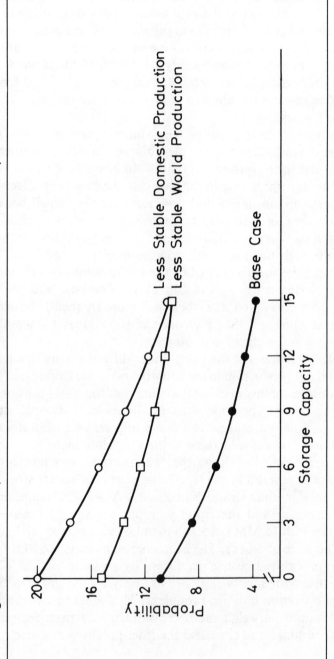

Figure 7-5. Probability that the Trade Deficit Exceeds 3 Percent of Normal Expenditures.

Table 7-10. Expected Annual Gains or Losses due to 6 MMT Buffer Stocks in a Closed and in an Open Economy
(as Percentage of Annual Expenditures in a Normal Year).

| | Economic Gains | | | | |
	Consumers	Producers	Storage Operating Costs	Storage Total Costs[a]	Total Economy
No trade	−.44	+.54	+0.2	−.19	−.09
Free trade					
Base case	+.03	+.02	−.03	−.24	−.19
With correlation	−.24	+.29	−.22	—	−.17
Large country	−.05	+.09	−.03	−.24	−.20
Very large country	−.37	+.44	−.02	−.23	−.16

[a]Including amortization costs.

Table 7-11. Expected Annual Gains or Losses due to 6 MMT Buffer Stocks at Different Levels of Production Variability
(As Percentage of Annual Expenditures in a Normal Year).

	Economic Gains				
	Consumers	Producers	Storage Operating Costs	Storage Total Costs[a]	Total Economy
Free Trade					
Base case	+.03	+.02	-.03	-.24	-.19
Less stable world	+.13	-.09	-.05	-.26	-.22
Less stable country					
No trade	-.61	+.74	+.17	-.04	+.09
Free trade	+.26	-.21	-.02	-.23	-.18

[a]Including amortization costs.

Figure 7-6. Stability and Trade Effects of Buffer Stocks with Supply Response. ■ = Volume of Imports as Percentage of Normal Production. □ = Trade Deficit as Percentage of Normal Expenditures.

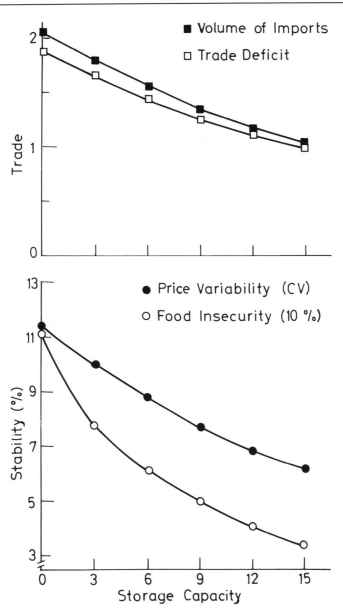

THE SUBSIDY PROGRAM
IN AN OPEN ECONOMY

Internal price programs are designed to solve group-specific problems, problems unique to a specific target group. Thus, for instance, the subsidy program is designed to solve the food security problem, defined as the exposure of low-income people in urban areas to malnutrition and famine. Two issues involving the internal price programs will concern us in this section. First, what are the dimensions of the group-specific problems in an open economy? In other words, to what extent would these programs be necessary if the country were to pursue a policy of free trade? Second, what are the direct and indirect effects of these programs in an open economy?

Let us consider first the subsidy program. As explained in Chapter 5, this program, which allows the low-income consumers to increase their consumption at every level of the market price, effectively raises the country's demand and thus when free trade is permitted, the program would raise its excess demand for imports. Hence, while in a closed economy the program works by shifting consumption from the nonbeneficiary to the beneficiary consumers, in an open economy it works also by supplementing domestic food supply with imported food. Under foreign exchange constraint these imports would have to be at the expense of other programs and other uses. Hence, whereas in the closed economy the program would effectively redistribute more favorably the available food supply among consumers, in the

Table 7-12. Expected Annual Gains or Losses due to 6 MMT Buffer Stocks with Supply Response
(As Percentage of Annual Expenditures in a Normal Year.)

	Economic Gains			
	Consumers	Producers	Storage Costs[a]	Total Economy
Marginal gains from storage	+0.7	+0.3	−0.2	+0.8
Total gains from storage and trade	+8.1	−3.3	−0.2	+4.6

[a]Including amortization costs.

Table 7-13. Effects of the Subsidy Program: Stability, Food Security, and Balance of Payments.

| | Food Security Indicators | | Stability Indicators | | Balance of Payments Indicators | | |
| | Food Insecurity (10%)[a] | Food Insecurity (5%)[a] | Price Variability CV (%) | Farmers' Income Variability CV (%) | Volume of Imports[b] | Average Trade Balance[c] | Probability That Deficit Exceeds 3% of Annual Expenditures, % |
Policy							
No trade							
No subsidy	17	32	18	11	—	—	—
With subsidy	0	5	23	15	—	—	—
Free trade							
No subsidy	6	26	11	6	0.98	−0.23	11
With subsidy	0	0	12	7	1.45	−0.78	11

[a]Probability that the quantity consumed by the urban poor falls by more than 10 (or 5) percent below their normal consumption.
[b]As percentage of annual production in a normal year.
[c]As percentage of annual expenditures in a normal year.

open economy it would also involve a redistribution of resources between consumption and other uses; for example, the foreign exchange resources set aside for food imports could be allocated instead to investments. At the same time, however, shifting part of the extra demand created by the program to foreign markets moderates the indirect effects of the program on the market price and thus on other consumers and on producers.

Table 7-13 presents the main effects of the subsidy program in the closed and the open economies. A number of things stand out. First, in the open economy the dimensions of the food security problem are much smaller. Thus, for instance, the probability that the consumption of the urban poor falls by more than 10 percent below their normal consumption is 17 percent in the closed economy but only 6 percent in the open economy.

Second, if this level of food security is still considered unacceptable (and noting that, even with free trade, once every four years consumption of the urban poor falls by more than 5 percent below normal) a special subsidy program may still be necessary. The simulation results demonstrate that with a subsidy program, food insecurity can be eliminated altogether.[3] Third, the variability of the market price, which in the closed economy rises by 28 percent as an effect of the subsidy program rises only by 9 percent in the open economy. Fourth, the added security provided by the subsidy program in the open economy would lead to an increase of 85 percent in the average volume of imports and an almost threefold increase in the average trade deficit.

In the open economy only a small part of the extra consumption of the urban poor permitted by the subsidy program represents consumption foregone by the other consumer groups and the rest comes

Table 7-14. Economic Gains and Losses from the Subsidy Program
(As a Percentage of Annual Expenditures in a Normal Year).

Economic Sector	Closed Economy	Open Economy
Beneficiary consumers	+ 1.53	+ 1.17
Nonbeneficiary consumers	− 3.00	− 0.66
Producers	+ 4.30	+ 0.94
Government	− 2.96	− 1.48
Total economy	− 0.13	− 0.03

from imports. As a result the income transfers associated with the redistribution of consumption are much smaller in the open economy, as shown in Table 7-14 (noting, however, that the analysis is carried out in a partial equilibrium framework). The gains of the beneficiary consumers in the open economy are not much smaller than their gains in the closed economy while the losses of the nonbeneficiary consumers in the open economy are only one-fifth of their losses in the closed economy. This is because the beneficiary consumers continue to enjoy the subsidized price even when the market price is determined by the import price. In that case, however, the program is not affecting the price, the nonbeneficiary consumers, or the producers. Government expenses on the program in the open economy are one-half of those in the closed economy. The total economic losses are so small that they can be disregarded in assessing the desirability of the program.

Also to be considered are the gains from trade, when a subsidy program is effective. These gains or losses, presented in Table 7-15, represent mainly a reduction in the gains or the losses from the subsidy program. The large gains of the nonbeneficiary consumers are due to the shift of the extra demand created by the program to foreign markets instead of taxing their own consumption. The losses of producers reflect a reduction in their gains from the subsidy program as an effect of free trade. Government gains reflect its savings on the subsidy payments. Governments committed to a subsidy program thus have a strong incentive to permit free trade.

MULTIPLE POLICY COMBINATIONS

Different policy combinations have different effects on stability, food security, income distribution, and balance of payments. The policies considered here are the solid subsidy program, the floor price support program, the government procurement program, and buffer stocks. (See Table 7-16.) The most noteworthy observation is the strong stabilizing effect of free trade, which provides a level of food security and price stability that no internal program or combination of programs can match. In the open economy and when the relevant policy combinations are in operation food insecurity is entirely eliminated; the variability of the price is reduced by 40 to 45 percent; the variability in farmers' income is cut by half. However, whether

Table 7-15. Economic Gains and Losses from Trade
(As a Percentage of Annual Expenditures in a Normal Year).

Economic Sector	No Subsidy Program	With Subsidy Program
Beneficiary consumers	0.01	−0.36
Nonbeneficiary consumers	0.14	+2.50
Producers	0.03	−3.33
Government	0.00	+1.48
Total economy	0.18	+0.29

free trade is a viable option for the country politically, economically, or otherwise depends on two factors: one is the effect it has on the balance of payments, taken together with the ability of the country to mobilize the foreign exchange needed, and the other is the effect it has on income distribution. The consequences to the balance of payments are presented in Table 7-16. Whether the country can finance such a deficit depends on its overall foreign exchange position. This question has important implications for the country's trade policies, as well as for international food aid programs, which will be discussed later. Table 7-17 presents the total gains from the different policy combinations (which also include, in the case of the open economy, the gains from trade) and their distribution among consumers, producers, and the government. The total gains are very small compared with the income transfers involved. The beneficiary consumers gain under all policy combinations, since all of them include a subsidy program. For the same reason the nonbeneficiary consumers lose, although their losses are considerably smaller in the open economy. Notice, however, that under the government procurement program their losses are 2.5 times larger than under the other policy options. Producers gain from these policies, largely on account of the subsidy program, but their gains are much smaller in the open economy. This may explain why producers are often reluctant to accept free trade and sometimes strongly oppose it. Their reluctance, however, is not because of the negative effects that trade would have on their welfare. In a self-sufficient country, which by definition has neither an advantage nor a disadvantage in the production of foodgrains, free trade itself will be beneficial to the farmers, as seen earlier in this chapter. Their losses from trade in the present

Table 7-16. Stability, Food Security, and Balance of Payments Effects of Different Policy Combinations.

Policy Combination	Food Insecurity (5%)	Stability		Balance of Payments	
		Price Variability, CV (%)	Farmers' Income Variability, CV (%)	Volume of Imports[a]	Balance of Trade[b]
Subsidy + 6 MMT stocks					
No trade	3.1	18	11	0	0
Free trade	0	10	5	1.2	−0.8
Subsidy + support price + 6 MMT stocks					
No trade	3.1	18		0	0
Free trade	0	10	5	1.2	−0.8
Subsidy + government procurement + 6 MMT stocks					
No trade	2.6	15	9	0	0
Free trade	0	9	5	1.2	−0.6

[a]Expressed as a percentage of annual production in a normal year.
[b]Expressed as a percentage of annual expenditures in a normal year.

Table 7-17. Economic Gains and Losses from Different Policy Combinations (as Percentage of Annual Expenditures in a Normal Year).

Policy Combination / Economic Sector	Beneficiary Consumers	Nonbeneficiary Consumers	Producers	Government[a]	Total Economy
Subsidy + 6 MMT stocks					
No trade	+1.01	-2.53	+3.72	-2.39	-0.19
Free trade	+0.95	-0.25	+0.66	-1.41	-0.05
Subsidy + support price + 6 MMT stocks					
No trade	+1.01	-2.53	—	—	-0.12
Free trade	+0.95	-0.25	+1.25	-2.00	-0.05
Subsidy + government procurement + 6 MMT stocks					
No trade	+0.67	-2.85	+4.28	-2.35	-0.25
Free trade	+0.77	-0.60	+1.19	-1.45	-0.09

[a]Including $3.5 annual amortization costs per ton capacity.

context are only a *reduction in the gains* they would obtain from the other policies. The government saves substantially on expenses associated with the programs, and these savings may provide yet another incentive for free trade.

SUMMARY AND CONCLUSIONS

The static theory of international trade emphasizes the role of trade in increasing a country's resources. The theory of trade policies emphasizes the country's ability to shift its internal disequilibria to its trading partners via trade. In this chapter we have examined yet another aspect of international trade. In a world characterized by substantial and continuous aberrations, free trade allows the country to moderate the adjustments made necessary by the instability in its supply and demand. Supply problems in years of crop failure can be avoided via compensating imports; sharp falls in price in years of plentiful harvest can be moderated via exports.

In this chapter the theoretical analysis of the previous chapter is extended to a more complex and thus more realistic model of a country. It considers the self-sufficient country as well as the generally importing and the generally exporting countries; the small country and the large ones, whose excess supply or demand affects the world price. The simulation analysis confirms that free trade can offer a highly efficient outlet for internal adjustments. Trade enables the country to reduce its price variability by 40 percent and its food insecurity (at the 10 percent level) by 65 percent. If free trade is allowed, considerable trade flows would be created as a result of the domestic and foreign instability, and through these avenues the internal adjustment problems would be shipped abroad. Even the self-sufficient country, which by definition has neither advantage nor disadvantage in grain production, would be actively engaged in trade. For this country the volume of exports and imports, during periods that grain was imported or exported, would be more than 4 percent of the normal annual expenditures on these products. Because of their instability the exporting and importing countries would trade far more than they would have if domestic and foreign production were completely stable.

The stabilizing effects of free trade appear to be much more substantial and perhaps also more significant than the economic gains on which the static trade theory concentrates. The total gains from trade for the self-sufficient small country (the base case) are less than one-fifth of one percent of annual expenditures in a normal year. However, trade would have a considerable impact on the income distribution, although this impact depends very much on the specific country case. Thus for instance, in the small self-sufficient country both consumers and producers would enjoy gains, albeit small, from trade; if the country is very large producers would have substantial losses and consumers substantial gains.

For both exporting and importing countries the gains from trade would be more than 2.5 times larger under instability than under stable conditions of production. The income distribution effects, normally very substantial in these countries, would be even larger under unstable conditions.

The ability of the country to shift its internal adjustments to other countries through trade leads in turn to very significant changes in the role and effects of its domestic policies. Thus, for instance, no reasonable amount of storage can provide the same level of food security as that secured by free trade, and the stabilizing effects of buffer stocks are markedly smaller in an open than in a closed economy. Hence, in considering buffer stocks and trade liberalization as alternative ways of promoting stability, the latter is revealed to be by far the more efficient.

Free trade also changes the effects of the subsidy program. Whereas in a closed economy the program works by shifting food consumption from one consumer group to another, in an open economy, once every four years the urban poor are likely to suffer a supplied from abroad. If the subsidy program is implemented in the open economy, the volume of imports increases by 50 percent and the trade deficit of the food sector more than triples. At the same time, however, in the open economy the program does not involve the massive income transfers from the nonbeneficiary consumers or the large government fiscal costs that exist in the closed economy.

The stabilizing effects of free trade, substantial though they are, do not dispel the need for a subsidy program. Even in the open economy, once every four years the urban poor are likely to suffer a drop in their consumption in excess of 5 percent of their normal consumption. Once every fifteen years the drop will be in excess of 10 percent of their normal consumption. If this level of food insecurity is regarded as intolerable a subsidy program would still be necessary; food insecurity can then be eliminated altogether.

These results suggest that domestic policies and free trade should not be thought of as two competing alternatives, but rather as complementing policies. The country by applying an appropriate combination of trade and domestic programs can thus secure its stabilization goals in the most efficient way.

NOTES

1. Normal price is defined as the *world's* stable prices. Note that for the non-self-sufficient country this price may differ from the country's stable price.
2. As an illustration consider the case in which domestic production is completely stable and the only source of instability is in the foreign price. Obviously, trade will in this case introduce an element of instability into the domestic market.
3. The subsidy program considered in the simulation analysis is the solid subsidy, which in the closed economy provides only partial security. See Chapter 5 for details of this program.

8 TRADE POLICIES AND DOMESTIC STABILITY

The long debate on trade policies with respect to agricultural products often reveals two diametrically opposed positions. One views the country's relative advantage as the centerpiece of its development and trade policy and thus supports trade liberalization and the preference of export or cash cropping. The other emphasizes the scarcity of foreign exchange, the exposure of the domestic market via trade to the instability of foreign markets, and the political vulnerability resulting from excessive dependence on food imports as reasons for promoting self-sufficiency and increasing government intervention to restrict trade.

Often missing in this debate are several important considerations. Significantly, even in a country that is normally self-sufficient free trade can play an important stabilizing role. In the previous chapter it was shown that with free trade, the country under consideration (which was assumed to be self-sufficient) could reduce its domestic price variability by 40 percent and its food insecurity by 65 percent. This process involved creating considerable trade flows both into and out of the country as vehicles for moderating temporary aberrations in supply or demand. Hence, self-sufficiency should not be taken to mean the elimination of all trade, nor can prohibitive trade restrictions be justified without taking into consideration the resulting instability of these measures.

From a practical point of view, even countries that place self-sufficiency at the center of their national development are often forced to use the trade outlet to supplement domestic supply in years of crop failure or to get rid of excesses in years of bumper crops. In India, for instance, self-sufficiency and a gradual elimination of the dependence on imports have long been the cornerstone of the government food policy. Whenever necessary, however, the government allowed imports on foodgrain to cover existing shortages. In the importing countries in the ASEAN region, self-sufficiency in rice is perhaps the most cherished government goal, and yet these countries have regular recourse to foreign trade for supplementing domestic production. In many other countries in Asia, Africa, the Middle East, and Latin America, fluctuations in domestic production are frequently countered by compensating movements of import or export that moderate the fluctuations in the domestic price and supply (see chapter 3 for more details). These practices are by no means unique to the developing countries; they are the centerpiece of the Common Agricultural Policy (CAP) of the EEC. (We shall return to this policy later on.)

The major problem with the conventional analysis of trade and agricultural policies is that it is essentially static; it lacks the elements relevant to a stochastic and dynamic world. In such a world self-sufficiency does not mean that the country should opt for supplying its own needs at all times, and in fact a rigid policy that prohibits all trade would badly serve the country's interests.

The purpose of this chapter is to analyze trade policies in agricultural food products (mostly with reference to foodgrains) in a nondeterministic world, where both domestic production and world price are subject to random and unpredictable fluctuations. We consider three types of trade policies: a conventional ad-valorem tariff, levied on imports or exports or both; a form of trade restriction that uses export tariffs as a means of preventing domestic shortages and import tariffs as a means of avoiding critical falls in price; and a policy of variable levies designed to stabilize the domestic market via trade.

Variable levies have a long history in trade policy; they were employed in England (under the Corn Law) and in France more than 150 years ago. Today they are the centerpiece of the CAP of the EEC. Their objective is to maintain stable prices within the community by providing protection against low world prices via sliding-scale import levies and by preventing sharp falls in domestic prices by assuring the exports of any excesses via sliding-scale export subsidies. When surplus production occurs it is acquired and stored for future disposition or exported with whatever subsidy is needed to sell it abroad. For deficit products, the main import controls are levies that vary according to the difference between the guaranteed target or threshold price and the world market price (CIF Europe). Sampson and Snape (1981) analyzed the quantitative significance of variable levies and demonstrated that in a single year (1977) the range of variation for the tariff rates on grain (the percentage difference between the maximum and the minimum rates) was 68 percent for hard wheat, 53 percent for soft wheat, 225 percent for barley, and 145 percent for corn. High guaranteed farm prices, which are maintained within the community by government intervention and import controls, secure a high degree of self-sufficiency in grains, dairy products, meats, fruits, and vegetables.

In the developing countries, the main role of variable levies is to assure a stable flow of supply in the food-deficit countries and a stable price in the exporting countries. In a food-deficit country the government often purchases foodgrains abroad at the high world prices to supplement domestic supply and sells them to domestic consumers at a lower price. Government losses on these sales form an effective subsidy on imports, which varies according to the difference between the world price and the domestic target price. We can thus term this policy a "stabilizing trade policy."

The gains or losses from this policy are hard to assess, and the conventional measure of welfare losses associated with trade intervention is sometimes inappropriate. The overriding concern of governments in most less developed countries is the security of food supply. They cannot afford, for instance, unrestricted exports of basic foodstuffs in times of a favorable world market and must give precedence to domestic demand. William Corden once commented, in this connection, that international trade theory does not even recognize the concern over food security, yet gains from free trade can be reaped only by the living, not by the dead. The scope of this book will not permit a detailed consideration of the operation and various effects of the different trade policies; I will therefore only highlight the main conclusions.

TRADE POLICIES:
MODEL, DATA, AND PARAMETERS

We consider several types of trade policies, the most important of which are fixed ad-valorem tariff and variable levies. The ad-valorem tariff can be imposed on imports or exports or both. The variable levies policy stabilizes the domestic market by means of a tax-cum-subsidy system, which is readjusted from year to year according to the specific domestic and world prices. The principles of the policy, in the form considered here, are as follows: in a year of domestic crop failure and high world price, the government subsidizes imports or directly purchases the product in the world market and sells it in the domestic market at a loss, thereby lowering the domestic price to the prespecified target price. In a year of domestic bumper crops and high world prices, the government taxes exports in order to prevent the domestic price from rising to the high levels of the world price. The policy of complete stabilization via foreign trade which we have considered in Chapter 6 is a special case of the variable levies policy, which, in general, is designed to secure only partial stabilization. The specific decision rules of the variable levies policy for imports and exports are illustrated in Figures 8-1 and 8-2, where DD is the market schedule and TT is the target schedule. If the import price is P_1^I the target price would be P_1^T and a subsidy of $(P_1^I - P_1^T)$ is given to each unit of imports to ensure that the quantity Q_1^T will be available in the domestic market. If the import price is P_2^I, the target price will be P_2^T and a tariff $(P_2^T - P_2^I)$ is imposed on imports. In Figure 8-2 if the export price is P_2^X, the target price will be P_2^T and a subsidy of $(P_2^T - P_2^X)$ will be given to exports. If the export price is P_1^X, the target price will be P_1^T and a tax of $(P_1^X - P_1^T)$ is imposed on all exports.

The economic gains from the variable levies policy for each sector depend on the extent to which the policy alters the price that is relevant for that sector. It depends also on the type of internal price policy that is in effect, as will now be shown. Figure 8-3 illustrates the gains from an import subsidy when no internal price program is in effect. If P_1^I is the free market import price then P_1^T would be the subsidized import price. Consumers' gains from the policy are given by the shaded area A and producers' losses by the area $(A + B)$. Government subsidy payments are given by the area C. An additional quantity $(Q_2 - Q_1)$ is imported due to the policy.

Figure 8-4 illustrates the *marginal* gains from an import subsidy to eligible consumers when an internal subsidy program is in effect. With free trade, the import price is P^I and the subsidized price effective for the beneficiary consumers is P_S^I. With an import subsidy the market price would be reduced to P^T and the subsidized price to P_S^T. The effective reduction in price for the beneficiary consumers would therefore be from P_S^I to P_S^T, and their gains from the *import subsidy* (given that a subsidy program is in effect) would be given by the area

Figure 8-1.   Stabilizing Trade Policy: Import Decision Rules.

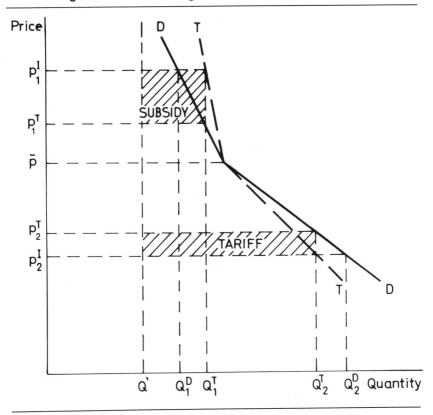

$(A + B)$. If an import subsidy is in effect, their (*marginal*) gains from a *domestic subsidy program* is given by the shaded area A. For comparison, the gains of the beneficiary consumers from the domestic subsidy program under free trade is given by the area C. The subsidy payments involved in the domestic subsidy program under free trade is given by the area $(C + E)$, whereas if an import subsidy is already in effect these payments would be $(A + D)$.

The specific parameters of the models are those detailed in the previous chapters, with the following additions that define the trade policies:

1. We consider three rates of fixed ad-valorem tariff: 10, 15, and 20 percent of the value.

2. A policy of *restricted trade* is defined as a policy in which an ad-valorem tariff of 10 percent is imposed on all imports and exports.

Figure 8-2. Stabilization Trade Policy: Export Decision Rules.

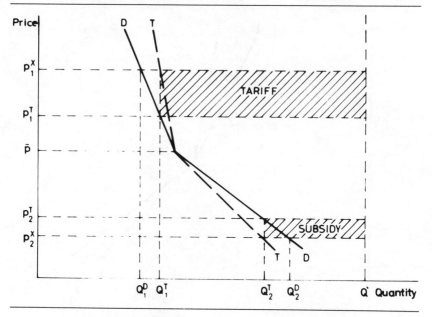

Figure 8-3. Gains and Losses from the Stabilizing Trade Policy: Subsidy to Imports.

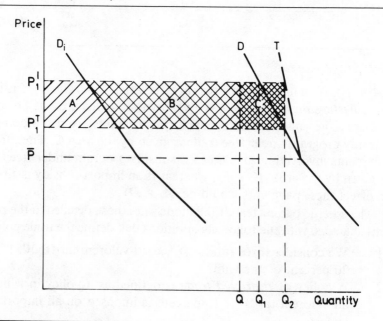

Figure 8-4. Marginal Gains from Stabilizing Trade Policy.

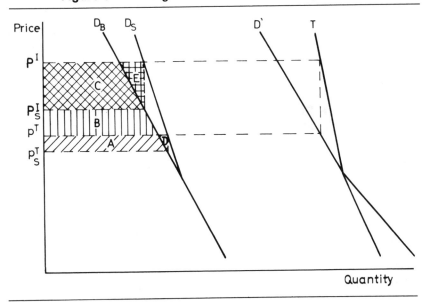

3. The policy of variable levies is determined by the elasticities of the target demand schedule. Three levels of intensity at which this policy can raise domestic stability through trade are "partial," "solid," and "complete" stabilizing trade. (These terms should not be confused with the terms "partial," "solid," and "complete" food security used to describe the intensity of the internal subsidy program.) Table 8-1 summarizes the price

Table 8-1. Price Elasticities of Demand with Policies for Stabilizing Trade
(Calculated at P = 100).

Policy	Left Segment P > 100	Right Segment P < 100
Total demand		
Without internal subsidy	0.36	0.43
With solid food security internal subsidy	0.225	0.43
Target demand		
Partial stabilizing trade	0.20	0.30
Solid stabilizing trade	0.10	0.15
Complete stabilizing trade	0.00	0.00

elasticities of the original demand curve with and without an internal subsidy program (assuming that the solid food security program is implemented) and the elasticities of the target schedules corresponding to the three policies for stabilizing trade.

TRADE POLICIES IN A SELF-SUFFICIENT COUNTRY

Since free trade helps to increase stability in the country, any restrictions on trade through import or export tariffs will only reduce domestic stability. This reduction in stability represents another burden on the economy resulting from tariffs, and this is added to the conventional burden revealed in a comparative static analysis and represented by the consumers' and producers' welfare losses. The former can only be revealed in a stochastic world, however. Figure 8–5 illustrates the rising instability associated with rising tariff rates.

Consumers would gain and producers lose from a tariff on exports, and conversely with respect to a tariff on imports. The end result depends largely on the price elasticity of demand in the country and the probability distribution of the world price. If demands in the country and in the world become less elastic at smaller quantities, as assumed in the simulation experiments, then consumers may lose and producers gain from the trade restrictions. Noteworthy also is the effect on the government tax revenues: in a static world, whether the government gains or loses from increasing the tariff rates depends solely on the price elasticity of demand. In a stochastic world it would depend also on the probability distributions of the country's production and the world price. In the country under consideration the simulation experiments show that the government would *lose* from increasing the tariff rates; its revenues would be reduced to half their value as the rate has risen from 10 to 20 percent. These effects of an import tax are presented in Table 8–2.

The policy of stabilizing trade through variable levies is the antithesis of the ad-valorem tax policy. Whereas the latter is an example of trade-restricting policy that reduces domestic stability, the former represents the country's potential for increasing domestic stability via trade. Indeed, with appropriate levels of variable levies the country can achieve any degree of domestic stability desired. The burden

Figure 8-5. Instability Consequences of Different Tariff Rates.

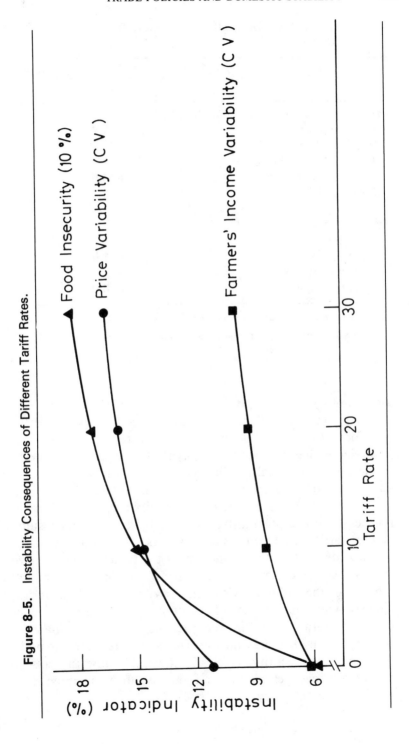

Table 8-2. Main Effects of Import Tax in a Self-Sufficient
Country.

	Tariff Rate	
	10%	*20%*
Percentage change		
Average price[a]	+ 1.7	+ 2.5
Price variability[a]	+ 17.0	+ 26.8
Average farmers' income[a]	+ 1.6	+ 2.3
Farmers' income variability[a]	+ 14.5	+ 25.8
Balance of Trade[b]	+ 0.7	+ 1.0
Economic gains and losses[b]		
Consumers	− 1.70	− 2.42
Producers	+ 1.63	+ 2.33
Government	+ 0.04	+ 0.02
Total Economy	− 0.03	− 0.07

[a]Percentage change relative to the level in free trade.

[b]Expressed as percentage of annual expenditures in a normal year.

associated with the policy—its opportunity cost—is revealed, however, in the balance of payments; this policy effectively transforms the internal price and supply instability into an instability in foreign exchange receipts and payments. The ability of the country to increase its internal stability via trade depends, therefore, on its ability to command the necessary foreign exchange.

Table 8-3 summarizes the main stability effects of different trade policies. As noted previously, the restricted-trade policy assumes a 10 percent tariff on all imports and exports. The solid stabilizing trade policy is defined by the elasticities of the target demand curve. The results clearly illustrate the stabilizing power of free trade and even more so of the variable levies policy. With solid stabilizing trade the country would be able to reduce its price variability by 55 percent compared with the level in free trade and entirely eliminate food insecurity. Figure 8-6 presents the effects of different trade policies on domestic food security. It clearly illustrates how the country can reduce and even eliminate its food insecurity by intensifying the stabilizing trade policy.

Table 8-3. Stabilizing Effects of Trade Policies.

	No Trade	Restricted Trade	Free Trade	Solid Stabilizing Trade
Price variability, CV (%)	18	16	11	5
Probability that price falls by more than 20 percent below normal price	11	7	2	0
Food insecurity (10%)	17	15	6	0
Variability of farmers' income, CV (%)	11	8	6	5

Thus far we have assumed that the country is small, that it has no effect on the world price. If the country is large, however, its excess demand or supply affects not only the level of the world price but also its variability. As a consequence the stabilizing effects of trade and of the variable levies would be somewhat weaker in the large than in the small country. Figure 8-7 demonstrates the effects of different trade policies on the domestic price variability in the small, large,[1] and very large[2] countries. It shows that with trade, the level of instability would be roughly 5 percent higher in the large and 15 percent higher in the very large country compared with its level in the small country. However, even the very large country can achieve complete stability though appropriate variable levies.

As the large country transfers its internal adjustment problems associated with instability to its trading partners, it will magnify their instability. Thus, for instance, if the country were to stabilize its domestic markets totally, via the complete stabilizing trade policy, it would cause the variability of the world price to rise by 7 percent if the country is large and by as much as 35 percent if the country is very large. Figure 8-8 demonstrates the effect of trade policies in the large and the very large countries on the variability of the world price. It shows that with free trade not only the country but also the world would enjoy greater price stability. However, as the country increasingly stabilizes its own domestic market via trade and appropriate tariffs and subsidies for imports and exports, the world

Figure 8-6.   Food Insecurity with Different Trade Policies.

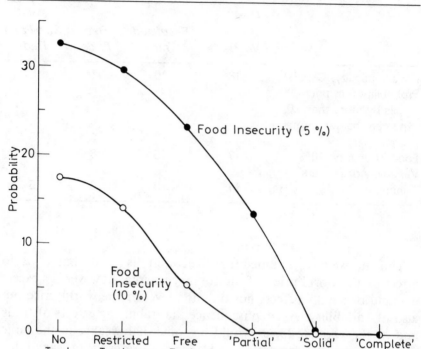

market becomes increasingly unstable. Whether the country would be able to achieve its stabilization goals via this trade policy thus depends also on whether its trading partners would be willing to accept these consequences of the policy. (See also Bale and Lutz 1979 for an analysis of the effects of other trade intervention policies on international price stability.)

The stabilizing trade policy would substantially intensify the country's import and export activities. With the solid stabilizing trade, for instance, the volume of imports and exports would more than double and the trade deficit almost quadruple. The process by which domestic instability is traded off against a larger volume of imports through the trade policies is displayed in Figure 8–9.

Even more important, however, is the effect of the policy on the stability of foreign exchange receipts and payments. With imperfect

Figure 8-7. Variability of Country Price with Different Trade Policies.

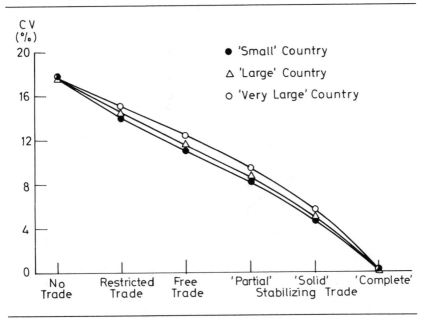

capital markets, the need to draw on large holdings of foreign exchange or on large loans in order to meet extreme situations may limit the country's ability to supplement its supply via trade. Under the solid trade policy, for example, the trade deficit on account of foodgrain imports would exceed the critical level (assumed to be 3 percent of normal expenditures) once every six years, compared with once every ten years under free trade. This proves again that foreign exchange constraints or a limited access to the international financial markets may be severely detrimental to the country's ability to secure a stable flow of supply via trade.

In addition to its stabilizing and balance of payments effects, the trade policy would also have significant effects on the economy's welfare and income distribution. These effects are summarized in Table 8-4, which presents the *total* gains or losses from the policy (calculated against the closed economy case) as well as its *marginal* gains or losses (calculated against the free trade case). The table shows that the stabilizing trade policy would involve considerable

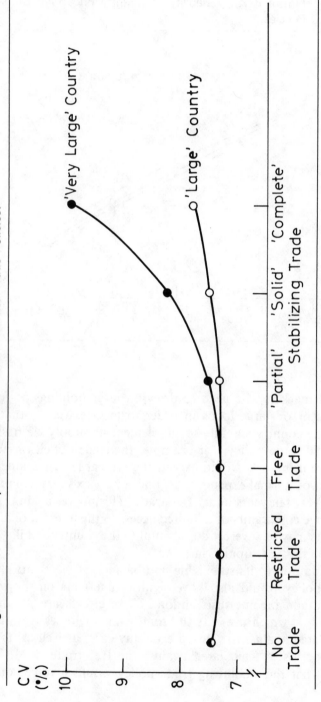

Figure 8-8. Variability of World Price with Different Trade Policies.

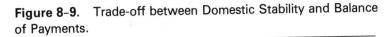

Figure 8-9. Trade-off between Domestic Stability and Balance of Payments.

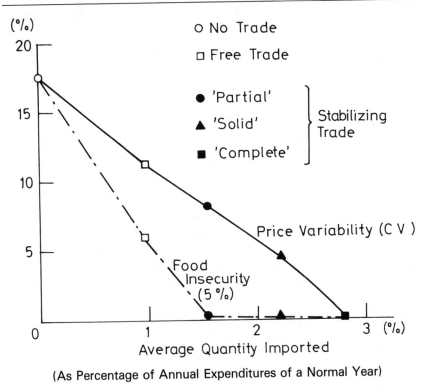

(As Percentage of Annual Expenditures of a Normal Year)

changes in income distribution and a substantial burden on the fiscal budget. Consumers would gain and producers lose from a trade policy that reduces price fluctuations originating mostly from the domestic production. As a result of the government's net subsidy payments, the net *marginal* gains to the private sector (consumers and producers) due to the policy would be turned into a net loss to the economy at large.

Figure 8-10 presents the cost effectiveness of the various trade policies in reducing the domestic price variability. Several things stand out. First, consumers' gains and producers' losses from the stabilizing trade policy (which include also their gains from trade) would start to decline beyond a certain level of intensity of the policy.

Table 8-4. Expected Gains and Losses from Trade Policy
(As Percentage of Annual Expenditures in a Normal Year).

| | Total Gains | | Marginal Gains |
	Free Trade	Solid Stabilizing Trade	Solid Stabilizing Trade
Consumers	0.15	0.95	0.80
Producers	0.03	− 0.54	− 0.57
Government	0.00	− 0.37	− 0.37
Total economy	0.18	+ 0.04	− 0.14

Thus, for instance, consumers' gains and producers' losses from the complete stabilizing trade policy would be, respectively, 11 and 70 percent smaller than their gains and losses from the partial trade policy. The gains of the private sector would monotonically increase with trade and the stabilizing trade policies, but government losses on account of the import and export subsidy payments would rise more rapidly, turning the economy's net gains from free trade into a net loss from the complete stabilizing trade.

We conducted sensititivity analyses in order to examine the robustness of the results with respect to the assumed structure of the model. Table 8–5 summarizes the outcome of some of these analyses. It shows that while some of the trends would be accentuated under larger variability in either the country or the world, the main conclusions emerging from the base case analysis would by and large remain unchanged.

Finally, Table 8–6 summarizes the effects of the partial stabilizing trade policies when risk-averse producers respond to the greater stability under the policy by increasing their output. It shows that, with the parameter values assumed in our model, despite the slight decrease in the average price, the larger reduction in its variability would induce producers to increase their output and the country would become *more* self-sufficient than before. As a result, the increase in imports and in the trade deficit associated with the stabilization policy would be smaller than if producers were risk-neutral. The ensuing increase in output would also secure substantial economic gains to consumers, and these would outweigh the losses of producers as an effect of the price decrease. The economy as a whole

Figure 8-10. Total Costs and Benefits by Economic Sector of Price Stabilization with Different Trade Policies.

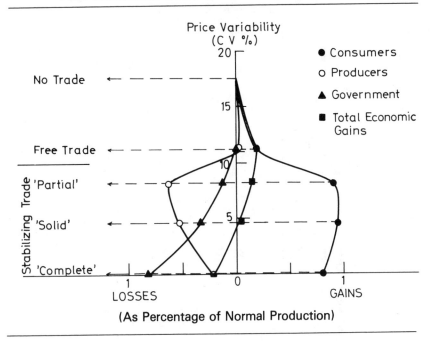

(As Percentage of Normal Production)

would now gain from the trade policy, whereas under risk neutrality it would have lost.

EXPORTING AND IMPORTING COUNTRIES

The main purpose of trade restrictions in an exporting country is to lower food prices to the urban population. Producers in the rural sector suffer considerable losses as a result of these restrictions that lower the price on their produce and thus also depress their income. To a large extent this policy, which is quite common in exporting developing countries, amounts to an income transfer from producers in the rural sector to consumers in the urban sector, despite the fact that in many of these countries the average income of the latter is higher than that of the former. In contrast to these policies we consider also a policy of stabilizing trade, which in an exporting country would have the effect of promoting exports by assuring a stable

Table 8-5. Effects of Partial Stabilizing Trade Policy: Sensitivity Analysis.

	Base Case	Country-World Correlation[a]	Adaptive Expectations	Less Stable Country[b]	Less Stable World[b]
Price variability, CV (%)	8	10	8	9	9
Food insecurity (5%)	14	22	14	15	17
Variability of farmers' income, CV (%)	5	5	5	6	7
Quantity imported[b]	1.6	1.3	1.7	1.7	3.1
Quantity exported[b]	1.3	0.8	1.4	1.5	2.6
Balance of payments[c]	−0.6	−0.8	−0.7	−0.4	−1.2
Trade subsidy net payments[c]	0.1	0.2	0.1	0.1	0.3

[a]A correlation coefficient (R^2) of 0.3 between the country's and the world's productions.

[b]Percentage of normal production.

[c]Percentage of normal expenditures.

Table 8-6. Effects of Partial Stabilizing Trade Policy: Supply Response.

	Free Trade	Partial Stabilizing Trade
Country's Price		
Mean	105	102
CV (%)	11	8
Quantity available for consumption		
Mean	98	99
CV (%)	4	3
Quantity imported[a]	2.1	2.6
Balance of trade[b]	−1.9	−2.4
Economic gains from policy[b]		
Consumers	. . .	+2.6
Producers	. . .	−1.3
Government	. . .	−0.2
Total economy	. . .	+1.1

[a]Percentage of normal production.

[b]Percentage of normal expenditures.

price to producers in the face of fluctuating world prices through appropriate restitution payments.

In the importing country the purpose of trade restrictions is to prevent cheap imports from dumping the domestic market and hurting domestic producers. The resulting economic losses that the country would suffer are regarded by many governments as insurance payments to assure a greater degree of self-sufficiency in food supply.

Tariffs

In this framework we consider only the effects of an ad-valorem export tax in an exporting country. Table 8-7 summarizes the main effects of this tax. The results indicate that for the country under consideration a 20 percent export tax would cause a reduction in the quantity exported by as much as 60 percent. This quantity would be diverted to the domestic market and thus raise domestic supply by

Table 8-7. Main Effects of Export Tax in an Exporting Country.

	Tariff Rate	
	10%	*20%*
Rates of change, %		
Price[a]	−9.3	−15.1
Domestic Supply	+2.4	+4.7
Farmers' income[a]	−10.8	−18.1
Price instability[a]	+6.7	+51.7
Quantity exported	−36.1	−60.3
Trade surplus	−36.3	−60.5
Economic Gains or Losses[b]		
Consumers	+7.0	+11.8
Producers	−13.1	−20.1
Government	0.8	1.0
Total economy	−5.8	−7.3

[a]Rate of change relative to the level in free trade.

[b]Expressed as percentage of annual expenditures in a 'normal' year.

close to 5 percent and lower domestic price by 15 percent against their level in free trade. These effects are illustrated in Figure 8-11.

Equally significant is the effect of this policy on domestic stability. With a 20 percent export tax, price variability would increase by more than 50 percent and the variability of supply by 30 percent. As for the variability of farmers' income, low tax rates would bring it down from its level under free trade because the changes in domestic production would be compensated by changes in the opposite direction in the price. At higher tax rates farmers' income would become less stable as the stabilizing effects of trade would diminish. These effects are illustrated in Figure 8-12.

Trade Restrictions

The purpose of this policy is to prevent sharp falls in price or in the quantity available for consumption due to fluctuations abroad. In the

Figure 8-11.   Effects of Ad-Valorem Export Tax on the Level of Price, Supply, and Farmers' Income (as Percentage of Their Level in a Normal Year).

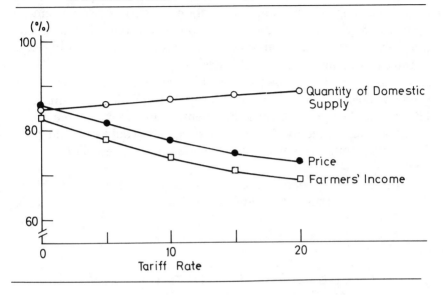

Figure 8-12.   Instability Effect of Ad-Valorem Export Tax in an Exporting Country.

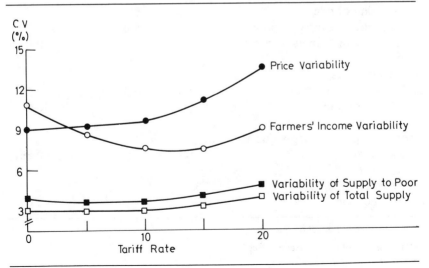

importing country the policy would have the meaning of an antidumping policy. It does not allow the import price in any given year to lower the market price below a critical level, assumed to be 95 percent of its long-run average. There is no intervention to restrict price movement up to that level. The instrument for enforcing this restriction is an import levy that may vary from year to year according to the world price.

Table 8-8 summarizes the main economic effects of this policy in an importing country. It shows that with these restrictions the country would be able to reduce its price and supply instability by as much as 13 percent. At the same time the quantity imported and the trade deficit would decline by 7 percent. Consumers would lose and producers gain from this constraint, while the tax revenues will be rather small.

In the exporting country the purpose of this policy is to stabilize the flow of domestic supply and in particular to prevent sharp falls

Table 8-8. Effects of Stabilizing Trade Restrictions in an Importing Country.

	Free Trade	Stabilizing Import Restrictions
Stability indicators, CV (%)		
Variability of price	6.5	5.7
Variability of supply to poor	4.5	4.0
Variability of farmers' income	10.3	9.6
Trade indicators		
Quantity imported[a]	10.3	9.6
Balance of trade[b]	11.7	10.9
Economic gains or losses due to policy[b]		
Consumers		−0.85
Producers		+0.78
Government		+0.07
Total economy		0.00

[a]Percentage of normal production.

[b]Percentage of normal expenditures.

below a certain critical level. The government intervenes to restrict exports and divert certain quantities to the local market whenever the quantity available for domestic consumption falls by more than 5 percent below its normal level. An export tax, which may vary from year to year, is imposed to prevent any export in excess of the critical amount. Table 8-9 summarizes the main economic effects in the exporting country. It shows that with this tax the government would be able to reduce domestic instability by 15 to 20 percent but at the expense of a reduction in the trade balance by 6 percent. Consumers would gain and producers lose from these restrictions on exports.

Stabilizing Trade Policies

In the exporting country the stabilizing trade policy would have the effect of variable export subsidies aimed at assuring the exports of

Table 8-9. Effects of Stabilizing Trade Restrictions in an Exporting Country.

	Free Trade	Stabilizing Export Restrictions
Stability indicators, CV (%)		
Variability of price	8.9	7.1
Variability of supply to poor	3.9	3.1
Variability of farmers' income	10.8	9.1
Trade indicators		
Quantity exported[a]	12.1	11.4
Balance of trade[b]	10.6	9.9
Economic gains or losses due to policy[b]		
Consumers		+1.06
Producers		−1.46
Government		+0.17
Total economy		−0.23

[a]Percentage of normal production.

[b]Percentage of normal expenditures.

any surpluses through appropriate restitution payments, thus securing stable prices for domestic producers. Table 8–10 summarizes the main effects of this policy. It shows that with the partial stabilizing and export promoting program the mean price would rise by 4 percent. As a result domestic production would expand, while the quantity demanded by domestic consumers would decline. The end result would be an increase in the quantity exported and the trade surplus by more than 16 percent. These trends would be even more accentuated with the solid program, under which the quantity exported and the trade surplus would rise by as much as 40 percent.

In the importing country the stabilizing trade policy would have the meaning of variable import subsidies aimed at increasing as well as stabilizing the flow of foodgrain supply to domestic consumers in the face of high world price and lagging domestic production. Table 8–11 summarizes the main effects of this policy. It shows that with the partial stabilizing and consumption-promoting policy, the quantity available for domestic consumers would rise by 2.3 percent after an increase in imports and in the trade deficit by approximately 40 percent, which is offset in part by a *decrease* in domestic production

Table 8-10. Stabilizing Trade Policies in an Exporting Country.

| | Free Trade | Variable Export Subsidies | |
		Partial	Solid
Price			
Mean	86.3	89.5	95.0
CV (%)	8.9	5.0	2.7
Quantity available for consumption			
Mean	84.7	83.5	81.7
CV (%)	3.1	1.9	1.1
Farmers' income			
Mean	83.5	87.3	93.9
CV (%)	11.0	8.3	7.5
Quantity exported[a]	12.1	14.1	17.1
Balance of trade[b]	+ 10.6	+ 12.2	+ 14.7
Export subsidy payments[b]	. . .	0.5	1.6

[a]Percentage of normal production.

[b]Percentage of normal expenditures.

Table 8-11.   Stabilizing Trade Policies in an Importing Country.

	Free Trade	Variable Import Subsidies	
		Partial	*Solid*
Price			
Mean	114.8	108.7	104.3
CV (%)	6.5	3.7	2.0
Quantity available for consumption			
Mean	113.6	116.2	118.1
CV (%)	2.9	1.5	0.1
Quantity imported[a]	10.3	14.3	17.2
Balance of trade[b]	− 11.7	− 16.4	− 19.8
Import subsidy payments[b]	0	0.9	1.9

[a]Percentage of normal production.

[b]Percentage of normal expenditures.

by 1.4 percent due to the reduction in price. At the same time the variability of the market price and domestic supply would decline by 40 and 50 percent respectively.

CONCLUDING REMARKS

In the past decade international trade was dominated by mounting protectionist tendencies on the one hand and floating exchange rates on the other. In agricultural products the new protectionism was characterized by trade policies designed to achieve greater self-sufficiency and to protect domestic producers and consumers from price fluctuations originating in foreign countries. These policies include export taxes and trade restrictions on the one hand and import and domestic tariffs or subsidies as well as quotas, licensing, and so on on the other hand. This chapter illustrates the concomitant instability consequences of various trade policies in addition to their resulting effects on the volume of trade, the balance of payments and the income distribution. Thus, for instance, a 20 percent import tariff in a self-sufficient country would raise the average price and consequently also farmer's income by about 2.5 percent. As an effect of this tariff, however, price variability and the variability of farmers' income would rise by more than 25 percent. Whether or not such tariffs would be desirable from the producers' point of view depends on their subjective preferences and particularly on their degree of risk aversion. In any event, these results clearly demonstrate that a comparative static analysis of trade policies that concentrates on the welfare effects only may be entirely inappropriate for assessing their desirability since it ignores the instability consequences.

The chapter far from exhausts this subject, which is likely to gain even greater importance in the years ahead. Among the topics that deserve special attention are the effects of trade policies in one group of countries (such as the EEC) on the Third World countries or the role of direct aid as well as indirect assistance through trade concessions.

NOTES

1.   Normal production in the large country is one-third of the world's normal production.
2.   Normal production in the very large country is equal to the world's normal production.

REFERENCES

Adams, F.G., and S.A. Klein (eds.). 1978. *Stabilizing World Commodity Markets.* Lexington, Mass.: Lexington Books.

Afif, S., and C.P. Timmer. 1971. "Rice Policy in Indonesia," *Food Research Institute Studies* 10 (2):131–59.

Ahmed, R. 1979. "Foodgrain Supply, Distribution and Consumption Policies within a Dual Pricing Mechanism: A Case Study of Bangladesh." Research Report 8. Washington, D.C.: International Food Policy Research Institute.

Alderman, H. 1978. "The Potential to Influence Food Consumption by Price Policy: The Indonesian Example." Cornell University. Unpublished.

Bale, M.D., and E. Lutz. 1979. "The Effects of Trade Intervention on International Price Stability." *American Journal of Agricultural Economics* 61:512–16.

Baron, D.P., and R. Forsythe. 1979. "Models of the Firm and International Trade under Uncertainty." *American Economic Review* 69: 565–74.

Batra, R.N. 1975. "Production Uncertainty and the Heckscher-Ohlin Theorem." *Review of Economic Studies* 42:259–68.

Baumol, W.J. 1963. "An Expected Gain-Confidence Limit Criterion for Portfolio Selection." *Management Science* 9:174–82.

Benito, C. 1979. "Patterns of Food Production and Consumption in Underdevelopment: The Case of a Peasant Community in Mexico." *Journal of Policy Modeling* 1:383–98.

339

Bigman, D. 1980a. "Trade Strategies of Stabilization in Agricultural Primary Products." In D. Yaron and C. Tapiero (eds.), *Proceedings of Operations Research in Agriculture and Water Resources.* Amsterdam: North-Holland, pp. 159–73.

———. 1980b. "Stabilization and Welfare with Trade, Variable Levies and Internal Price Policies." *European Journal of Agricultural Economics* 7:185–202.

———. 1981. "Buffer Stocks Operation with Different Supply Specification: A Simulation Analysis." A paper presented at a conference on Simulation of Agricultural Hydrological and Ecological Systems. Rehovot, Israel.

———. Forthcoming. "Buffer Stocks and Domestic Price Policies." In A. Chickan (ed.), *Proceedings of the International Symposium on Inventories.* Budapest: Hungarian Academy of Science.

Bigman, D., K. Knapp, and S. Reutlinger. 1978. "National Policies for Stabilization: Objectives and Trade-offs." A paper presented at the meeting of the Southern Economic Association, Washington, D.C.

Bigman, D., and S.P. Leite. 1978. "Welfare and Trade Effects of Exchange Rate Uncertainty." *Southern Economic Journal* 45:534–42.

Bigman, D. and S. Reutlinger. 1979a. "National and International Policies toward Food Security and Price Stabilization." *American Economic Review* 69:159–63.

———. 1979b. "Food Price and Supply Stabilization: National Buffer Stocks and Trade Policies." *American Journal of Agricultural Economics* 61:657–67.

Bigman, D., and H. Shalit. 1980. "Applied Welfare Analysis for a Consumer with Commodity Income." Working Paper No. 8002. The Center for Agricultural Economic Research, The Hebrew University of Jerusalem.

Boulding, K.E. 1965. "The Population Trap." In *The Meaning of the 20th Century.* New York: Harper & Row.

Bultin, M. 1976. "The Welfare Effects of Price Stabilization: A Simple Multi-Market Extension." *The Economic Record* 52:483–96.

Burmeister, E. 1978. "Is Price Stabilization Theoretically Desirable?" In Adams and Klein (eds.).

Burns, M.E. 1973. "A Note on the Concept and Measure of Consumer's Surplus." *American Economic Review* 63:335–44.

Candler, W., and U. Lele. 1980. "Food Security: Some East African Considerations." In Valdez (ed.).

Carlyle, T. 1915. "Charitism." In *English and Other Critical Essays.* New York: pp. 172–73.

Carter, C., and A. Schmitz. 1979. "Import Tariffs and Price Formation in the World Wheat Market." *American Journal of Agricultural Economics* 61:517–22.

Chambers, R.G., J.M. Letiche, and A. Schmitz. 1979. "The Gains from International Trade." In Hillman and Schmitz (eds.).

Chou, M., D.P. Harman, Jr., and S.H. Wittwer. 1977. *World Food Prospects and Agricultural Potential.* New York: Praeger.

Cochrane, W.W. 1980. "Some Nonconformist Thoughts on Welfare Economics and Commodity Price Stabilization." *American Journal of Agricultural Economics* 62:508-11.

Colman, D. 1978. "Some Aspects of the Economics of Stabilization." *Journal of Agricultural Economics* 29:243-56.

Corden, W.M. 1974. *Trade Policy and Economic Welfare.* Oxford: Clarendon Press.

Council on Environmental Quality (CEQ). 1980. *The Global 2000 Report to the President.*

Crosson, P.R., and K.D. Frederick. 1977. *The World Food Situation.* Resources for the Future. Research Paper R-6. Washington, D.C.

Cuddington, J.T., and R.I. McKinnon. 1979. "Free Trade versus Protectionism: A Perspective." In Institute for Contemporary Studies, *Tariffs, Quotas and Trade: The Politics of Protectionism.* San Francisco.

Cuddy, J.D.A. 1978. "Commodity Price Stabilization." *Resources Policy* 4:25-30.

Currie, J.M., J.A. Murphy, and A. Schmitz. 1971. "The Concept of Economic Surplus and Its Use in Economic Analysis." *Economic Journal* 81:741-99.

Dahrendorf, Ralf. 1968. *Essays in the Theory of Society.* Palo Alto, Calif.: Stanford University Press.

Davis, J.M. 1977. "The Fiscal Role of Food Subsidy Program." *IMF Staff Papers* 24, pp. 100-26.

Dumont, R. 1975. "The Biggest Famine in History Has Just Begun." In S. Aziz (ed.). *Hunger, Politics, and Markets: The Real Issues in the Food Crisis.* New York: New York University Press.

Eaton, J. 1980. "Price Variability, Utility and Savings," *Review of Economic Studies* 47:513-20.

Eaton, D.J., and W.S. Steel (eds.). 1976. *Analysis of Grain Reserves.* U.S. Department of Agriculture, Economic Research Service 634.

Eckholm, E. 1976. Worldwatch Paper 9.

Edwards, R., and C.P. Hallwood. 1980. "The Determination of Optimum Buffer Stock Intervention Rules." *Quarterly Journal of Economics* 94:150-66.

Enzer, S., R. Drobnick, and S. Alter. 1978. *Neither Feast nor Famine.* Lexington, Mass.: Lexington Books.

Feder, G., R. Just, and A. Schmitz. 1977. "Storage with Price Uncertainty in International Trade." *International Economic Review* 18:553-68.

Fleming, J.M. 1951. "On Making the Best of Balance of Payments Restrictions on Imports." *Economic Journal* 61:48-71.

Food and Agriculture Organization of the United Nations (FAO). 1976. *Food and Population.* Rome.

———. *Current Status of National Cereal Stock Policies and Targets.* UN FAO CFS 77/7. Rome.

Fox, R. 1979. "Brazil's Minimum Price Policy and the Agricultural Sector of Northeast Brazil." Research Paper No. 9. Washington, D.C.: International Food Policy Research Institute.

Garcia, J.G. 1981. "The Nature of Food Insecurity in Colombia." In Valdez (ed.).

Gavan, J.D., and I. Sri Chandrasekera. 1979. "The Impact of Public Foodgrain Distribution and Food Consumption and Welfare in Sri Lanka." Research Report 13. Washington, D.C.: International Food Policy Research Institute.

George, P.S. 1979. "Public Distribution of Foodgrains in Kerala—Income Distribution Implications and Effectiveness." Research Report 7. Washington, D.C.: International Food Policy Research Institute.

George, S. 1976. *How the Other Half Dies: The Real Reasons for World Hunger.* London: Penguin Books.

Goldman, R.H. 1975. "Staple Food Self-Sufficiency and the Distributive Impact of Malaysian Rice Policy." *Food Research Institute Studies* 14 (3):251–93.

Gotsch, C., and G. Brown. 1980. "Prices, Taxes and Subsidies in Pakistan Agriculture, 1960–1976." World Bank Staff Working Paper No. 387.

Goueli, A.A. 1980. "National Food Security Program in Egypt." In Valdez (ed.).

Grennes, T., P.R. Johnson, and M. Thursby. 1978. *The Economics of World Grain Trade.* New York: Praeger.

Hanoch, G. 1974. "Desirability of Price Stabilization or Destabilization." Harvard Institute of Economic Research.

Hardin, G. 1981. *Newsweek.* October 26.

Hathaway, D.E. 1976. "Grain Stocks and Economic Stability: A Policy Perspective." In Eaton and Steel (eds.).

Hazell, P.B.R., and P.L. Scandizzo. 1975. "Market Intervention Policies when Production Is Risky." *American Journal of Agricultural Economics* 57:641–49.

———. 1977. "Farmers' Expectations, Risk Aversion, and Market Equilibrium under Risk." *American Journal of Agricultural Economics* 59:204–9.

Heidhues, T. 1979. "The Gains from Trade: An Applied Political Analysis." In Hillman and Schmitz (eds.).

Helmberger, P., and R. Weaver. 1977. "Welfare Implications of Commodity Storage under Uncertainty." *American Journal of Agricultural Economics* 59:639–51.

Helpman, E., and A. Razin. 1978. *A Theory of International Trade under Uncertainty.* New York: Academic Press.

Hesse, M. 1980. "Export Restrictions as a Means of Avoiding 'Critical Shortages'." A paper presented at the Theodor Heidhues Memorial Seminar, University of Gottingen.

Hillman, J.S. 1981. "The Role of Export Cropping in Less Developed Countries." *American Journal of Agricultural Economics* 63:375-83.

Hillman, J.S., and A. Schmitz (eds.). 1979. *International Trade in Agriculture: Theory and Policy.* Boulder, Colo.: Westview Press.

Howell, L.D. 1945. "Does the Consumer Benefit from Price Stability?" *Quarterly Journal of Economics* 59:287-95.

Hueth, D., and A. Schmitz. 1972. "International Trade in Intermediate and Final Goods: Some Welfare Implications of Destabilized Prices." *Quarterly Journal of Economics* 86:351-65.

Hueth, D.L., R.E. Just; and A. Schmitz. 1982. *Applied Welfare Economics and Public Policy,* Englewood Cliffs: Prentice-Hall.

Hwa, E.C., and N. Kulatilaka. 1979. "Stabilizing World Commodity Markets through Buffer Stocks: A Simulation Experiment with the Fixed Band Rule." International Monetary Fund DM/79/71.

International Food Research Institute. 1977. *Food Needs of Developing Countries: Projection of Production and Consumption to 1990.* Research Report No. 3, Washington, D.C.

Johnson, D.G. 1975. "World Agriculture, Commodity Policy and Price Variability." *American Journal of Agricultural Economics* 57:823-28.

_____. 1976. "Increased Insurance." *World Development* 4:977-87.

_____. "Food Production Potentials in Southeast Asia and Other Developing Countries." University of Chicago, Office of Agricultural Economic Research, No. 77.

Josling, T.F. 1974. "Agricultural Policies in Developing Countries: A Review." *Journal of Agricultural Economics* 25:229-64.

_____. 1980. "International Trade and World Food Production." In D. Gale Johnson (ed.), *The Politics of Food*, Chicago Council on Foreign Relations, pp. 36-59.

Just, R.E. 1975. "Risk Response Models and Their Use in Agricultural Policy Evaluation." *American Journal of Agricultural Economics* 57:836-43.

_____. 1976. "The Welfare Economics of Agricultural Risk." In *Market Risks in Agriculture: Concepts, Methods and Policy Issues.* Texas Agricultural Experiment Station, Department Technical Report No. 78-1, pp. 1-19.

Just, R.E., and A. Hallam. 1978. "Functional Flexibility in Analysis of Commodity Price Stabilization Policy." *Proceedings of the American Statistical Association,* pp. 177-93.

Just, R.E., and D.L. Hueth. 1979. "Welfare Measures in a Multimarket Framework." *American Economic Review* 69:947-54.

Just, R., E. Lutz, A. Schmitz, and S.J. Turnovsky. 1977. "The Distribution of Welfare Gains from International Price under Distortion." *American Journal of Agricultural Economics* 59:652-61.

———. 1978. "The Distribution of Welfare Gains from Price Stabilization: An International Perspective." *Journal of International Economics* 8:551-63.

Just, R.E., A. Schmitz, and D. Zilberman. 1979. "Price Controls and Optimal Export Policies under Alternative Market Structures." *American Economic Review* 69:706-14.

Kataoka, S. 1963. "A Stochastic Programming Model." *Econometrica* 31:181-96.

Knudsen, O., and P.L. Scandizzo. 1979. "Nutrition and Food Needs in Developing Countries." World Bank Staff Working Paper No. 328. *World Development Report.* Washington, D.C.

Krishna, R. 1974. "Unemployment in India." In *Agricultural Development Council Teaching Forum, Development Processes and Planning* 38.

———. "Government Operations in Foodgrains." In Wadhva (ed.).

Krishna, R., and G.S. Paychandhuri. 1980. "Some Aspects of Wheat and Rice Price Policy in India." World Bank Staff Working Paper No. 381.

Ladejinsky, W. 1974. "Food Shortage in West Bengal: Crisis or Chronic." World Bank memo.

Leland, H.E. 1972. "Theory of the Firm Facing Uncertain Demand." *American Economic Review* 62:278-91.

Leontief, W. 1974. "Sails and Rudders, Ship of State." In L. Silk (ed.) *Capitalism: The Moving Target.* New York, pp. 101-4.

Letiche, J.M. 1959. *Balance of Payments and Economic Growth.* New York: Harper Bros.

Lewis, A.W. 1978. *The Evolution of the International Economic Order.* Princeton, N.J.: Princeton University Press.

Little, I.M.D. 1957. *A Critique of Welfare Economics.* Oxford: Clarendon Press.

Lloyd, P.J. 1980. "The Effects of Trade Interventions on International Price Instability and National Welfare." Seminar Paper No. 146, Institute for International Economic Studies, University of Stockholm.

Lucas, R.E. 1976. "Econometric Policy Evaluation: Critique." In *Phillips Curve and Labor Market,* K. Brunner and A.H. Meltzer (ed.) Vol. 1 of the Carnegie-Rochester Conference Series on Public Policy. Supplementary Series to the *Journal of Monetary Economics.*

Lutz, E. 1978. "The Welfare Gains from Price Stabilization under Risk Response." *Zeitschrift fur Volkswirtschaft und Statistics* 2:115-30.

Massell, B.F. 1969. "Price Stabilization and Welfare." *Quarterly Journal of Economics* 83:284-98.

———. "Some Welfare Implications of International Price Stabilization." *Journal of Political Economy* 78:404-17.

Mayer, W. 1976. "The Rybczynski, Stopler-Samuelson and Factor-Price Equalization Theorems under Price Uncertainty." *American Economic Review* 66:797-808.

McCalla, A.F. 1978. "North American Food and Agricultural Policy: Conflict and Cooperation—A General Introduction." *American Journal of Agricultural Economics* 60:782-84.

Meade, J.E. 1955. *The Theory of International Economic Policy.* Oxford England: Clarendon Press.

Minhas, B.S. 1976. "Towards National Food Security." *The Indian Journal of Agricultural Economics* 31:8-19.

———. 1977. "Design of Economic Policy and the Phenomenon of Corruption: Some Suggestions for Economic Reform." In Wadhva (ed.).

Mishan, E.J. 1977. "The Plain Truth about Consumer Surplus." *Zeitschrift fur Nationalekonomie* 37:1-37.

Muth, J.F. 1961. "Rational Expectations and the Theory of Price Movements." *Econometrica* 29:315-35.

Nerlove, M. 1958. "Adaptive Expectations and Cobweb Phenomena." *Quarterly Journal of Economics* 73:227-40.

Newbery, D.M.G., and J.E. Stiglitz. 1979. "The Theory of Commodity Price Stabilization Rules: Welfare Impacts and Supply Responses." *The Economic Journal* 89:799-817.

———. 1981. *The Theory of Commodity Price Stabilization.* Oxford, England: Clarendon Press.

Oi, W.Y. 1961. "The Desirability of Price Instability under Perfect Competition." *Econometrica* 29:58-64.

———. 1972. "The Consumer Does Benefit from Feasible Price Stability: Comment." *Quarterly Journal of Economics* 86:494-98.

Okun, A. 1975. *Equality and Efficiency.* Washington, D.C.

Plato, 1966. *The Republic.* Translated by F.M. Dornford. New York: Oxford University Press.

Prasad, K. 1977. "Foodgrains Policy: 1966-1976." In Wadhva (ed.).

Raymer, A.J., and G.V. Reed. 1979. "Domestic Price Stabilization, Trade Restrictions and Buffer Stocks Policy: A Theoretical Policy Analysis with Reference to EEC Agriculture." *European Review of Agricultural Economics* 5:101-18.

Reutlinger, S. 1976. "A Simulation Model for Evaluating Worldwide Buffer Stocks of Wheat." *American Journal of Agricultural Economics* 58:1-12.

Reutlinger, S., and H. Alderman. 1980. "The Prevalence of Calorie-Deficient Diets in Developing Countries." *World Development* 8:399–411.

Reutlinger, S., and D. Bigman. 1981. "Feasibility, Effectiveness and Costs of Food Security Alternatives in Developing Countries." In Valdes (ed.), pp. 185–212.

Reutlinger, S., D. Bigman, and D. Eaton. 1976. "Should Developing Countries Carry Grain Reserves." In Eaton and Steel (eds.), pp. 12–38.

Reutlinger, S., and M. Selowsky. 1976. *Malnutritional Poverty: Magnitude and Policy Options.* World Bank Occasional Paper No. 23. Baltimore: The Johns Hopkins University Press.

Roy, A.D. 1952. "Safety First and the Holding of Assets." *Econometrica* 19:431–449.

Sampson, G.P., and R.H. Snape. 1981. "Effects of the EEC's Variable Import Levies." *Journal of Political Economy* 88:1026–1040.

Samuelson, P.A. 1947. *Foundations of Economic Analysis.* Cambridge, Mass.: Harvard University Press.

––––––. 1972a. "The Consumer Does Benefit from Feasible Price Stability." *Quarterly Journal of Economics* 86:476–93.

––––––. 1972b. "Rejoinder." *Quarterly Journal of Economics* 86:500–3.

Sandmo, A. 1971. "On the Theory of the Competitive Firm under Price Uncertainty." *American Economic Review* 61:65–73.

Sarris, A.H., and L. Taylor. 1978. "Buffer Stock Analysis for Agricultural Products. Theoretical Work or Empirical Resolution." In Adams and Klein (eds.).

Scandizzo, P.L., P.B.L. Hazell, and J.R. Anderson, 1980. "Producers' Price Expectations and the Size of the Welfare Gains from Price Stabilization," The World Bank. (Unpublished)

Scandizzo, L., and G. Swami. 1981. "Benefits and Costs of Food Distribution Policies: The India Case." AGREP Division Working Paper No. 35, World Bank.

Schmitz, A., H. Shalit, and S.J. Turnovsky. 1981. "Producer Welfare and the Preference for Price Stability." *American Journal of Agricultural Economics* 63:157–60.

Schultz, T.W. 1977. "On Economics, Agriculture and the Political Economy." In T. Dams and K.E. Hunt (eds.), *Decision Making in Agriculture,* Lincoln: University of Nebraska Press.

Segal, J.A. 1970. *Food for the Hungry: The Reluctant Society.* Baltimore: The Johns Hopkins University Press.

Selowsky, M. 1979. 1979. "Target Group-Oriented Food Programs: Cost Effectiveness Comparison." *American Journal of Agricultural Economics* 61:988–94.

Sen, A. 1977. "Poverty and Economic Development." In Wadhva (ed.).

––––––. 1981. *Poverty and Famines: An Essay on Entitlement and Deprivation.* Oxford: Clarendon Press.

Shalit, H. 1980. "Who Should Pay for Price Stabilization?" Working Paper No. 8006, The Center for Agricultural Economic Research.

Shei, S.Y., and R.L. Thompson. 1977. "The Impact of Trade Restrictions on Price Stability in the World Wheat Market." *American Journal of Agricultural Economics* 59:628-38.

Siamwalla, A. 1980. "Security of Rice Supplies in the ASEAN Region." In Valdez (ed.).

Silberberg, E. 1972. "Duality and the Many Consumer's Surpluses." *American Economic Review* 62:942-52.

Smith, G.W. 1978. "Commodity Instability and Market Failure: A Survey of Issues." In Adams and Klein (eds.).

Srinivasan, T.N. 1977. "Income Distribution: A Survey of Policy Aspects." In Wadhva (ed.).

Subotkin, A., and J.P. Houck. 1976. "Welfare Implications of Stabilizing Consumption and Production." *American Journal of Agricultural Economics* 58:13-20.

Swami, G. 1979. "Public Food Distribution in India." AGREP Division Working Paper. World Bank.

Swamy and Binswanger. 1980. "Income and Price Elasticities for Foodgrains in India." World Bank memo.

Taylor, L., S. Horton, and D. Ralf. 1980. "Food Subsidy Programs: A Survey." Massachusetts Institute of Technology. A report prepared for the Ford Foundation.

Telser, L.G. 1955-56. "Safety First and Hedging." *Review of Economic Studies* 23:1-16.

Thiesenhusen, W.C. 1978. "Reaching the Rural Poor and the Poorest: A Goal Unmet." In H. Newly (ed.), *International Perspectives in Rural Sociology*. Charleston: John Wiley & Sons, pp. 159-82.

Timmer, C.P. 1975. "The Political Economy of Rice in Asia: Indonesia." *Food Research Institute Studies* 14.

Tisdell, C. 1963. "Uncertainty, Instability and Expected Profit." *Econometrica* 31:243-47.

Turnovsky, S.J. 1973. "Optimal Stabilization Policies in a Market with Lagged Adjustment in Supply." *Economic Record* 49:31-49.

_____ . 1974. "Price Expectations and the Welfare Gains from Price Stabilization." *American Journal of Agricultural Economics* 56:706-16.

_____ . 1976. "The Distribution of Welfare Gains from Price Stabilization: The Case of Multiplicative Disturbances." *International Economic Review* 17:133-48.

_____ . 1978a. "Stabilization Rules and the Benefits from Price Stabilization." *Journal of Public Economics* 9:37-57.

_____ . 1978b. "The Distribution of Welfare Gains from Price Stabilization: A Survey of Some Theoretical Issues." In Adams and Klein (eds.).

_____. 1979. "Futures Markets, Private Storage and Price Stabilization." *Journal of Public Economics* 12:301–27.

Turnovsky, S.J., H. Shalit, and A. Schmitz. 1980. "Consumer's Surplus, Price Instability, and Consumer Welfare." *Econometrica* 48:135–52.

U.S. Department of Agriculture. 1974. "The World Food Situation and Prospects to 1985." Economic Research Service, Foreign Agricultural Economic Report No. 98, Washington, D.C.

U.S. Department of Agriculture. 1979. *Food and Nutrition for the 1990s: Moving Ahead.* Washington, D.C.

Valdes, A. (ed.) 1980. *Food Security for Developing Countries.* Colo.: Westview Press.

Viner, J. 1937. *Theory of International Trade.* New York: Harper Bros.

Wadhva, C.D. (ed.). 1977. *Some Problems of India's Economic Policy,* 2nd ed. New Delhi: Tata McGraw-Hill.

Wall, J. 1978. "Foodgrain Management in India, Pricing, Procurement, Distribution, Import and Storage Policy." World Bank Staff Working Paper No. 279.

Waugh, F.V. 1944. "Does the Consumer Benefit from Price Instability?" *Quarterly Journal of Economics* 58:602–14.

_____. 1945. "Reply." *Quarterly Journal of Economics* 59:301–3.

_____. 1966. "Consumer Aspects of Price Instability." *Econometrica* 34:504–8.

Whittemore, C. 1981. *Land For People.* Birmingham, England: Third World Publications.

Wilig, R.D. 1976. "Consumer's Surplus without Apology." *American Economy Review* 66:589–97.

World Bank. 1979. *World Development Report.* Washington, D.C.

_____. 1980. *World Development Report.* Washington, D.C.

_____. 1981. *World Development Report.* Washington, D.C.

Wortman, S., and R.W. Cummings, Jr. 1978. *To Feed This World: The Challenge and the Strategy.* Baltimore: The Johns Hopkins University Press.

Zucker, A. 1965. "On the Desirability of Price Instability." *Econometrica* 32:437–41.

Zusman, P., and A. Amiad. 1965. "Simulation: A Tool for Farm Planning under Conditions of Weather Uncertainty." *Journal of Farm Economics* 47:574–94.

INDEX

ABOUT THE AUTHOR

David Bigman is a senior lecturer and presently Chairman of the
Department of Agricultural Economics, Hebrew University of
Jerusalem. He has worked at the Ministry of Finance in Israel, the
World Bank, and the International Monetary Fund. He is the
author and co-author of numerous articles in mathematical eco-
nomics, international trade and development, and an editor (to-
gether with T. Taya) of the books *The Functioning of Floating
Exchange Rates: Theory, Evidence and Policy Implications* and
*Exchange Rate and Trade Instability: Causes, Consequences and
Policies.*